PRAISE FOR
THE WANDERING PALESTINIAN

"Anan Ameri's memoir is a valuable contribution to narratives of community organizing and grassroots activism especially on the question of Palestine. Weaving between heartbreak and personal and political triumph, her story sheds light on important solidarity work and organization building in the US."

— Dr. Sarah Gualtieri
Author of *Arab Routes: Pathways to Syrian California*

"…a riveting, 40 year-long journey through the streets of several American cities recounting tales, both humorous and heartbreaking, that illustrate the acculturation of an idealistic but restless Palestinian woman into American life. Ameri's writing is crisp and smooth, and I was hooked immediately. I couldn't put it down."

— Diana Abouali, PhD.
Director of the Arab American National Museum

"This is a gem in the archives of Arab America."

— Evelyn Alsultany, Associate Professor,
American Studies and Ethnicity, University of Southern California

"…a beautifully written book… This book is a joy to read."

— Louise Cainkar,
Scholar of Arab Americans and Professor, Marquette University

"…a masterful book capturing the intimate ways one woman's immigration story can contribute to the transformation of U.S. society at large …a must-read for anyone interested in immigration, feminism, activism, or Arab Americans."

Professor, University of Illin

"...Ameri tells captivating tales of youth, love, migration and the joys of struggling for dignity and justice. ...an Arab American saga, an enchanting web of stories."

— Khaled Mattawa
Poet, writer, and a creative writing professor, University of Michigan

"Like beautiful Middle Eastern tapestry she presents a personal narrative of immigration and activism woven into a story of institution building. Reading Anan Ameri's memoir one will be reminded that at the center of the fight for peace is the search for love."

— E. Ethelbert Miller
Literary activist and writer

THE
WANDERING PALESTINIAN
a memoir

ANAN AMERI

Livonia, Michigan

Edited by Jamie Rich
Proofread by Grace Nehls

THE WANDERING PALESTINIAN

Copyright © 2020 Anan Ameri

Published by BHC Press

Library of Congress Control Number: 2020933941

ISBN: 978-1-64397-130-8 (Hardcover)
ISBN: 978-1-64397-131-5 (Softcover)
ISBN: 978-1-64397-132-2 (Ebook)

For information, write:
BHC Press
885 Penniman #5505
Plymouth, MI 48170

Visit the publisher:
www.bhcpress.com

TABLE OF CONTENTS

To My Husband & My Friend
Noel Saleh

I never carried a rifle
On my shoulder
Or pulled a trigger
All I have
Is a flute's melody
A brush to paint my dreams
A bottle of ink
All I have
Is unshakable faith
And an infinite love
For my people in pain

Tawfiq Zayyad 1929-1994

FOREWORD
BY EVELYN ALSULTANY

D r. Anan Ameri is an icon in the Arab American community. She has invested her life to advancing the Arab American community and Palestinian rights. When Ismael Ahmed, another icon in the Arab American community, knocked on her office door in 2005 to introduce me, Anan took immediate interest. I had just moved to Michigan to become a professor at the University of Michigan. Soon after she invited me to her home for brunch, eager to find ways for us to collaborate. I have benefited enormously from her passionate commitment to mentoring Arab American women. She has that rare quality of generously offering advice while respecting the autonomy of others to make their own decisions. Over the years we became collaborators, friends, and writing partners. I have nothing but admiration for her extraordinary accomplishments, steadfast activism, and courage in speaking out for human rights for all.

Anan is invested in building institutions using a grassroots model. She understands that advancing the Arab American community and dispelling harmful stereotypes requires building institutions, but not elite corporate ones. Rather, such institutions must emerge from the community itself and reflect the diverse range of Arab American experiences and visions.

In 1997, Anan was hired at ACCESS, as the Director of the Cultural Arts program. A few years later, she led the organization's effort to establish the Arab American National Museum (AANM), the only cultural institution in the world that documents, preserves, and presents the history, culture, and contributions of Arab Americans. AANM opened in 2005 with Anan as its founding director—a position she held until she retired in 2013. Anan believes in the power of art and culture in empowering and building communities. This is the vision of the AANM: an institution that preserves and promotes history, art, and culture. In addition to her crucial role with the Arab American National Museum, Anan has published extensively on Arab American history, art, and institution building, contributing significantly to scholarship on Arab Americans.

I was standing outside the AANM on May 5, 2005, when it first opened its doors to an excited crowd of people. It was too packed for me to enter that day, but I've spent countless days there since, serving on the library committee to develop their collections, collaborating with Anan and museum staff on an online exhibit of Arab stereotypes (www.arabstereotypes.org), and attending academic, activist, and art conferences. It has become an essential hub for many Arab Americans, a place for us to be proud of who we are and what we have contributed to the United States.

The Wandering Palestinian serves as the prequel to the picture I've just painted, part of its rich origin story, if you will. In it, Anan recounts the journey of her younger self, trying to find her way as an Arab in the US. She moved from Beirut, Lebanon to Detroit, Michigan in 1974 for love. As she takes us through the challenges of adjusting to a new culture, being far from family, learning the language, and then, ironically, discovering that she has become too American to ever move back to Amman, Anan provides a vivid window into Arab immigrant life in the US in the late twentieth century. We learn how her personal encounters with injustice informed her commitment to solidarity and activism. She takes us through her role as the Founding Director of the Palestine Aid Society, to becoming a member of the Palestinian National Council (the legislative body of the Palestine Liberation Organization), and then the Founding Director of the Arab American National Museum.

When she retired in 2013, we became writing partners. We would meet regularly at the Ann Arbor Public Library and work on our respective writing projects. During this time, she wrote *The Scent of Jasmine: Coming of Age in Jerusalem and Damascus* (Interlink, 2017), which tells the story of her family's displacement from Palestine during the 1948 Nakba and her movement from west Jerusalem to Damascus, to east Jerusalem, then finally Amman.

THE WANDERING PALESTINIAN

The Wandering Palestinian picks up where *The Scent of Jasmine* left off, exploring Anan's adult life in the United States. Her early years in the US were not easy; she did not have a green card, spoke English poorly, did not have a driver's license, and deeply missed her friends and family. The stories from her life highlight the challenges immigrants face in adjusting to a new culture, from language and hospitality norms to learning about racism and inequality. After obtaining her Ph.D. at Wayne State University, her friends encouraged her to be an academic, but she was drawn instead to grassroots organizing that led her, along with other activists, to establish the Palestine Aid Society of America. Her activism took her from Detroit to Washington, DC; Cambridge, MA; Jerusalem; and back to Michigan. The short chapters, which bring us all the way up to the beginning of her work with ACCESS, include commentary about Palestinian activism in the US during the mid-70s to mid-90s, racial injustice in the US, Israeli injustice toward Palestinians, and Anan's ongoing commitment to solidarity politics. They also share her sadness following the death of her parents and relate funny anecdotes from her travels.

Those interested in Arab American history will be particularly intrigued by stories of her third-generation Arab American in-laws who participated in homesteading in North Dakota in the early 1900s and who preserve their culture by cultivating the land. She offers fascinating insight into Arab American activist groups like the Organization of Arab Students, the Association of Arab American University Graduates, and the Palestine Aid Society. Her experiences living in the Detroit area reveal a city marred by poverty and segregation that has become the capital of Arab America. Her life in the US takes place with the backdrop of a civil war in Lebanon, increased Israeli military occupation of Palestine, and the end of apartheid in South Africa.

I have marveled over the years at Anan's steadfast ability to calmly address controversial topics like the Israeli-Palestinian conflict and stereotypes about Arabs and Muslims. When giving public lectures about the Arab American National Museum, she was often asked where the museum gets their money. She would chuckle and point out the hypocrisy of the question that assumes that the funds come from illegitimate sources. She would in a matter-of-fact manner ask if the person would ask the same question to the Japanese American Museum, African American Museum, or the Jewish Museum. She would inform the person that all foundations and donors are listed on the wall in the lobby of the museum and she would be sure to underline the inherent stereotypes in the question. When she sees hypocrisy, double standards, and injustice she points it out and takes action to address it. We would chuckle at—as she would say—her inability to keep her mouth shut. This book provides insight into her moral compass and her fierce allergy to injustice and hypocrisy. She points out the everyday racism of the world we inhabit and is quick to question how people, especially those who have been oppressed, come to justify discrimination toward another group of people.

Like *The Scent of Jasmine*, *The Wandering Palestinian* is a vital contribution to the archives of Arab America. Though not technically an oral history conveyed from an interviewee to an interviewer, Anan's writing resonates with a similar intimacy and spirit of generosity. It is a deeply personal narrative that, at the same time, immerses readers in the wide-reaching political and cultural currents in which it is embedded. We learn about the experiences of an Arab immigrant to the US from the fraught 1970s to the present in Anan's own distinct voice and point of view. Anan uses her personal experience and insightful self-reflection to interrogate transnational social, political, and cultural norms. She shares her memories and experience so that others can document, preserve, and learn. Anan's life story stands in stark contrast to the many stories about Arab women as oppressed. This is a story about a fiercely independent Arab woman who worked as a journalist in Beirut, leads delegations to Israel and Palestine on fact-finding missions, builds a museum, and becomes an icon in the Arab American community.

Evelyn Alsultany, Associate Professor, American Studies and Ethnicity, University of Southern California and author of *Arab and Muslims in the Media: Race and Representation after 9/11*

THE WANDERING PALESTINIAN

CHAPTER 1
CAN YA MA CAN

ONCE UPON A TIME

I arrived in Detroit in July 1974 on a hot, muggy day. What brought me to Detroit was love.

Coming to the US was not on my radar. I never had the desire to come to America, not even for a visit, and definitely not to spend the rest of my life. But then, on a sunny spring day while living happily in Beirut, a charming Arab American fellow full of energy and enthusiasm crossed my path. It was love at the first sight—the kind of love and lust that sweeps you off your feet.

When I met Abdeen, I was twenty-nine years old. I had already gotten a master's degree in sociology from Cairo University. I was working as a researcher at the Palestine Research Center and had a side job as a freelance journalist. I was sharing a spacious apartment in the trendy Al Hamra neighborhood with my sister, Suad, who was attending the American University of Beirut. I enjoyed the freedom of living away from Amman and my parents. Life in Beirut—with its political and cultural activities, wonderful restaurants and cafés, and with its nightlife and the Mediterranean sun and beaches—seemed to be almost perfect. I had a politically active life and enjoyed a large circle of friends who, like me, came from other parts of the Arab world to be in Beirut, the center of revolutionary and progressive politics of the time. But love is blind, and I thought my life could become even better. I dropped everything and followed him to Detroit. Five months later, I uttered the words "I do."

Before coming to the US, as narrated in my book *The Scent of Jasmine: Coming of Age in Jerusalem and Damascus,* I lived in the cities of Jerusalem, Damascus, Amman, Cairo, and Beirut. I grew up in a politically and socially liberal household. Both of my parents were college graduates and were determined to give their three daughters the best education possible, and expected them to chart their own futures. Not going to college was not an option for any of their kids. I will forever remember my parents repeatedly telling me, "You can lose your money, your home, and your land, but no one can ever take away your degree." This was a lesson they must have learned in 1948 when they lost everything they owned and became, along with 850,000 other Palestinians, penniless refugees.

My father, a Palestinian from Jaffa, cherished books and spent most of his time reading and writing. People loved and respected him, not only for his intellect, but more so for his honesty and integrity, and his strong sense of justice and commitment to others. My mother, a Syrian from Damascus, was free-spirited, intelligent, and independent. She owned her own business, managed an all-male staff, and worked well into her seventies. Growing up, I was fortunate to be surrounded by strong and determined women who taught me, at a fairly young age, that I could be whoever I wanted to be, and that the sky was the limit when it came to my education and career choices.

I am also fortunate to have grown up when many Arab countries enjoyed a certain level of openness and acceptance. Although these countries had their own problems, including periods of political repression, they looked like paradise compared to their current sectarianism, intolerance, and civil wars. I came of age during the 1960s, the era of liberation movements, postcolonialism, Arab nationalism, and international solidarity. This was a time when we rebelled against male-dominated societies and oppressive regimes, and we rallied for women's liberation and, of course, for the liberation of Palestine.

When I came to America, I brought with me these values of activism and commitment to social justice. I also brought the values my parents instilled in me—to be independent and compassionate to those who are less fortunate. These values were my moral compass that guided me throughout my forty-some year journey in the US, and have influenced my personal and professional choices. They were part of who I was when I landed in this country and are part of who I am today.

To my surprise and disappointment, Detroit was a far cry from what I expected. It did not resemble what I saw on television or Hollywood movies. I couldn't believe that a major American city would pale in comparison to some Arab cities I lived in, including Beirut, Damascus, and Cairo. Although I was aware of the plight of African Americans, Detroit's 1967 rebellion, and the civil rights movement, these were not enough to prepare me to deal with Detroit's harsh reality. Overnight, I found myself unable to walk to a store to buy a loaf of bread because there was none within walking distance, nor was there dependable public transportation to get me anywhere. And I couldn't walk the streets of Detroit, especially after sunset, because it was not safe. But what shocked me the most were the abandoned and burned homes, and the poverty-stricken and racially segregated neighborhoods. It wasn't like I had never seen poverty before, especially in Palestinian refugee camps, and it wasn't like I couldn't see the resemblance of the injustice inflicted on both communities, but somehow Detroit's poverty and segregation seemed harsher and more hopeless.

As I reflect on my early years in Detroit, life was hard. Really hard. Love alone couldn't sustain me or save me from the loneliness, isolation, and even depression. In spite of my comfortable living, without speaking English, knowing how to drive, or a permit to work, I lost my independence, and I lost my identity and my pride. I felt uprooted, and much of what I took for granted was stripped away. I needed to create a different reality. I needed to reclaim myself and to reclaim some of my losses if I was to survive living in this country.

On the brighter side, Metro Detroit, especially Dearborn, had a large number of Lebanese, Palestinian, Yemeni, and Iraqi recent immigrants, with whom I shared a strong Arab identity and radical politics. It also had second- and third-generation Arab Americans who belonged to the anti-Vietnam War and civil rights movements, as well as other social justice issues. These two groups helped me break away from my isolation, resume my political activism, and find my own niche. They also paved the way for me to have a professional life that was in sync with my values and with issues I was most passionate about.

Like other immigrants, when I arrived, and to the distress of those who don't like immigrants, I couldn't shed my culture, identity, and sense of belonging. I was a proud young woman, full of hope and the promise that our generation could change the world. I was proud of my heritage, of my Arab-Palestinian identity, and of my people. Yet I was devastated by the bad image Arabs had in this country. This became much worse after 9/11. As an Arab Palestinian Muslim woman, I suddenly realized that to many people in this country, I was the embodiment of what was backward and evil in our world. I believe that I can also speak for many other immigrants who come from similar backgrounds. It was this very feeling of injustice that pushed me, and hundreds of others, to organize and build institutions to defend and support our people here and abroad. It was also what inspired me to tell my own story.

This book is rooted in the beautiful and rich tradition of storytelling, a tradition that has kept family and community histories alive by passing them from one generation to the next. During my childhood and adolescence, socializing was the main source of entertainment. Storytelling, as well as juicy gossip, was at the heart of these gatherings. I still recall many happy and sad stories told by my parents, aunts, and uncles. But the most vivid memory that continues to haunt me is seeing my father, along with his friends and relatives, grieve the loss of Palestine. While it pained me to watch them tell their stories, especially when I saw men, including my father, shed tears, I was captivated by their anecdotes. Their passionate conversations and stories ignited my curiosity. They taught me not only about the Palestinian tragedy of 1948, but also about the lasting impact and healing power of storytelling. I often wonder if that was what inspired me to commit most of my adult life to trying to bring peace and justice to Palestine. Or if that was what led me to work with immigrant communities, to hear and document their stories, and to demonstrate how our own individual stories are part of a larger American story.

The stories of this *Wandering Palestinian* are about the forty-three years I lived in the US. Writing some of them was sometimes painful, but memoirs require transparency and conveying the good, bad, and ugly. I want to honor the tradition of storytelling and to honor my readers. These are stories about my love and failed marriage to my first husband, my struggle with depression and therapy, and my activism that took me to Washington, DC; Cambridge, Massachusetts; and Jerusalem, then back to Detroit following my newfound love, and a new career opportunity that led me to play a vital role in the creation of the Arab American National Museum.

As the stories of this book reveal, my personal, social, and political life has been intertwined with Arab and Palestinian American activism. I hope these stories provide my readers a window not only to the challenges immigrants face, but also to their contributions and triumphs. I also hope that this book will encourage other activists from our community, especially women, to narrate their own stories. My parents used to tell me that no one can ever take away my education or college degrees. I look forward to the day when we, as well as other immigrants, will not be afraid to tell our own stories in our own voices and perspectives, so no one can take that away from us.

CHAPTER 2
THE INTERVIEW

BEIRUT, APRIL 1974

I was happily living in Beirut, the Paris of the Middle East, and the new home of the Palestine Liberation Organization (PLO). I moved there at age twenty-seven from Amman, Jordan to join thousands of global revolutionaries who flocked to the country to express their solidarity with the Palestinians. Luckily, I was able to find a full-time job at the Palestine Research Center. Life was good, really good, except for my meager salary. As radicals, we were supposed to shun materialism and live on very little.

But Beirut was a seductive city. It had a lot to offer: restaurants, bars, and cafés, as well as movies, concerts, and theaters, not to mention the beautiful Mediterranean beaches. You name it, Beirut had it, and I wanted it all. But I wasn't able to fully enjoy the city without a constant infusion of cash from my parents, from whom I was desperate to gain my independence.

Before moving to Beirut in 1972, I was living with my parents in Amman, Jordan. While they were thrilled to have me live with them, I wasn't. My other three siblings were in different parts of the world pursuing their university education. My sister Arwa was in the US, Ayman, my brother, was in England, and my younger sister Suad was in Lebanon. My parents couldn't wait to have one of their children come back home, who happened to be me after getting my MA in 1971 from Cairo University.

Although I wasn't that excited about living with my parents, with a few friends and a nicely paid job with Jordanian Television, I decided to stay in Amman, at least temporarily. But my job, which initially was glamorous and exciting, gradually became intolerable. The Jordanian government's censorship and repression was getting worse by the day. When one of my colleagues got fired for being a "PLO sympathizer," I decided to quit.

"I cannot take this anymore. I want to resign and go to Beirut," I told my parents while having dinner.

"Why?" my mother said. "You have a good job, and your dad and I love having you live with us."

"Mama, you know me. I cannot keep my mouth shut. Sooner or later, I'm going to say something they won't like. I better quit before they fire me."

I applied for a job at the Palestine Research Center, and before I heard back, I resigned, packed my few belongings, and left.

My parents weren't that excited about my decision. Had I opted to go for my PhD like my sister Arwa, they would have been delighted to see me leave. At the time, and in that part of the world, women did not leave their parents' home for a job. But since my liberal parents instilled in their daughters the need to be independent and chart their own lives, they had to live up to what they'd been preaching. Half-heartedly, they accepted my choice. Knowing I wouldn't be making enough money for a decent living, they managed to invent occasions that warranted cash gifts. Though not overjoyed to accept their subsidy, I swallowed my pride and took it.

My eighteen months of searching for an additional source of income finally led me to a part-time job as a freelance journalist with the Beirut-based Orient Press. Initially the owner wanted me to write articles about current issues. After submitting a few of them, he called me to his office, offered me a cup of coffee, and said, "I like your writing style. But I'd rather have you conduct interviews with famous people. That's what our readers want and that's what sells best."

"What kind of famous? Are you looking for politicians, artists, or writers? Do you have any in mind?"

"No. You can find them yourself. If I like what you give me, I'll pay you five hundred Lebanese lira for each interview."

That was twice as much as I was getting per article and more than half of my monthly salary at the Palestine Researcher Center. To my distress, however, the only semi-famous people I knew were within the PLO ranks, whose pictures were already on hundreds of walls, billboards, and magazine covers, and whose interviews saturated the press.

I left the office, wondering where I was supposed to find these people. My artist friend Kamal Boullata, a Palestinian American who unfortunately was not that famous at the time, was living temporarily in Beirut. He was working on an art project with Palestinian children in refugee camps. As we sat in a street café sipping gin and tonics, I shared my dilemma with him.

"The owner of the Orient Press wants me to interview celebrities. I don't know any and have no clue where to find them!"

A few days later, I got a call from Kamal suggesting I interview an Arab American who lived in Detroit, Michigan.

"What is his name?" I asked.

"Abdeen Jabara. He is a very good friend of mine."

"How famous is he? I've never heard of him."

"He is a rising star within the Arab American progressive community."

"What does he do? You need to tell me more so I can prepare my questions."

"He is a young civil rights attorney handling very important cases. He is also one of the founders of the Arab American University Graduates. You should meet him. I'm sure you'll find him interesting. But I need to warn you, his Arabic isn't that good. How is your English?"

"Not that good either. I wonder how I'll be able to interview him?"

"If you don't mind, we can meet at my apartment. I can help translate."

None of what I heard so far about the man seemed so glamorous. But desperate for cash, I agreed to at least give it a try.

I arrived at Kamal's one-bedroom apartment in al-Hamra neighborhood in the early afternoon. I quickly scanned the room while trying to adjust my vision from the bright sun outside. Two young men in their late twenties or early thirties, who were sitting on the couch, stood up to greet me. I spotted the Arab one right away. He had dark hair, brown eyes, and a gentle demeanor. I couldn't tell who the other man was with his sturdy body, fair skin, light brown hair, and hazel eyes. I assumed he was an American friend of either Abdeen or Kamal.

"This is my journalist friend, Anan Ameri. She will be conducting the interview. And this is my friend, Abdeen Jabara, and his friend, Dick Soble. They are traveling together."

"I am sorry, which one is Abdeen?" I asked.

"It is me," said the fair-skinned man with much enthusiasm.

I was taken by surprise since I assumed that Dick, who was in fact Jewish, was the Arab one. I should have known better not to make such an assumption. After all, my Syrian mother's family had many blonds with blue eyes, including my grandfather, a few aunts and uncles, as well as a handful of cousins.

Kamal's apartment was rather tiny with very little furniture. I sat on the floor in spite of the men's protest. I crossed my legs and placed my notepad on my lap and was ready for what seemed to be a new adventure. After exchanging a few pleasantries, I realized how poor Abdeen's Arabic was. I looked at Kamal and said, "Obviously I need your help. Are you still willing to be our translator?"

"Of course I am."

Abdeen leaned back in his seat resting one foot on his opposite knee, folding his hands across his well-built frame, and said in very broken Arabic, "I don't need a translator. I can do the interview in Arabic."

Between his broken Arabic and his nervous movements—constantly rearranging his hands and legs and pushing the long strands of hair away from his eyes—it was hard for me to concentrate. Every few minutes I would call on Kamal, "Please translate this one for me."

I took my disjointed handwritten notes home and stayed up all night, writing one draft after another trying to make sense of what I had. The image of the restless man with a contagious smile kept invading my vision, mind, and heart. I just couldn't stop thinking about him. Before submitting the article, I succumbed to my foolishness and called Kamal.

"Hi, Kamal. I have a question. Is Abdeen your friend's first or last name?"

"Abdeen is his first, Jabara his last."

"I'm wondering if he is still in town… Do you…?"

"Sorry, Anan." Kamal interrupted. "I was about to leave when you called. I'm late for a meeting. I'll call you when I come back."

"Just tell me where he is. Did he go back to the States?"

"No. He and his friend went to Syria, then they're heading to the West Bank."

"Do you—" Before I had a chance to finish my sentence, Kamal said, "I'm sorry, Anan, I have to go."

I was disappointed that our conversation was cut short. After I hung up the phone, I started to question myself. Why did I call Kamal? Why was I checking the whereabouts of Abdeen? What would I do if he was still in town?

Satisfied with my tenth draft, I put the few pages of the interview in a crisp new file folder and proudly walked into my boss's office.

"Here, I got you the first interview. It's a good one. I am sure you're going to like it." I placed the file on his desk and sat facing him, eager to hear his reaction.

"Abdeen Jabara? I never heard of him," said the boss as soon as he read the first line.

"Really! You don't know who he is?" I tried to sound as genuine as I could.

"No, I don't. Give me a couple days. I'll read it and get back to you," he said while leafing through the pages.

On my way out and before I had a chance to reach his office door, he yelled, "Anan, where are the pictures?"

I turned around to face him, "What pictures?"

"The pictures of this Jabara, the man you interviewed."

"You didn't tell me to get any," I protested.

"I didn't think I needed to. It's common sense. I cannot use this interview without photos. Next time, make sure to arrange with our photographer. I need professional pictures."

With my head buried deep between my shoulders, I left the Orient Press. Not only had I not done a good job, but I also doubted I would get the five hundred liras I had been fantasizing about.

To my surprise and delight, Kamal called me a week later to tell me that Abdeen was back in Beirut and would like to add a few things to the interview.

"There are a few important points he forgot to tell you. Is it too late?"

"No, of course not. I'm glad you called. I need to bring the photographer to take a few pictures of him. Can we still meet at your apartment?"

"You're more than welcome."

I was overjoyed to have found him. I tried to convince myself it was the prospect of getting paid once I had pictures of him, but my excitement was much more than getting the promised five hundred liras.

The rest is history. I spent the week with my newly found love and never made it to work. It was April, and everything was blooming in Lebanon, including me. A month later, we met in Paris. I flew to Detroit in July, and in November of that year, 1974, we were married.

CHAPTER 3
LOVE IS BLIND

DETROIT, JULY 1974

In the 1950s while in elementary school in Amman, Jordan, I learned that America was very big and far away. However, I never realized how far it really was until 1974 when I looked at my plane ticket from Beirut to Detroit: two days in the air, four different airlines, Middle East, Hungarian, French, then Northwest, with a ten hour layover in Budapest, a sleepover in Paris, and a final connection in New York City.

"This trip takes forever. Too many stops. Isn't there a better way to travel?" I asked the travel agent.

"Not if this is all you can afford."

What made the trip even longer and more complicated was my eagerness to meet my new love, and what it took to get there: three months of unpaid vacation when I could hardly afford it, lying to my parents about why I was going to Detroit, and borrowing money when I had no idea how I would pay it back. Adding to all of this was my anxiety of not knowing what to expect in America or from the man I had recently met, and in fact, hardly knew. A man with whom I spent only two weeks, one in Beirut when we first met, and another a month later in Paris. But I was totally captivated and more than willing to risk it all. Everything about him seemed so adorable, his sense of humor and laugh that shook his body head to toe, his childlike excitement, and his love of life, especially food. I was even charmed by his broken Arabic. Most importantly, he loved me like no man ever had, and, despite his bad singing voice, he sang to me "You are the sunshine of my life." When we met in Paris, he gave me a Stevie Wonder album, which I played day and night until my sister Suad, whom I was living with in Beirut, got sick of it.

"For God's sake, Anan, stop it or I will break that stupid album."

"How dare you? It is the most beautiful song I have ever heard."

A couple of days before leaving Beirut, I was meticulously packing my bag. Suad, who was more than six years younger and whom I treated like my own daughter since the day she was born, was trying to help me decide what to take.

"I can't believe what I'm doing. It's kind of crazy, isn't it?"

"Of course it's crazy. You hardly know the man. And what if he turns out to be one of those mass killers we hear about, luring women to rape then murder them?"

"Thanks, sister, for the encouragement. You better shut up before I murder you."

Regardless of my sister's worries, nothing was going to stop me. I was young and foolish, and as the old proverb goes, *elhub a'ama*, love is blind.

By the time I arrived in Detroit I was totally drained. I walked off the plane dragging my swollen feet and stiff back, and there he was, standing right by the airplane gate[1] with his big assuring smile. He gave me a warm bear hug and held me tightly. I had been dreaming of this reunion for three months, and wanted to stay there, held by him, forever. I melted in his embrace, and could feel my anxiety and exhaustion slowly leaving my body.

The drive from the airport to Abdeen's home in northwest Detroit took almost half an hour. It was still daylight, but there was hardly a soul on the streets. The place looked totally deserted even as we drove through the neighborhoods. Coming from Lebanon where strikes and curfews were daily occurrences, I naively asked, "Is there a general strike or some kind of a curfew?" Abdeen laughed so hard tears rolled down his cheeks. He thought I had a great sense of humor.

"Welcome home," Abdeen said as we entered his house. "Let me show you around." He walked me through the two-bedroom first-floor flat. It had a spacious kitchen, a breakfast nook, a dining room, a large living room with a fireplace, and a bay window with leaded glass.

"I hope you like it. I bought it three years ago with my friend Victor Papakian. He is an Armenian American attorney with whom I also share an office. His family immigrated to Michigan from Aleppo, Syria. He lives upstairs. You'll get a chance to meet him in the next few days."

Before we had time to settle in, we heard a gentle knock at the door. Abdeen opened the door. "Hi, Victor, what's up?"

"I came to meet and welcome Anan." He walked toward me stretching his hand, while looking sheepishly at Abdeen. "Don't worry, I'm not staying."

"Welcome to Detroit. I've heard so much about you. Since Abdeen met you, he hasn't stopped talking about you."

"Thank you. Abdeen told me about you too. You live upstairs, correct?"

"Yes, I do. Did he also tell you he's been cleaning this place for two weeks?" Victor said, with a big grin on his face.

"Get out of here," Abdeen said.

As Victor found his way out the door, I looked around. The house looked rather clean, but I couldn't help but wonder how the place looked before.

ABDEEN'S HOUSE, A corner duplex on Wisconsin Street, was on the northwest side of Detroit, only a block from McNichols street and Marygrove College. A few days after I arrived, Abdeen was working late and the weather had cooled down a little, so I decided to explore the neighborhood. The houses on our street and the nearby streets, which I had seen as we drove by, were mostly single-family homes. They were very well kept with small front porches, trees, and a plethora of flowers, some of which I had never seen before. Since I came from an area with little water, I was impressed with how lush and green the neighborhood was. Walking back home feeling happy, I heard someone saying, "You're not planning to get hurt, are you?" I looked around, and there was an older African American man sitting on his front porch. I thought he could not be talking to me, but no one else was around.

Eager to meet some of the neighbors, I approached the man with a big smile. "Hello. My name is Anan. I'm visiting from Lebanon and staying with your neighbor Abdeen," I said, assuming he would know him. "Were you talking to me?"

"Yes, ma'am. I was talking to you. I was wondering if you're planning to get hurt?"

"I don't understand. Why would I want to do that?"

"Young lady, you should know better than to walk by yourself this time of day."

"Why?"

"Because it's not safe for a young woman to walk by herself. That's why. The people you're visiting should've told you so."

It was hardly dark.

My dad had been in Detroit in 1967 shortly after the rebellion.[2] He gave me the same advice before I headed to America. I wasn't sure I believed my dad or my neighbor, and wondered what these old men were thinking. After all, I had lived in countries that had their share of poverty, wars, and conflict, but had never felt unsafe walking the streets of Cairo, Amman, Damascus, or Beirut.

Although I tried to dismiss what the old man told me, I kept recalling his words. When Abdeen came home, I said, "One of your neighbors saw me walking this evening and told me it's not safe to be out by myself. Is that true?"

"What neighbor?"

"He's an older man, lives a few houses down the street. I didn't get his name."

"I wouldn't worry about it. But to be on the safe side, maybe you shouldn't walk late by yourself."

Hearing that was unsettling. Detroit seemed to be peaceful and quiet, actually too quiet for my taste. Then I remembered the deserted streets when we drove from the airport and wondered if that was why.

ON A NICE early spring day, sixteen months after I arrived in Detroit, I learned my lesson about safety the hard way. By then Abdeen and I were already married. Someone broke into our home, stole all my jewelry, cash, and much more. They stole my wedding rings, which were a gift from my mother-in-law. They also stole the necklace my mother sent me as a wedding gift. But losing my mother-in-law's rings was the most devastating. Those rings were a twenty-fifth anniversary gift from her husband. Although Abdeen and I decided not to tell her, she did find out about it, but never said a word.

Only a few days before the break-in, I was elected the treasurer of ACCESS,[3] a nonprofit social service organization in Dearborn. ACCESS was located in the South End of Dearborn, a working-class neighborhood where a large number of Arab Americans including recent immigrants had settled. I had around six hundred dollars in cash from dues and donations collected at the organization's annual meeting. I kept the money at home, intending to deposit it in the bank. Discovering that the cash was gone, I panicked, and pleaded with my husband: "Please, Abdeen, don't tell them their money was stolen. They'll think I'm either negligent or a thief."

"Don't be silly, no one will think that."

My husband and I never said a word to anyone about it. Since I was not working and had no money of my own, Abdeen paid the money back, which made me feel more indebted to him, a feeling I was starting to resent.

They, whoever they were, didn't only steal, but left a big mess behind. They broke juice and beer bottles and smashed raw eggs on the walls including the big mirror over the fireplace. Even my wedding picture was all messed up with the gluey yellow stuff. I was terrified by the invasion, thanking God I was not there when they came.

"What if they come back while I'm home alone?" I asked Abdeen, who was working long hours.

"Don't worry, *Aini*, they took what they wanted. They left nothing worth coming back for."

Filled with fear and anger I spent the following day cleaning and putting the house in order, cursing the thieves and their mothers. With my radical tendencies, I could understand that poor people might get desperate, and I could forgive them for stealing my stuff. But why create such a mess? I kept crying while cleaning. I don't know if I was crying because I had to deal with the mess by myself while Abdeen insisted that he had to go to work, or because I was so scared.

Overwhelmed with all the mess the thieves left behind, I kept cursing while cleaning. "Why? You sons of bitches… Why? You bastards." I said it over and over again. The thieves must have heard me. They came back the following day and set the house on fire. The damage was so severe we had to stay at a hotel that night. Luckily neither Abdeen nor I were home, but I was in a state of shock, to say the least. Abdeen was just as devastated seeing his first home destroyed, but being the man, he repressed his own feelings to comfort me.

"Who are these people, and why would they burn our home? They stole everything we have, so why set the house on fire? Why?" I kept asking Abdeen.

"The police are investigating, but we may never know."

"But what if they come back after we fix the house? I'm terrified. I don't want to live in that house or even in this country anymore."

"*Aini*, I'm sorry you have to go through this. Don't worry. We won't go back to this house. We'll buy a nicer home. I promise."

"What if they burn our new home?"

"They won't."

"How do you know?"

"It's not like this happens every day. You have to trust me. It won't."

With Abdeen's activism, including his support for the Palestinian struggle and suing the FBI for spying on him, people started to wonder if the fire was politically motivated, which only reinforced my paranoia. For months I suffered from insomnia, stomachaches, neck and shoulder pain, and more severe migraines. It took me at least a couple of years to stop worrying about it.

At the time of the fire, I was already enrolled in graduate school at Wayne State University (WSU). When I asked my professor to give me extra time to finish a paper, he said, "You should have known better than to live in that neighborhood."

"How cruel and insensitive that was," I told Diane and Stuart, the two friends I had recently made at WSU. "And what exactly did he mean by 'I should have known better?'"

"What a fucking racist," said Diane. "He would say that about Detroit no matter where you live."

"I should've told him to go to hell, but I was shocked, and didn't know how to respond."

"I'm glad you didn't. Just let it go. Don't let him bother you," said Stuart.

By then, a lot about living in America was already bothering me. But I was in love, and love is blind.

For the next three months, we lived with my husband's friend Naser in the affluent suburb of Grosse Point. He had inherited the house from his mother and was trying to sell it.

Some days while staying at Naser's I would go for walks. His neighborhood was "safe," and I could walk alone as long and as late as I wanted. I couldn't believe how large and beautiful the homes were with their perfectly manicured yards and a wide variety of flowers, bushes, and trees. They looked so grand and so white, just as I expected America to be from all the TV shows I watched growing up. But unlike TV,

I hardly saw anyone in the yards or on the streets. It was just as deserted as my older neighborhood in Detroit. Once in a while a dog would bark at me.

"Where are all the people?" I kept asking Abdeen.

"They are inside or at work."

"Why do they have such nice yards if they don't sit outside and enjoy them?"

"They usually sit in their backyards."

I didn't see much of that either.

To entertain myself while walking, I used to count the number of people I saw on the streets or in their yards. Then I would come home and tell my husband, "Guess what? Today I walked around the neighborhood for a whole hour and I saw three people." Sometimes it would be two, or one, or even none. Whether walking or driving, forty-some years later, I still catch myself counting the number of people on the streets.

While staying at Naser's, an African American medical doctor and his wife came to look at the house. That same night a neighborhood delegation of men and women came by to talk to Naser. There were at least ten of them.

"You wouldn't sell your home to these people, would you?"

"I am a man of the law and I'm not about to break it," said Naser, a nonpracticing attorney. "If they pay my asking price, of course I will."

"We were so good to your mother. How could you do this to us?"

During the three months we stayed at Naser's, Abdeen and I were looking for a new house. We were also considering buying his house. After that encounter, I told Abdeen, "I'm not sure I want to have these people as my neighbors."

"I don't blame you."

"With my brown skin and dark hair, I wonder if they would question Naser about allowing me to stay in their fancy neighborhood."

When we finally found a house that we both liked on Detroit's east side, the owner was willing to sell it below the market price. It was around June, and he wanted to get out of the neighborhood before the school year started. He did not want his daughter to be bussed to school with black kids.

The day we moved in, my new next-door neighbor, a widow of a policeman, said to me, "I'm glad you bought the house. I was afraid that some of those colored people would buy it. I'm too old to move."

My early lessons about racism in American were sinking in. Although an immigrant with a heavy accent and dark skin, to my new neighbor, I wasn't colored the same way as those other "colored" people.

CHAPTER 4
PRESERVING *OROOB* CULTURE

MANCELONA, MICHIGAN, SUMMER 1974

The two-hundred-and-forty-mile drive from Detroit to Mancelona took more than six hours. We kept hitting congested traffic on I-75, with so many people heading north to spend the weekend. Abdeen and I had not yet decided to get married. Nonetheless, he was dropping me at his mother's, while he went to Canada on a hunting trip with his two brothers. Hunting was not part of the culture I grew up with, but neither was a lot of American culture I had to learn and adjust to.

Abdeen was driving and listening to the radio while I was watching the road, admiring nature along the way. Although I had been on this road once before, I was still taken by the large size of the trees and the plethora of lush vegetation.

"Those are beautiful. What kind of trees are they?" I asked Abdeen.

"Different kinds. See those," he said, pointing. "They're oak trees...and those are maple...look how beautiful those pines are, and..." He got so excited, explaining and pointing, I was worried we might end up having an accident.

I don't know if I was really interested in learning the names of the different trees as much as wanting to distract myself from feeling anxious about spending ten days with Abdeen's mother, whom I hardly knew. The first time I saw her I was touched by her kindness and warmth. She kept telling me, "I'm so happy you and Abdeen met."

However, staying with someone I had visited only once in a small town of 1,200 people with no way out was rather nerve-wracking.

"You know my mother loves you, and so do my aunt and uncles. You're going to enjoy being with them."

"I'm sure I will," I said, trying to be polite. "But ten days is a lot of time. I hope I'm not imposing on them."

"Imposing? Don't be silly. They love having you. The days will go by real fast."

I could have chosen to stay at Abdeen's house. But I had no friends or family in Detroit, and had no car. On the other hand, I didn't want to ask Abdeen to cancel a trip he was looking forward to, so I agreed to spend the time with his family.

"How much longer do we have to drive? I'm getting restless and hungry," I told Abdeen after four hours of driving.

"Not long. We should be there in a couple of hours at the most. No later that 6:00."

"Two more hours? We could've driven from Amman to Beirut in less time," I said. "I'm hungry. Can we stop at a restaurant?"

"My mom and aunt are getting dinner ready. They'll be disappointed if we don't eat with them."

I knew better than to argue. I would have felt the same if I spent time cooking, only to have the expected guests tell me they had already eaten.

I had been to Mancelona once before and was overwhelmed by the hospitality of Abdeen's family. His mom, Mymonie, who was a gentle, tiny woman with hazel eyes and rosy cheeks, was living by herself. Her husband had died in a car accident almost twenty-five years ago when Abdeen was only ten. All of her kids, three girls and four boys, had already left home. Aunt Thahabiya, a good fifteen years younger than Mymonie, was a vibrant middle-aged woman, with a heart of gold that fit her name, which literally means "made of gold." She had a full house with her husband Mohammad and three sons. Her brother in-law Fayze, who never got married, was also living with them.

We arrived in Mancelona a little past 6:00 in the evening, heading first to Thahabiya's home. Mymonie and her two brothers were in the backyard, working in the large vegetable garden. They greeted me with warm hugs and kisses, as if they had known me forever.

"I'm so happy you're going to spend a few days with us," said Mymonie.

"Thanks. Me too," I said, trying to sound as genuine as possible.

Fayze and Mohammad said the same. Within minutes Fayze and Abdeen were joking, patting each other on the back, and laughing really loud. Thahabiya must have heard us. She came hurriedly from the kitchen with her apron and a large wooden spoon in her hand to greet us.

"*Ahlan wa Sahlan*… Welcome. Happy you're here." After giving us hugs and kisses, she said, "Come on in. Dinner is ready. You must be starving."

"Let me show them the vegetable garden first," Fayze said.

"They can see it later."

"It'll be dark after dinner."

"As you like. But don't be late. The food will get cold," Thahabiya said as she walked inside the house.

My stomach was growling and the prospect of not eating right away did not suit me. Hunger tends to trigger my migraines and alter my mood. But as a guest, I kept quiet, hoping it wouldn't be long before we ate.

The two worlds-apart brothers were competing to show us their garden. Mohammad, the older brother, who was still working as a school custodian, was a quiet soft-spoken man. He smiled a lot and said little. His gentle demeanor resembled that of his sister. Fayze, a retired car dealer, was loud, opinionated, and had a large presence. In many ways, he and Abdeen were alike. I couldn't help but notice the special bond between them. As we walked through their garden, both brothers were proudly pointing to what they had. "See this *kussa*, the small Arabic zucchinis, we got the seeds from the old country. Look how beautiful they are, just the perfect size. I picked some this morning and Thahabiya cored and stuffed them with rice and meat. We'll have some for dinner. You are going to love them. And these cucumbers, we also got the seeds from the old country. We pick them small while they're still tender. Here, taste one."

"How do you manage to get seeds from the old country?" I asked.

"Whenever someone we know goes back to Lebanon, we ask them to get us some, and we have our own. See these huge *kussas* and cucumbers? We let them grow so we can use the seeds for the next season."

The two brothers went on and on, talking about their garden's different kinds of tomatoes, okra, green beans, and the variety of herbs, picking leaves of mint, rosemary, and sage, and having me smell them. They talked about their plants with as much pleasure as if they were talking about a piece of art. But Fayze dominated most of the conversation. He was also arguing with his sister about whose garden was more beautiful. I was enthralled by the level of their passion and pride, and by the not-so-subtle competition between Fayze and Mymonie.

I was starving and getting bitten by mosquitos, but embarrassed to walk away from their enthusiasm. Luckily Thahabiya came yelling, "Come on in. Let's eat. The food is getting cold."

The large dining table was covered with platters of *kibbeh, mujadarah,* rice, green beans, stuffed grape leaves, stuffed *kussa,* tabbouleh, and yogurt-cucumber salad. There was enough to feed an army.

"My God, Thahabiya. This looks just beautiful. You must've spent days cooking. You didn't have to do all this."

"I don't mind. Mymonie helped me. We're happy to have you."

"I cannot believe this. Here I am, thousands of miles and oceans away from home, only to find the freshest and finest Arabic food one can dream of."

"It all came from the vegetable garden you just saw," Fayze said.

"Wait till you taste it," Abdeen said. "Thahabiya and my mom are the best cooks ever."

"My mother never cooks like this," I said.

"No? How come?" Abdeen asked.

"She hates cooking and housework. But she loves working at her print shop and bossing around the men who work for her."

After dinner the three men, Abdeen and his two uncles, moved to a smaller table to play cards, while Thahabiya and Mymonie started clearing the dining table, putting the food away, and washing the pots and dishes. I was exhausted but felt embarrassed not to join the women, both much older than me. Meanwhile, the men kept asking for more coffee and desserts. Although I am used to seeing women serve men, I was a little taken aback. I grew up and came of age in the 1960s and had watched American women on TV demanding equality and burning their bras. I assumed some of that rebellious spirit would have reached Mancelona. But obviously it didn't.

Once the cleaning was done, I found a comfortable chair and sat waiting to go to Mymonie's house to sleep. The two women sat on the couch next to each other. They pulled their knitting bags and started to work on what seemed to be small blankets or scarves. I wanted to ask them what they were making, or act curious and interested, but I was too tired. The three men were engrossed in their game, arguing and laughing. When Abdeen saw me dozing off, he said, "Let me finish this one. It won't be long." But it must have been two or three games later when he said, "Let's go." When I opened my eyes, Mymonie and Thahabiya were sound asleep on the couch with their knitting resting on their laps.

By the time we got to Mymonie's it was almost midnight. We entered the house from the attached two-car garage. She had no car. I don't think she ever drove. The garage was filled with all sorts of things: pillows, newspapers, coffee tables, chairs, pots, clothes, garden tools, and fruit. You name it, it was there. Except for a narrow pathway leading to the kitchen, there wasn't an empty inch. Her three-floor, six-bedroom house, which she occupied alone, was as packed as her garage. All her children had left years ago, but she kept every single item of their belongings since they were born, and much more. Although I had been at her house once before, I was still fascinated by the amount of stuff she had piled up over the years.

Mymonie, who was only three years old when she arrived in the US, grew up poor on a North Dakota farm. Her father, Ahmed Melhem, first immigrated to Mexico in 1894. A few years later, he came to the US and homesteaded in North Dakota, following in the footsteps of earlier Lebanese immigrants. At the time, the government was giving 160 acres to anyone who was willing to farm the land for five consecutive years. Once he secured the title to the land, Ahmed went back to Lebanon to get married. After his first child, Mymonie, was born in 1906, he came back to the US by himself. His wife and daughter followed him in 1909. Mymonie's other four siblings, three boys and one girl, were born in North Dakota.

Life on the big farm was unforgiving, as Mymonie describes it. "Winter was terribly harsh and the snow drifts were very high—one could hardly see anything but white stuff. We had to tie a rope between the barn and the house so we didn't get lost." The combination of isolation and poverty made it hard for Mymonie to get rid of things. As she used to say, "I'll never know when I'll need it."

Mymonie directed her son and me to separate bedrooms, as she had in our previous visit, although she knew we had been living together for the last two months. I kissed Abdeen good night and walked to my assigned room, smiling, and remembering her telephone call the day I came to the US. After asking Abdeen if I had arrived safely, she wanted to know where I would be staying. When Abdeen said, "She is staying with me," her response was, "What are people going to say about us?"

"I'm surprised to hear your mom say this. She lived all her life in the US, and she's still concerned about what people might say?" I told Abdeen.

"Well, my grandparents brought the old country with them and passed it along to their kids."

"And they managed to preserve their Lebanese village culture for three generations! That's impressive."

The following morning, I woke up after 10:00 to an empty house. I went to the yard looking, and there she was, with her apron, scarf, and a sweater on, working in her vegetable garden. The weather was cool and refreshing.

"Good morning, Um Khalid."[4] Not sure how to address her, I called her by her oldest son's name, mother of Khalid, as is tradition in the Arab world.

"Good morning. I'm glad you had time to rest. You must be hungry. Let me fix you something to eat."

"Don't worry about it. I'll take care of myself. Where is Abdeen?"

"He went to see his Uncle Fayze. He asked me to call him as soon as you woke up."

Mymonie took off her gloves, rinsed her hands with the hose, and came in the house. I followed her. The kitchen was as packed as the rest of the house. There was hardly a spot for a single plate. She handed me a cup of coffee while I sat at the kitchen table, uncomfortable with being served. I wanted to fix my own breakfast but I didn't know how. It was impossible to find anything. She must have read my mind when she said, "I'm sorry the kitchen is a mess. I wanted to straighten the house before you came but I had no time. The yard is a lot of work."

"I know. Don't worry about it."

For the next ten days, I watched with fascination how Abdeen's family was trying so hard to protect their extended family and preserve their culture, even after three quarters of a century. Other than their sister Mary and her family, they were the only Arab Americans living in Mancelona. At one point, another

Lebanese family, the Jajays, also lived in Mancelona but had left when Abdeen was only seven. Mymonie saw her brothers and had dinner at their home almost daily, and they all seemed to be content with each other's company. Most of the time, Thahabiya cooked while Mymonie helped clean and wash the dishes. After dinner, the men retreated to read the newspaper, watch TV, or when they had company, play cards. The women on the other hand, were always busy washing dishes, cleaning, making cheese or yogurt, canning fruit and vegetables, or baking. I don't recall seeing them visit friends, go for a walk, or sit down for a coffee without doing something. Resting or idle hands for these two women were alien concepts. When too tired to do physical labor, they crocheted blankets of all sizes and colors without having a clue what to do with them. They had handmade blankets on every single couch and bed, and they were gifting them to people whether they wanted them or not. I still have at least three of them, and so do their children, grandchildren, and great grandchildren.

Some days, while Mymonie was busy with her vegetable garden, I would walk to Thahabiya's. Her home was livelier with many people stopping by, including the neighbors, her sons' classmates, Mohammad's coworkers, or Fayze's friends. She had coffee percolating all day long, and food ready to feed whomever stopped by her house. She would also insist that people take some of the garden's vegetables. Later, with so many people coming and going, I started to tease Thahabiya, calling her home "the Mancelona train station."

Fayze also spent a few hours a day tending to his vegetable garden. Sometimes he would drive Mymonie, Thahabiya, and me to an orchard to pick berries, peaches, or grape leaves. We would come back with huge amounts, only to spend the evening or the following day canning or making jam. Other days the two women would send Fayze to the store to buy milk to make yogurt and cheese. And of course, they picked vegetables from their own gardens to cook all summer long. They stacked the endless shelves and multiple freezers in their basements with homegrown canned and frozen food as if the world was about to be hit with the worst famine.

Then came making the *marqook,* a traditional paper-thin bread. Thahabiya, who worked as hard as Mymonie but kept her house in much neater shape, had a stove and a *saj* in her basement that was especially designed to make bread. While I never baked before, I enjoyed the company of the two women as they spent hours baking, talking, and laughing. Thahabiya would stretch the dough with a circular hand movement, similar to making pizza, but to a much thinner and larger size. After baking it on top of the hot *saj*, she would hand it to Mymonie to cool on long sheet-covered tables. They would pause once in a while to brush each loaf with melted butter. Once the bread cooled, they would carefully fold each loaf several times, then pack a dozen loaves in a plastic bag. After watching them do that a couple of times, I joined them brushing and folding the bread. It smelled delicious, and I couldn't resist the temptation.

"This looks so good. Can I have some?" I asked.

"Of course you can," said both women in unison.

As I started tearing a loaf, Thahabiya said, "Wait. Let me go get you some cheese and marmalade."

"Please don't. I like it just like this."

The two women spent a whole day making enough bread to give to all of Mymonie's seven children and still had enough to feed people who would pass by Thahabiya's home.

"I've been trying to teach my daughters and granddaughters how to make *marqook*, but no one is interested. I'm hoping you'll keep the tradition," Mymonie said as they started making the bread, hinting that I would end up marrying her son.

"But I never baked bread," I said.

"How come? Did your mother not teach you?"

Little did she know about my mother! I laughed just imagining my mom in the kitchen baking with flour covering her clothes, the counters, and the floor, while cursing her family and husband for making her work so hard.

"My mother never baked bread. We just bought it. Most people did."

"You bought bread in the old country? For real?" She stared at me, bewildered. Her eyebrows moved upward, and her eyes doubled their size. She was also surprised by the fact that we never made jam, cheese, or yogurt. I, on the other hand, was amazed how and when they learned to make all that food.

"Did Thahabiya teach you how to make the *marqook*?" I asked. Thahabiya grew up in a Lebanese village, and came to the US in her early twenties.

"No, I learned it from my mother. In North Dakota, where my family settled, there were no nearby stores. We had to bake our own bread and make our own cheese and yogurt. We also had to milk the cows. My dad managed to make a *saj* for my mother. There were no gas stoves then, so we used wood to bake."

Due to North Dakota's isolated living, Mymonie's parents never learned English. They managed to pass on to the children, not only the language, but also their village culture. It was 1974, and they were still holding on to what was most dear to them—the *oroob* ways.

Abdeen's father, Mohammad, or Sam as he was called, also came from a small village in Lebanon. Upon arrival to the US in 1910, he went to Boyne City, Michigan, where a number of men from his village were working on the railroad or a tannery. They helped him find a job in a tannery, and suggested he take an American name, Sam.

"No one can pronounce Mohammad," they told him. "You better choose a simple name." And he did.

Sam also joined his fellow villagers, all single men, and lived in a boarding house. After a few years he was injured at the tannery, so he quit his job and bought the boarding house he was living in. When WWI broke out, he joined the US Army along with his Lebanese friends. But Sam was soon discharged because of his health. He sold the boarding house and moved to Mancelona to work at a friend's grocery store, which he ended up buying. After thirteen years of being in the US, Sam was ready to settle down.

"My dad was determined to marry a Lebanese Muslim girl," Abdeen told me once.

"But how did he and your mother meet? It's not like Michigan is next door to North Dakota."

"My dad knew some Lebanese peddlers who traveled throughout the country. They were the ones who led him to my mom."

After getting married, Sam asked Mymonie if she would like to live in Detroit or Mancelona. For someone whose closest neighbor in North Dakota was miles away, Mancelona, with a population of 1,200, was large enough.

Mymonie and all seven kids worked in the family store. Like his wife, Abdeen's father was adamant about teaching the children Arab culture, or the *oroob* ways, as they used to call it, including speaking the language. As Abdeen described it, "We used to get embarrassed when my father spoke to us in Arabic in front of our friends or the store's customers. One time, my brother Khalid asked him not to talk to him in Arabic in front of other people. My dad got so mad, he told him, 'I'm going to speak to you in Arabic in the store, in the street, and at home.'"

After Mymonie's mother died, her father, two brothers, and sister followed her to Mancelona. Gradually the Jabara-Melhems created their own community with aunts, uncles, and many children and cousins. Life was good as long as they were able to speak their language, grow their own vegetables, cook their food, and socialize with each other. Among the most important part of the culture they preserved was that men were men and women were women. And each understood and performed his or her assigned gender roles.

One morning while Mymonie and I were having breakfast, I asked her, "How did the people in Mancelona react when you and your siblings moved here?"

"What do you mean?"

"You are the only Arab Muslims in this town. Were people ever hostile to you?"

"No, never. They were all nice to us. Most were our store customers."

That was a far cry from what Arab American immigrants were experiencing in Dearborn, Michigan. I wondered if their small number and fair skin with light-colored eyes made them more welcome.

By the end of my ten-day visit, Mymonie realized that I wouldn't be the one who was going to preserve much of the *oroob* culture she was trying hard to pass on to her daughters and granddaughters.

"Sorry, Um Khaled. I wasn't able to help you make *marqook* or cheese. I hope you still love me," I said kiddingly as I was saying goodbye to her.

She laughed. "You're a city girl, but I haven't given up on you learning."

In spite of my shortcomings in the area of making bread and cheese, Mymonie was still excited that her charming Abdeen had found a woman from the "old country," who would hopefully soon be wedded to her favorite son.

CHAPTER 5
THEY MARRY A LOT AND DIVORCE A LOT

DETROIT, FALL 1974

"Abdeen," I pleaded, "I need to find something to do, a paid or volunteer job. I'm going out of my mind staying home by myself most days."

"*Aini*, you're on a visitor visa. You can't work."

"How about volunteering?"

"Your English is not that good. Please be patient."

"I simply can't live like this."

"This won't last forever. Once we get married, you'll get your green card as the wife of an American citizen, and your English will get better with time." He paused for a few seconds then said, "We do plan to get married. Don't we?"

"Of course. But first, I need to muster the courage to tell my parents. I'm not sure they're going to like it. Remember, I haven't told them about you yet."

"But sooner or later you need to do it."

"I know, *wallah*, I know," I said trying to hide my anxiety.

Abdeen got off his seat and gave me a hug. "*Aini*, you worry too much. Trust me, everything is going to be fine."

When I came to the US, I told my parents my trip was work-related. As liberal as they might have been and as much as they wanted me to be independent, I was not ready to tell them the real story. *I met him in Beirut. We fell madly in love and spent a week together. A month later we spent another week in Paris. He sent me money to buy a plane ticket to visit him in Detroit, and I will be staying with him.* I was so infatuated with my new love that I wasn't about to let anything or anyone keep me away from him.

Our wedding date was set for November 23, 1974, my thirtieth birthday. I wrote a letter to my parents claiming I met Abdeen in Detroit. I could have called, but I was not ready to lie to them directly or deal with their reaction over the phone.

In my letter I made a point to elaborate on all of his credentials, his charm and pure Lebanese Arab bloodline. I also wrote kiddingly, "He is blond with hazel eyes." I thought that would make him more appealing to my mother since she used to tell me, "If you ever get married, be sure he is fair. Otherwise your kids will be too dark." My mother told me this often, which infuriated me. Although most Arabs are dark, and my mother claimed to have married my dad because he looked like Gandhi, she, like most people in our region, favored light skin.

"I am afraid they're not going to like me getting married so far away, or not knowing the man who is soon to be their son-in-law. I don't think being fair or even blond will go that far with my mother," I told Abdeen, teasing, trying to make light of my apprehension while waiting to hear from my parents.

A week or so later my parents called. As expected, they were not thrilled about the news. Actually, my mother freaked out.

"What do you mean you are getting married in America? People who go there don't come back. We will never see you again." Then she started crying.

"Mama, please don't cry. You should be happy for me. Of course you will see me. It is only a plane ride away."

"It is too far. Look at me, I forever regret marrying far from my family."

My mother was always complaining about living in Amman away from her Damascene family, which was only 125 miles away. I believe what she missed most was the luxury of her rich family. She felt cheated out of a good life by being married to my father. "I should have stayed single like Suad and Nahida. They're much happier than me," she said, referring to her two older sisters.

"But, Mama, I want to get married."

"You don't expect me to say yes before I even meet the man? We have to know him, to learn about his background and his family. Let him come here and ask for your hand like a real gentleman. Your dad and I have to know who you're getting married to. You have your wedding here, where your family and friends are, not in America, not like an orphan who has no family or knows no one."

I started telling her about all the great and unique characteristics of my future husband, and then some. I went on to tell her how much of a gentleman he was and how wonderful and welcoming his family had been.

"Mama, I'm not that young anymore. We plan to get married on my birthday."

"On your birthday! That's too soon. You mean to tell me you're getting married in less than two months?" She started crying again.

"Why can't you understand? I love him."

"Love doesn't last. Trust me. You will regret it later." Then she added, "When you get old, and you *will* sooner than you think, you're going to be so lonely away from your family and friends."

"Mama. Please. You don't have to be so dramatic. I know what I'm doing."

Our conversation went back and forth for a while, and the phone bill was getting bigger by the minute. When my mother realized that I wasn't about to change my mind, she found a new frontier of attack.

"How old is he? Your father is too old for me."

In spite of my frustration with the way our conversation was going, I smiled. My mother never missed a chance to complain about my dad.

"He is thirty-four. Only four years older than me."

"He must have been married before. Americans marry young. Does he have any children?"

"No, Mama. He has no children and was never married."

"If I were you, I would double-check. These Americans, they marry a lot and divorce a lot."

Poor mother, little did she know that in the future, two of her three daughters would end up divorced.

My dad, on the other hand, told me, "I trust you, Anan, but this has come as a surprise to us. We need time to think about it. I want to ask my friend who lives in Detroit to check him out, to find information about him. As you can tell, your mom is very upset. We need to give her time."

"So, when will I hear from you?

"Soon, *Inshallah*."

Three weeks later, I received a letter from my dad, blessing my choice. "You're old enough to make your own decisions and I trust your judgment. The only thing I want from you is to have the right of divorce. This is the only thing I asked of your sister Arwa when she got married. I hope you will never need it, but just in case." My dad was not aware of the no-fault divorce law in Michigan, which allows either spouse to get a divorce without the consent of the other partner.

After the wedding, my parents called to congratulate us. At the end of the conversation my dad said, "Your mom and I always wanted you to get your PhD like your sister Arwa. Take advantage of the great universities in America. Getting married shouldn't stop you from pursuing your education."

IT WOULDN'T HAVE bothered either one of my parents if none of their three daughters got married. But when it came to our education, they were on a mission. This was virtually the only thing my mother and father saw eye to eye on. I remember my mother telling us over and over again, "In our culture, your brother"—her only son and the apple of her eye—"can sell vegetables on the street corner, and that would not be *eib*. As a woman, what can you do without a good education?"

Who ever thought sexism could be useful sometimes!

As a teenager, I didn't really care for school, and I wasn't a particularly good student. I was not interested in boys that much either. But when it came to politics, demonstrations, and rebellion, these were my passion. After all, I came of age in the early 1960s, and the whole world was rebelling and demanding freedom. I wanted my freedom too, including coming and going as I pleased. My mother made it crystal clear that I had no chance of getting my freedom before getting my university degree no matter how much I cried or argued. To her that was the natural order of progression. To put it in her own words, "Get me that *kartooneh*"—referring to a university degree—"then you can put one foot in the East and one foot in the West, and I'll never ask you where you're going, or what you're doing."

I got my BA from the University of Jordan in 1968 and was ready to declare my independence. I was so happy to hand my mother "that *kartooneh*."

"A BA? In this time and age? It barely amounts to a high school diploma in my time. What kind of a job are you going to get with a BA in sociology? You need to go to graduate school."

"But you said…."

"I didn't mean a BA. No daughter of mine is going to settle for such little education."

I went to Cairo University and got my MA in sociology. A year after I came back to Amman, I decided to quit my job at the television station and go to Lebanon. Not only did I want to get away from the increasing political repression in Jordan, but I also wanted to get away from my parents. I was missing the taste of freedom I enjoyed in Cairo. When my mother failed to convince me to stay at my job or find another job in Amman, she starting nagging me about my education. "Don't you want to get your PhD? Wouldn't it be wonderful to be called *doctora*? You can find a job as a university professor. Look at your sister, Arwa—"

"No, no, and no. Please, Mama, Stop. I'm leaving for Beirut. I plan to find a job and settle there."

Soon I left for Beirut. I only had her partial blessing and some cash to help me start my new life. But whenever I saw her or my dad, they would ask me if I had given more thought to getting my PhD.

Unlike most women of her generation, my mother rarely wore makeup or jewelry other than her wedding ring and a set of gold bracelets, a gift from her mother. For special occasions, she would wear lipstick and a pearl necklace. I particularly liked one of her necklaces, a choker with five strings of seed pearls. Like my mother, I didn't wear much makeup or jewelry. However, occasionally I would ask her if I could have her pearl choker.

"You can have it after I die."

"But I don't want it after you die. I might feel too sad to wear it. And what if I die before you?"

"You're not going to die before me."

"How do you know?"

"I know. Besides, I got this from my mother as a wedding gift. I'm not ready to give it up."

My mother and I had this conversation more than once, but to no avail. She was not giving it up.

A FEW MONTHS after I got married, I received a phone call from a friend of my mother who was visiting her brother in Michigan. She was bringing me a wedding gift from my mother.

"What is it?' I asked anxiously.

"A necklace. It is very beautiful and looks rather expensive. I don't want to carry it around. I'd like you to come and get it as soon as you can."

I was thrilled to finally get the necklace. My mother's mother had given it to her as a wedding gift and she was giving it to me. I could not wait to get it. I started describing the necklace to Abdeen, telling him how long I had been asking for it. To my surprise, it was not her necklace, the one I had been wanting for so long. Instead it was a new one she must have bought for me. *How selfish can a mother be? I never asked her for much,* I thought to myself. In fact, I was so upset I wished she had never sent me a wedding gift. I stuck it in my dresser and never wore it. But I was heartbroken when it was stolen along with other jewelry when our home in Detroit was robbed. After all, it was my mother's wedding gift. At the same time, I was happy my mother never gave me her necklace. At least with her it was safe.

In the US, away from my parents' pressure, I decided to get my PhD in sociology from Wayne State University. Soon after I graduated in 1981, my mother came to visit. When I met her at the airport, she hugged me so tight, her eyes swelled with tears. *"Mabrook, Doctora.* You have no idea how happy and proud you make me."

Once we settled in at home she opened her purse and said, "I have a gift for you." From the box I could tell it was another piece of jewelry. To my utter surprise it was her necklace, the choker I always wanted.

"Oh, Mama, this is a real surprise. I expected you to give it to me when I got married, but when you didn't, I thought I'd never get it."

She looked me straight in the eye and said, "Marriage is not an accomplishment. A PhD is."

CHAPTER 6
WE DO NOT THINK LIKE THIS IN MANCELONA

DETROIT AND MANCELONA, 1974

"Hi, Mother," I heard Abdeen saying. It was almost midnight. "I'm fine... Anan is fine... No, you didn't wake us up... We were out... Mom, stop worrying. Everything is taken care of... Mother, why can't you understand? I told you, she doesn't want a wedding ring. I've already asked her... No, she's not only saying that... Fine, fine. I'll take care of it. Don't worry... I will... I will."

I believe Mymonie was more excited about the wedding than I was. Every night she would call to inquire about the big day's plans. She wanted to be sure we were not missing any important details like inviting her sister Mary, although she and Mary were not that close. She wanted to be sure that every guest had a place to stay. She wanted us to approve her choice of the wedding cake. Then there was the music, the food, and of course there was the wedding dress and the ring. The list of what needed to be taken care of was endless. "Just because she has no family living here doesn't mean she shouldn't get the best wedding," she kept telling her son. "If you don't have the money, I'll pay for it."

One night, Abdeen's mom called to check if we had booked Imam Kharoub. "Did you call him?" she asked. Before Abdeen had a chance to answer, she went on, "He's a busy man. You need to give him enough time to arrange his schedule so he can travel to Mancelona."

"Mother, we don't need Imam Kharoub. We're planning to have a civil marriage."

"Your dad would be very upset if you don't have a Muslim wedding," Mymonie protested.

"But Anan and I would rather go to City Hall, get married, then come up north for the wedding reception."

"Imam Kharoub married all your brothers and sisters, and I want his son to marry you." By then the father had passed away and his son became the new imam.

"If that would make your mother happy, it's fine with me. It's not worth her getting upset," I told Abdeen. I, however, was amazed by her wish. I wasn't sure what being a Muslim meant to her or to her family, since no one practiced or even knew much about it.

While I was happy to be getting married to Abdeen, I was not into religious ceremonies or traditional weddings with a ring, cake, and a white bridal dress. I was also quite indifferent about the wedding food, guests, and venue. I didn't have a single friend or relative in the US to invite, and no one in my family was able to come. True, I had met Abdeen's family and friends, but I hadn't been in the US long enough to feel close to any of them. The only two people I felt some bond with were Mymonie and Abdeen's friend Dick, who was traveling with him when we first met in Beirut. In spite of the outpouring of love from everyone, I couldn't escape the sadness and loneliness that engulfed me on my wedding day. I kept wondering if I should have listened to my mother and gone home to get married.

THE DAY BEFORE the wedding, we arrived in Mancelona in the early afternoon. Abdeen's mother, Mymonie, was waiting for us in her front yard. Although I had met her before, I was still amazed by her small size, especially after she had given birth to seven children, all big and stocky. She hugged me and held on to me. I could smell dirt and sweat. She must have been doing what she liked best, working in the yard. It was an unusually warm day for late November.

"Welcome to our family. This is a happy day for me. I was afraid he would never get married, just like his Uncle Fayze."

"Come in, have a seat," she said. I looked, but couldn't find a single empty spot to sit. The house looked just as packed as when I first saw it. She moved quickly to empty part of the sofa. I was amazed by her energetic, flexible small body. She did not act or look seventy-one. She had a few age lines surrounding her small eyes. Her face was tanned and her cheeks were red, even in November. Her light brown hair had a few strands of gray, and she smiled a lot.

"I meant to straighten the house before the wedding, but I haven't had the time. Please excuse me."

"Don't worry about it," I said, "I only need a small space."

After she secured a spot for me, she went to the kitchen and brought two folding chairs. She struggled to find a couple of spots for them. Abdeen tried to help. Finally, the three of us were seated.

Soon Abdeen's nephew Jim came by to greet us, and Mymonie had to fetch a chair for him. After we settled in, she said, addressing her grandson, "I'm so happy your uncle found a wife from the old country. Anan is so smart. Can you believe it? She can read and write Arabic." Then she turned to me and said, "Am I correct?"

"Of course I can," I responded, not understanding the source of her amusement. After all I grew up, lived, and worked in Arab countries until I came to the US.

When it was time to go to bed, she put us, Abdeen and me, in separate rooms, as she had during our previous visits. I thought that was funny, but said nothing. She knew I was living with her son, and we were getting married the following day. But I learned about denial when it comes to premarital sex from the society I grew up in, including my liberal parents. Not only would they never talk about sex with their children, they would never acknowledge that premarital sex even existed. I should have expected that Mymonie would definitely keep the tradition of sex-denial very much alive.

The morning of the wedding, I sat drinking a cup of coffee on the corner of the sofa she had emptied for me the night before. As I was about to finish my coffee, Mymonie came down the stairway. She took the pile of clothes next to me, put it on the floor and then sat down. "I have something for you," she said, while putting one arm around my shoulders. The softness of her voice and the warmth of her touch triggered emotions I had never experienced before. I felt affection, happiness, and sadness all at the same time. I felt the kind of unconditional love not even my own mother was ever able to give me. I struggled not to cry.

Mymonie must have felt the intensity of my emotions. She sat there still for a few minutes, then reached in her apron pocket and pulled out an old wrapped handkerchief. She had a hard time taking off the rusty safety pin. Curious, I watched as she carefully unwrapped it. To my surprise, she unveiled what seemed to be an expensive set of wedding rings, one with a large diamond, and a matching band with five small diamonds.

"My husband gave me these for our twenty-fifth anniversary. I've had them wrapped since he died. They're yours now," she said as she handed me the rings.

I was totally taken aback. I had not known Mymonie but for a few months, and I had visited her only twice before, but I was so overwhelmed and humbled by this simple woman's kindness and generosity.

"No. No, Mother. I can't take them. Please. I just can't."

"But this is my wedding gift to you."

"Abdeen didn't get me a ring because I didn't want one. Otherwise he would have."

"I'm giving these to you because I want you to have them."

"You ought to give them to one of your daughters or granddaughters. I don't feel right taking them."

"You're my daughter, and I love you more than you know."

"I love you too," I said, wiping a couple of escaping tears. I wondered what I had done to deserve this woman's love.

I wanted to give the rings back, but Abdeen said, "Please don't. If you do, she will be really hurt." I wore the rings twice, once on my wedding day, and once when she visited us a few months after we got married. By her second visit, the rings, along with my other jewelry, had been stolen. I felt guilty and sad, as if part of me had been ripped away. Abdeen and I never mentioned the theft to Mymonie, but one of my sisters-in-law did, although she was sworn to secrecy. I often wonder if she did that because she was upset that I was the one to get the ring rather than her, her daughter, or one of her other two sisters.

BY THE THIRD year of our marriage, Abdeen and I started to host family Thanksgiving dinners. Mymonie, or Mother, as I called her, would come a few days earlier to help. By the time she left, every windowsill, counter, and table would be packed with bowls, cups, and small plates filled with spices. She would spend her time, while Abdeen and I were at work, trying to straighten my kitchen by emptying all the half-full spice jars with the intention of putting them in smaller ones. To her, putting the spices in the right size jar was like an unsolved puzzle that I had to solve after she left. "I'm sorry I didn't have time to take care of the spices. I just couldn't find the right size jars. Next time I will bring a few empty ones. I have a lot in my house." I had no doubt she had all the right sizes for everything one could think of. I was hoping she wouldn't start bringing any to my home!

On one of her Thanksgiving visits, I came home early from work, only to find her tackling the spice jars again. "You're home early," she said. "Are you all right? You must be hungry. Let me fix you something to eat. How about something to drink?" Being raised by a mother who hated housework and taking care of kids made it hard for me to deal with so much affection and love.

"Mother, I am feeling fine," I interrupted. "I came home early to take you with me to the grocery store. You've been stuck home all day. It's nice out. Why don't you put your coat on and come with me?"

"No, honey, I can't go. I will have the kitchen counters clear by the time you come back."

I had learned not to push her. While Mymonie was extremely gentle, she was also very stubborn. I had a cup of coffee with her and then left. By the time I came back, she was still working at it. She, however, helped me cook dinner and as always, insisted on washing the dishes. After we ate, I started preparing for Thanksgiving dinner. Cooking for thirty or so people, all with healthy appetites, required at least a couple of days.

"Mother, you must be tired. Why don't you join Abdeen in the living room?"

"Honey, I'm not going to leave you alone in the kitchen. Maybe I'm not much help, but at least I can keep you company."

During the entire time I cooked, Mymonie would give me her instructions: "Honey, don't waste that much of the parsley." "Honey, don't peel that much of the onions." "Honey, don't keep the water running." After a while I would go to Abdeen, who was watching TV, begging him to take his mother out of the kitchen.

"But I have to help her. She can't cook all this food by herself," she would say protesting. Once in a while she would go to the living room to ask Abdeen if he wanted something to eat or drink.

Around 11:00, Abdeen came to the kitchen to say good night. Mymonie followed him upstairs only to come back a few minutes later.

"Mother, it's getting late. Why don't you go to sleep too?"

"No. I won't go to sleep before you. I just went upstairs to use the bathroom. To my surprise I saw Abdeen fixing the bed. Had I noticed the bed was not made, I would've fixed it."

"Why should you? He can fix the bed. After all, he sleeps in it."

"Honey, I know he can. But poor son, he works so hard. It's late, and he must be very tired."

"I know he's your baby, but even if he worked hard all day, he has done nothing since he came home. I've been working all day. You too. Don't you think we're more tired than he is?" I tried my best not to sound irritated.

She was quiet for a while. Then she said, "I guess you're right. But, honey, we don't think like this in Mancelona."

CHAPTER 7
AINI IN WONDERLAND

DETROIT, 1975

"Good morning, *Aini*. Can you please get up?" said my husband. His cheerful voice told me it wasn't that urgent. I pretended not to hear him.

"Please, *Aini*, get up. I need your help," he insisted.

"What do you want? It's too early. It's dark and cold. Leave me alone, I want to sleep."

"*Aini*, my shirt button came loose. Can you please fix it?"

"You're kidding me. You woke me up for this? You have tons of shirts. Wear another one," I said as I covered my head and turned my back on him.

"But I want to wear this one. How about if I bring you a cup of coffee and you fix my shirt?"

Not wanting to get into an early morning discussion about shirts, I said, "Fair enough. Let me first have my coffee, then get me a needle and white thread."

"We don't have any."

"I'm not a magician. How do you expect me to sew a button without that? You go ahead and wear another shirt. Later, I will go to a store and buy some."

"Go to Hudson's," he said excitedly. "You might find other things you like. They have everything."

I had already been to Hudson's. How could I not? It was one of the first places Abdeen pointed out to me while driving through downtown Detroit. "See that building? That is Hudson's. It is the largest department store in the world. It has everything. You name it, they have it. We'll go there soon."

Sure enough, Abdeen took me to Hudson's shorty after. He wanted to buy new sheets and towels in honor of my visit. I was wondering how he could find what he wanted in such a huge place, but he did.

Recalling that visit, I asked Abdeen, "Isn't there a store close by I can walk to? Hudson's is too far and too big. How am I going to find needles and thread there?"

"I'm not aware of any nearby store. Besides, Hudson's is a fun place. People come from near and far to shop there. If you can get ready within fifteen minutes, I can take you. But we have to go to my office first. I don't think they're open this early."

"It's too early for me too. Don't worry, I'll manage."

While shopping or sewing weren't my favorite activities, I was happy to be on a mission that would take a few hours and break up the monotony of my day.

When I got on my first bus, I asked the driver for a transfer, and sat watching the passengers as they came on and off the bus. Except for two young men who looked like students, all the other passengers were African Americans. I was wondering if white Americans actually rode buses, or just drove their own cars. My thoughts were interrupted when the bus arrived at my transfer stop at Woodward and McNichols. As I was leaving, I noticed an older woman with a bunch of grocery bags struggling to get off the bus. Her heavy weight did not help. She would carry a couple of bags, put them down by the bus entrance and then go back to get more. Without even thinking, I grabbed the grocery bags from where she left them. When I saw her jaw drop and her bewildered eyes grow big, I said, "I'm trying to help you carry your bags to the ..."

Before I could finish my sentence, she started screaming, "Give me back my bags. Leave them there." Then she looked desperately at other passengers and said, "Get her away from me."

The bus driver looked at the old woman and said, "Ma'am, the young lady is trying to help you."

She looked at me and yelled, "I don't need your help."

I stood at the corner of Woodward and McNichols waiting for a downtown bus, shivering from the cold while wondering if the old woman really thought I was trying to steal her groceries. A strong flood of emotions took hold of me. I wasn't sure if I was sad, furious, or embarrassed to be yelled at in public.

The Woodward bus dropped me across the street from Hudson's. I stared at the unbelievably humongous building. With so many display windows and entrances, I tried to figure out which door I should take. After a few minutes of considering my options, I decided to take the one closest to the bus stop. Once inside, I made sure to pay close attention to the entrance's location, marking it by the nearby merchandise. With my bad sense of direction, I was terrified of not being able to find my way out or to the bus stop. Being in big cities with large department stores, including Paris and London, was not enough to prepare me for this.

Once inside, I wasn't sure where to go, or which elevator or escalator to take. Shopping for a needle and thread in this thirty-two-floor building seemed like looking for a needle in a haystack.

Of course, the store had a large and easily visible directory, but a needle and thread were not among what they listed. Reluctantly, I approached the first salesperson, and asked, while trying to use my best possible English, "Excuse me, ma'am, where would I find needles and thread?"

"I'm not sure. Try the twelfth floor."

"How do I get there?"

"Take one of the elevators or escalators," she said, sounding annoyed.

Looking around, overwhelmed by the number of signs for escalators and elevators, I just got into the closest one.

"What floor?" asked the elevator operator, an African American woman all dressed up in a navy blue uniform and white gloves.

"Twelve, please."

I walked out of the elevator. After taking a few seconds to get my bearings, I slowly walked around, searching. There were pillows and more pillows, sheets of all sizes and colors, shelves packed with towels and more towels. There was every kitchen gadget humanity had invented. There were plates, and pots and pans to feed the whole population of Jordan. I started to question my sanity looking for a needle and thread in the middle of all this.

I had no choice but to ask another salesperson. Luckily, she was a little kinder.

"You might want to try the lower levels," she said.

"Lower level, please," I told the elevator operator.

"Which one?" she asked.

"How many are there?"

"Ma'am, we have four basements. Which one do you want?"

After visiting two basements and getting more disoriented from so much stuff, I decided to leave. I had been carrying my heavy coat and scarf for a while, not knowing if I was getting suffocated and dizzy from the overheated place, the perfume smells attacking me, or from frustration and anger.

"I cannot believe this. I have been here almost two hours going from one floor to another looking for a needle and thread, but I can't find any," I told the elevator operator.

"You're better off going to Woolworths across the street," she said whispering. There was no one else in the elevator.

Exhausted, I left Hudson's and walked around the block, not yet ready to go into another store. It was snowing and the cold air felt refreshing. Despite shivering from the sudden change in temperature, I was overjoyed to be outside.

Woolworths was another huge store on Woodward, but compared to Hudson's, it was not that bad. It was only two floors.

"I need some sewing needles and white thread," I told the first salesperson I saw.

"They're downstairs."

I went down, only to find aisles filled with pillows, sheets, bedcovers, dishes, cups, pots, and all kinds of other merchandise. It was not as large or fancy as Hudson's, which made me feel a bit more optimistic that I might find what I wanted.

"Where can I find a needle and thread?" I asked another worker.

"Try aisle nine."

"Where is that?"

"There," she pointed.

When I finally got to the right spot, I found boxes with dozens of spools with all colors of thread and large packets of needles.

I took what I found to the cashier and said, "I need only one spool of white thread and a couple of needles." When she gave me an astonished look, I said, "I will take white and black spools and six needles."

"Ma'am! You have to buy the whole thing."

I did.

Victorious, I held my new acquisition close to my chest. In spite of my throbbing head and aching knees, I smiled all the way home, imagining the old lady telling her neighbors about her encounter with a thief who was trying to steal her food during daylight in front of so many people. I could also envision the Woolworth's saleswoman sitting around her dining room table telling her family about the stupid brown customer with funny English who wanted to buy only one spool of white thread and a couple of needles.

Believe it or not, forty-three years and seven homes later, I still have some of the spool of thread I bought that day. It sits in the drawer of my coffee table. I often smile when I see it.

I got home five hours later, exhausted but happy not to have spent the day at home. When Abdeen came from work he asked me, "*Aini*, how was your day? Did you go to Hudson's? Did you like it? Isn't it a fun place? Did you buy anything?"

"I had a great day, but can you believe it? It took most of my day just to buy needles and thread."

"Did you not buy anything else from Hudson's?"

"No. I couldn't wait to get out of that crazy place. Guess what else happened to me today?"

"What?"

"I tried to help an old woman get her groceries off the bus but she started yelling at me. I think she thought I was about to steal her groceries."

"Did you ask her if she needed your help?"

"No. Why should I? If one is sincere about wanting to help, he or she should just do it."

"Well, *Aini*, that doesn't work here. Next time you should ask if someone needs your help."

That is one of the many cultural lessons that, for good or bad, I often forget.

CHAPTER 8
THE CHICKEN OR THE EGG

DETROIT, 1974-75

When I fell in love, my sister said to me, "You hardly speak English and he hardly speaks Arabic. How do you understand each other?"

"We don't. Maybe that's why we fell madly in love."

Truth be told, I did study English for six years, which was mandatory for all middle and high school students in Jordan. I suppose we had to learn the colonizer's language, which in our case was Great Britain. Had I been raised in Lebanon, it would have been French. When I came to America to be with my new love, it was more than ten years since I had graduated from high school, and whatever English I had learned was almost forgotten. Learning the language was the first thing I needed to do. Or so I thought.

Life in my new world turned out to be much more complicated than I anticipated. Before long, I found out that I needed to learn how to drive and to have a car in order to get to an English class. To afford a car, I needed to have a job. To have a job I needed to improve my English. Most importantly, I needed to have a green card. It was like the chicken and the egg. I tried to figure out which had to come first, but I was told over and over again that driving was the most critical skill if I was to survive in Motown.

When it came to my English, most people appreciated that I spoke some. They were also impressed that English was mandatory where I went to school. Learning a second language is not required in America. Why should it be? Had

Jordan been a superpower, it wouldn't have required its students to learn another language. But not knowing how to drive! That was a totally different story. Driving and owning a car was almost like a religion or a national duty with status and moral values attached to it.

"How can you be twenty-nine years old and not know how to drive?" was a question I was asked by Abdeen's family, his friends, and everyone I met, even kids. Soon I felt inadequate and backward for lacking such a basic human skill.

Whenever the subject of driving came up, which happened all the time, I felt under attack. My response to the drilling was "How can you live in a city that has too little or no public transportation?" Or "How can you think of your country as the best when it takes forever to get anywhere? And what if someone cannot afford a car?" My counter arguments didn't make me feel any better. Once in a while someone would tell me, "If you don't like it here, why don't you go back to your country?" To them, the US was the place where everyone should be thankful to land on its shores. After all, this is the real land of milk and honey. As for me, I didn't come for the milk; in fact I don't digest milk. But I did come for the honey. My honey!

I grew up in Amman, Jordan, and my middle-class family always had a car, but we used public transportation for our daily movement. I don't recall when or how I learned to use the bus or the *serveece*, a shared taxi that ran certain routes. We used public transportation within cities, between cities, and even between countries. It was simply how we moved from one place to another. It was rather hard to comprehend why every American adult needed a car, or how they could afford one. In fact, it took me a while to really understand how little public transportation existed in Michigan. I remember arguing with Abdeen, telling him, "Don't try to convince me that there is no public transportation between Detroit and Plymouth," a town twenty-some miles west of Detroit where three of his siblings lived. I honestly thought he was trying to stop me from going places on my own. I didn't believe him until my sister Suad came to the University of Michigan for her MA. She had to decline an internship opportunity in Plymouth when she realized that there was no public transportation to take her there.

BEING IN DETROIT without a job or anything to occupy my days was driving me out of my mind. Not having a car or knowing how to drive, I decided to look into taking English classes at Marygrove College, which was only two blocks from Abdeen's home. Although Abdeen and I had not decided to get married yet, I figured learning English would be useful regardless of the outcome of our relationship, though we kind of knew where it was heading. As the beginning of the school year approached, I walked to the college and picked up a copy of their course catalogue. Sure enough they had an English course that would prepare me for TOEFL, the proficiency language test requirement for foreign students in order to get accepted at universities, which I hoped to pass.

After filling out the application form, I proudly took it to the registrar's office with twenty dollars in cash. To my surprise, the tuition was two hundred dollars. I must have missed a very important zero.

"That can't be true," I told the man behind the registration desk.

"I'm sorry, it is. Here," he said, pointing to the catalogue.

"I'm registering for only one class. How could it be that much?"

"It costs that much to provide a good education."

"But…"

"Lady, if you can't pay then you need to move out of the way. There are other students waiting behind you."

He was speaking to me slowly and loudly. People stared at me. I was so embarrassed I wished I could just disappear, or as we say in Arabic, I wished the ground would open up and swallow me.

I took the form and walked home searching my pockets and purse for tissues to wipe my runny nose and foggy eyes.

"I can't live here. I hate this country," I told Abdeen the minute he entered the house.

"Why, *Aini*? What happened?"

"The guy at Marygrove was trying to rip me off. He thinks I am stupid because I don't speak good English. He wanted to charge me two hundred dollars instead of twenty."

"*Aini*, there is no university class for twenty dollars, let alone a private university."

"But that is more than what I paid for my BA at the University of Jordan and my MA at Cairo University combined."

Of course, there were other places where I could have taken an English class for much less. But without a car, I would have to take two buses that often ran late, and spend at least ninety minutes each way with no guarantee to make it to class on time. Finally, I had to come to my senses and realize that no matter how much I protested the lack of dependable public transportation, no quick remedy was about to happen just to accommodate me. People were right. If I was to live in Motown, I needed first and foremost to learn how to drive. I could worry about owning a car later.

Shortly after the wedding, Abdeen suggested I start learning how to drive.

"Maybe I should wait until spring. There is too much snow on the roads. It's scary to learn driving now."

"*Aini*, snow is part of life in Michigan. Sooner or later you'll have to drive on snow, even ice."

My dear husband found me Samir, a recent Palestinian immigrant instructor. My fear evaporated the minute I met Samir—he not only spoke Arabic, but was also interested in Palestinian politics (I have yet to meet one that is not). Between teaching me how to drive and discussing politics, the lessons took twice as long. What did I care? I had nothing but time on my hands.

"I'll tell Samir to give you one or two more lessons, then I can help you drive."

Enjoying my instructor's company, I said, "I'm not ready to drive yet. Samir should give me a few more lessons."

"I think you're fine. I'll take you out to practice and you'll learn in no time."

But when it came to it, I realized that was not the best idea. I would be nervously driving when, out of nowhere, Abdeen would start yelling and jumping in his seat. "Anan…Anan…watch it…watch it." Or he would scream, "Oh my God, Anan, don't do that!"

I would slam my foot on the brake with my heart pounding. "What did I do now?" I would say. "You are making me nervous. Why are you screaming?"

"You were about to total the car." Or worse, "You almost killed that woman."

"Forget it, I don't want to learn how to drive."

It didn't take a genius to realize that I needed a different approach if I were to keep loving this man.

One evening Abdeen's friend Dick invited us for dinner. Dick was not only witness to the birth of our romance, but also the best man at our wedding. We sat around the dining room table to have what I had hoped to be a peaceful dinner. As if there was nothing else to talk about, the topic of my driving came up. Frustrated by it all, I said, "Leave me alone, I don't want to learn how to drive or even to stay in this country." I left the table and sat on the couch.

There was a moment of tense silence. Both men were perplexed by my outburst. A few minutes later, Dick quietly got up from his chair and sat next to me.

"Please don't be upset. Everything is going to be just fine."

"Nothing is fine. Everything in this country is so complicated and expensive. I don't think I'll ever learn how to drive."

"Of course you will. Come here." He gave me a big hug and whispered in my ear, "You're going to be the best driver in Detroit. You can practice with me."

Sure enough, Dick made me a good driver, except for going in reverse. Forty some years later, I still occasionally hit something with my car when I back up. I blame it on him. He must have been so concerned about me moving forward that he forgot to teach me how to reverse.

CHAPTER 9
THE ELUSIVE GREEN CARD

DETROIT, 1974-75

Once we became husband and wife, Abdeen assured me that he would immediately start the process of filing for my green card application. Being an American-born attorney, I trusted he was more qualified to do it than myself. All I had to do was sign the application, which I did without even reading it.

A few days later, my husband came home from work with a big grin on his face. "I have great news. Today I submitted your green card application."

"Can I start looking for a job now?"

"No, *Aini*, you have to wait until you get it."

"How long will that take?"

"Only a few months. At the most six."

"Six months? It has been six months since I arrived. You mean to tell me I have to spend a whole year not working? That'll drive me crazy."

I think by that time I was already halfway there.

"Well, I wish I could do something about it, but who knows, maybe you'll get lucky and get it sooner."

"How soon? I want to find a job, and I want to go visit my family. I can't seem to do either before getting the fucking green card."

"*Aini*, I promise you we will go see your family as soon as you get your green card. Also, you're already studying English. By the time you get your green card your language will be good enough to be able to work. A green card alone won't get you a job. You need to have very, very good English."

Determined not to pay the two hundred dollars to Marygrove College for an English class, I was already taking classes at the much cheaper International Institute, located in Detroit's Cultural Center next to the Detroit Institute of Arts (DIA), and only a few blocks from Wayne State University (WSU). Twice a week Abdeen would drop me at the Institute on his way to work. After class, I would stay there to study and have lunch, or walk one block to have lunch at the DIA. Some days I would take the bus home or walk to Abdeen's law office in the New Center area and stay there studying until the end of his workday.

"It is a nice day. Why don't you go to Wayne State's campus? You can have lunch at the Student Center," Abdeen said as he dropped me off at the International Institute.

"How far is it?"

"Not that far. It's much closer than my office. A ten-minute walk at the most."

As soon as I entered the second floor of the Student Center, my ears, eyes, and heart were drawn to an Arabic-speaking group of students. About a dozen of them were sitting at three adjacent tables eating, smoking, and passionately discussing politics. Without giving it much thought, I rushed toward them introducing myself. In return, they invited me to join them for lunch. The majority of them were recent arrivals from Lebanon and Palestine. It was as if I had found some lost cousins!

"You should come to our OAS[5] activities. They are open to the public," said one of the students.

"What is OAS, and what kind of activities?"

"It is the Organization of Arab Students. It has chapters on campuses all over the country. We have a very active chapter here at Wayne. We hold regular activities like lectures, seminars, and movies, most of them about Palestine. You should come."

Little did he know his words were music to my ears. It was at that moment when I started to consider going to WSU for my PhD.

Meeting these Arab students was more than enough to have me walk to WSU twice a week in spite of the cold weather. After my English class, I would sit in the Student Center spending my time studying and talking to students. Some days, even when I didn't have a class at the International Institute, I would take the two ninety-minute bus rides to be with my newly found friends.

As the inhumane, freezing weather of December seeped into my Mediterranean bones, it became almost impossible for me to walk the distance between the International Institute and WSU, or to take the bus to Wayne on days I did not have classes. I would just stay home studying and reading newspapers, magazines, and novels with the help of an English-Arabic dictionary that became attached to my body. When my eyes became blurry from too much reading, I would take a break to watch one or two episodes of soap operas, like "All My Children," "The Young and the Restless," or "Return to Peyton Place," which, although more risqué, were just as dramatic as the Egyptian ones I used to watch before coming to the US.

THE COLD, MISERABLE weather that seemed to last forever added to the list of my complaints about life in America. My yearning for my previous life in Beirut was getting stronger by the day. I missed the Mediterranean sun and the al-Hamra apartment I shared with sister Suad. I missed my family and friends, and I missed my job. Most importantly, I missed my independence. It didn't take much to realize that I was gradually sinking into depression. To no avail, I spent my time fighting tears, trying to swallow the lump in my throat and lift the heavy weight off my chest.

Poor Abdeen, he couldn't wrap his head around my sadness, and was trying hard to figure out what he could possibly do to alter my mood. One day as he dropped me at the International Institute, he said, "How about joining me for lunch with the ACCESS director, Aliya Hassan. I'm sure you'll like her. In many ways, she's like my mother." That was encouraging, since l liked his mother a lot.

"What do you mean, she's like your mother?"

"My mother's family as well as Aliya's were among the Lebanese Muslim immigrants to homestead in North Dakota in the early 1900s. Both Aliya and my mother grew up there."

"Do they know each other?"

"No. They never met," said Abdeen

Aliya, or *Hajja* Aliya, as people called her, did match Mymonie in her tiny size, glittery small eyes, and kindness, and her life was most fascinating. She had held many interesting jobs, including being a private detective in New York City. Her activism was far-reaching, extending beyond the Arab American community. She managed to establish strong relationships with African Americans and led a civil rights delegation on a trip to Egypt to meet with the Egyptian leader Gamal Abdel Nasser. As a close friend of Malcolm X, she organized his first trip to Mecca. Aliya was also one of the founders of ACCESS, and its first director. Although thirty-five years my senior, it was natural for me to feel a special affinity toward her. Before leaving, I asked Aliya if she would be interested in having me volunteer at ACCESS. "It would be great to have you," she said. "I could use some help."

While driving back to Abdeen's office, I said, "Guess what? I just landed a volunteer job working with Aliya Hassan. Thank you for introducing me. You are absolutely correct. She's great."

"Glad you liked her, but you need to focus on your English."

"I have classes only twice a week for a couple of hours each. I have a lot of time on my hands and I want to be with people. Who knows, maybe volunteering will help me find a job."

"If that's what you want, it's fine by me. But we need to figure out the transportation. I can't drop you there like I do at the International Institute. ACCESS is too far from my office."

I didn't quite understand what he was referring to. ACCESS was in Dearborn's South End neighborhood, only two blocks from Wyoming Avenue, and so was our home on Wisconsin Street in northwest Detroit.

"But I can walk two blocks to Wyoming, then take it to ACCESS. It can't be that far."

"*Aini*, you can't walk. It is almost ten miles."

Since we drove from the International Institute, I wasn't aware how far from our home ACCESS was. Coming from cities where only a few of the main roads have names, the longest of which was hardly a couple of miles, I couldn't envision a single street stretching ten miles long.

At ACCESS, I was assigned to fill out intake forms of Arabic-speaking clients, which included information about their families and what kind of services they were looking for. With my poor English, I was unable to immediately translate the information and fill out the forms. After a couple of days, I decided to complete the forms in Arabic, and translate them later. Some days I would take them home to translate, violating clients' privacy rules. Since I was good at math, I also volunteered to help in accounting, but even that required reading inventories. Soon I realized that with my poor English and lack of dependable transportation, my skills as a volunteer were not that impressive. I decided to save my pride and quit, rather than getting fired. Was it not for Abdeen, an active founding member of ACCESS, by the second week they probably would have told me, "Thank you for your help, but we no longer need your services."

"I can't believe this," I told Abdeen. "With all my education and work experience, I can't even do a good job as a volunteer. How depressing is that?"

"*Aini*, be patient. Your English will improve faster than you think. You're already learning how to drive, and I plan to get you a car soon."

I wished I could believe him or have some of his optimism rub off on me. Between my poor language skills, no job, and no car, I tried very hard to see the light at the end of tunnel, but it was nowhere to be found.

"MABROOK. YOU GOT your green card. You're lucky. It only took three months. Much faster than I thought," said my husband as he marched into the house with a big smile stretching to his ears. I loved his enthusiasm. He embraced life with the excitement of a five-year-old.

I jumped out of my seat, matching his enthusiasm. "Say, *wallah*…I have been waiting for this for ages. Give it to me. Let me see it!"

Although the card came by the end of February, much earlier than expected, it had been almost eight months since I arrived in the US. With Abdeen working long hours and traveling to meetings over weekends, I felt very isolated. I was desperate to have a job, to get out of the house, to travel out of the country. The green card was my only salvation.

I snatched the card from Abdeen. To my surprise, it was not green as I expected. I don't remember what color it was, but that didn't really matter. I looked at my picture. It was a nice one. I looked at my name, looked again, then grabbed the card with both hands and drew it closer to my face and stared at it: "Anan Mohammad Jabara."

"Jabara? Really? You must be kidding."

"I don't understand. Kidding about what?"

"How did my name become Anan Mohammad Jabara?"

"What do you mean?"

"My name is Anan Ameri, in case you haven't noticed." My voice was shaking and I was getting more resentful by the second.

"It is your father's name and my family name," he said with a perplexed look on his face.

"But who said I wanted to change my name?"

"Women change their names when they get married. Besides, it was like this on the application you signed."

"I should have read the application before signing. I'm sorry I didn't."

"I thought you would be happy to have my name."

"I'm not."

"Why? What is wrong with Jabara?"

"Nothing is wrong with your name, it is just not mine. How would you like your name to become Abdeen Ameri without being asked?" I said, almost ready to strangle him.

"You're not going to give me this feminist shit, are you?"

I never thought of myself as a feminist. All I knew was that my name was my name. To me it was that simple.

As a compromise, I changed my name to Anan Ameri Jabara, following in the footsteps of my mother Siham Jabri Ameri. At Wayne State University, where I got my PhD, however, I kept my name as Anan Ameri. This would be my degree. It would have my name.

I should have predicted trouble down the road, but as the proverb goes: *elhub a'ama.*

ONCE I GOT my green card, I began nagging Abdeen to help me find a job. March was around the corner and the promise of spring was warming my heart.

"I want to start working, to make my own money and my own friends," I told Abdeen. All my parents' grilling about being independent came back to haunt me.

"Be patient. It takes time to find a job."

"How patient do you expect me to be? It's been over nine months. I can't spend more time not working."

To my surprise, a couple of weeks later, I received a call from Aliya Hassan.

"I'm looking for someone who speaks Arabic to do some research in the community. Would you be interested?"

Recalling my disastrous volunteering experience at ACCESS, I asked, "What kind of research?"

"We need to have a better understanding of new immigrants' needs. You did work as a researcher in Lebanon, am I correct?"

"Yes, yes, I did. But my English, as you know, is not that good."

"You don't have to worry about that. We're looking for someone who speaks Arabic well and knows how to do research. We have a small grant. We can pay you."

"Thank you for thinking of me." My heart was pounding so hard I was worried she could hear it through the phone lines.

"When can you start?"

"Well," I said reluctantly, "Abdeen and I are going to visit my family in Jordan in early April. You know my family never met Abdeen. I'll be gone for three weeks, maybe a month. Can this wait?" I asked, concerned my trip back home, which I had been yearning for since I came to the US, would cost me my first job.

"Yes. Yes. No problem. We can wait."

"Can we meet before I leave to talk about it?" I asked, hoping such a meeting might secure me the job.

"Of course. When can you come?"

"Tomorrow."

The minute Abdeen walked into the house, I jumped out of my seat, greeting him with a big hug and a passionate kiss.

"Wow. What did I do to deserve this?" said Abdeen, smiling, surprised by my gesture.

"Aliya offered me a paid job. I told her about our trip. She said that it's fine." For a change, I was the one with a big grin on my face.

"What kind of job?"

"She needs someone to do research about Arab immigrants. It sounds like a needs assessment. I'll know more tomorrow. I need to borrow the car."

"Not tomorrow. I have to be in court early."

I was not that happy to call Aliya and change the meeting date, but the excitement of the prospect of having a job was much greater. Aliya agreed that I would start as soon as I came back from my trip. Meanwhile, Abdeen agreed to work out the logistics of sharing his car. Although I had no idea how much I would be paid, I started dreaming about the kind and color of the car I would soon buy.

CHAPTER 10
THE LONG ROAD TO INDEPENDENCE

DETROIT, 1975

For the first time since I landed in this country of milk and honey, life in America started to taste sweet. I was married to the love of my life and had acquired all the needed skills to survive in America: a driver's license, a green card, and a reasonable command of the English language. And now I had a real job that I liked. With the speed of a bullet, I designed the research and started to interview new immigrants, who came mostly from Yemen, Lebanon, and Palestine.

My job provided me with an opportunity to meet some of ACCESS's clients and learn about their challenges and hardships, as well as their apprehension and fears of not actualizing the dreams that drew them to the US. Suddenly I found myself being the one to say, "Be patient. Trust me, life will get better soon."

At work, I also cherished meeting other ACCESS volunteers, all of whom were activists. Those born in the US were involved in local social justice issues like poverty, racism, labor, and unemployment. On the other hand, some, like myself, were recent immigrants who were influenced by Arab nationalism, the Non-Aligned Movement, and third world liberation struggles. They were concerned with social and political issues back home, specifically the Palestinian struggle and the Civil War in Lebanon, which started shortly after I arrived in Detroit. While we, new immigrants, learned from those born in the US about American progressive politics, they learned from us about Arab world struggles, which ignited their Arab identity. I believe that the combined efforts of these two groups, with their different backgrounds, had shaped and continue to shape Arab American activism locally and nationally, including my own.

Among the female activists I met at ACCESS was Helen Atwal, a volunteer who was heavily involved in establishing the Southeast Dearborn Community Council, which had regular meetings at ACCESS.

"Tell me more about the Council. I'm not sure I understand what it's all about," I asked Helen one time.

"It's a grassroots organization led by the residents of the South End to save their neighborhood from the City of Dearborn and Ford Motor Company's urban renewal plans."

"What kind of plans?"

"They want to transform this area from residential to industrial. Since the late 1960s the city has been evicting families and demolishing their homes."

"Demolishing their homes? Can they do that?"

"They can try but they won't succeed. This is a politically active working-class neighborhood with a strong labor movement. We will do everything we can to stop them."

Helen also told me that many Arab immigrants, mostly Syrian and Lebanese, used to live in Highland Park, a small town adjacent to Detroit, which was home to Ford Motor Company's Model T plant. They had established a lively neighborhood with stores, coffee shops, and restaurants as well as other small businesses. In 1923, the community was able to build their own mosque. But when Ford built its new Rouge Plant[6] in the South End of Dearborn, most of the community moved to work in the new plant. By 1937 they built a new mosque on Dix Avenue, not far from ACCESS. They also established a strongly knit community with all kinds of stores and services, including their own doctors, dentists, travel agents, newspapers, and community organizations. Evicting the residents and transforming such a vibrant neighborhood did not make much sense to me either.

"I don't understand. Why would they want to destroy this neighborhood?" I asked Helen.

"Because this neighborhood is adjacent to Detroit. By transforming it into an industrial area they will hit many birds with one stone: destroy the activists' neighborhood, block Blacks from moving to Dearborn, and get rid of Arab immigrants."

"You think you can stop them?"

"We are determined to legally challenge their plans. This is our neighborhood and we're not going to sit still watching it being destroyed."[7]

This was a lot of information for me to comprehend, but I found the community's fight against their city government and their employer, Ford Motor Company, rather fascinating. So, I did hang around Helen to learn more whenever I could.

One day, as we were having lunch and chatting, she casually said, "It is nice of Abdeen to pay for the research you are doing."

"What do you mean Abdeen is paying for the research?"

"You don't know? I think he asked Aliya to give you a job and said he would pay for it."

I could feel the heat spreading from my chest to my neck and face. Even my ears were burning.

"Does this include my salary or just the cost of the research?"

Realizing that I was not aware of the arrangement, Helen tried to retract what she said. "I'm sorry, I shouldn't have said anything. I'm not really sure. Actually I am wrong, maybe it's someone else..."

"Don't worry about it," I said, but everything about me said otherwise.

All that excitement I had about having a job evaporated in seconds. I swallowed my tears along with my pride and went home. I was ready to tell Abdeen to forget it, to pack my few belongings, and just leave.

The minute Abdeen walked in the house, I burst into tears.

"How could you do this to me?" I screamed, getting out of my chair and going into the bedroom.

"What did I do now?" he said as he followed me.

"You lied to me. There is no real job. You gave Aliya money to pay me."

Abdeen stood by the bedroom door staring at me. "I'm trying to help. What difference does it make who is paying for the research?"

"You and Aliya made the whole thing up. This is insulting," I said.

Dizzy, I sat down on the edge of the bed wiping my nose and tears with the back of my hands.

"I just don't know what's so insulting about it."

"Lying to me is insulting. Making me your charity is insulting." Abdeen looked hard at me, then he raised his hands in resignation. "You go ahead and find your own job. I'm getting tired of this. It is so frustrating. I just don't know what I can do to make you happy."

While I couldn't fathom how he would lie to me, he, on the other hand, couldn't grasp why I was so upset or ungrateful for all that he was doing. Neither he nor Aliya would give me a straight answer if the research was needed or invented. Feeling betrayed by the two people I loved and trusted, I decided to quit.

Angry and frustrated, I went back to square one, trying to figure out how to chart my own path in the US, to have my own friends, and establish my own identity. I also found myself resenting Abdeen as he continued to have his job, family, and friends, and live in his familiar terrain, while I had to give it all up to be with him. Losing the first hope to gain some independence reinforced my feeling of the unfairness and disparity between the two of us—this was not what I had envisioned my marriage to be.

As upset as I was by the research ordeal, I had to admit that both Abdeen and Aliya helped me meet community activists. Before long, I started to volunteer again at ACCESS, and in March 1976 I was elected to the organization's executive committee as the treasurer of the organization. Fate does indeed work in a mysterious way. Little did I know that in 1997, almost twenty-one years later, I would become ACCESS's Cultural Arts Director and the founding director of the Arab American National Museum.

CHAPTER 11
LOVE, POLITICS, AND FEMINISM

DETROIT, 1974-76

When I look back at how and why I came to the US, I am amazed by my sense of adventure, or maybe my foolishness. I didn't know much about Abdeen or his family and friends. And I didn't know much about Detroit either. The little I knew came from our mutual friend Kamal Boullata, and from my interview with Abdeen for the Orient Press where I worked as a freelance journalist. The interview focused mostly on Abdeen's political activism. However, I had no clue about the depth of his involvement or the extent to which he was idealized as a rising star within the Arab American community, as well as with non-Arab progressives, both locally and nationally.

Only two days after I arrived, Abdeen asked me if I wanted to join him for a lunch meeting at Ford Motor Company's headquarters in Dearborn. "I want you to meet my friend Barbara Aswad. You'll really like her. She's a professor of Anthropology at Wayne State University. She does lots of work with Arab immigrants."

Like Abdeen, Dr. Aswad was also on ACCESS's board of directors. Because of her name and the kind of activism she was involved in, I assumed she was an Arab American. I was surprised when I met her. Barbara was European American, and Aswad was her married name.

Most of the drive from Abdeen's home to Dearborn was on the highway, and I had little chance to see much. Soon after we exited, Abdeen said, pointing,

"You see that big green glass building in front of us? That's Ford's headquarters. That's where we're going."

"It's beautiful."

Being at Ford Motor Company was most impressive. Lunch was served in a fancy restaurant on the top floor. Tables were elegantly set with white tablecloths and napkins, and multiple plates and lots of glasses. I felt important just being there. I was taken by the view of the building's lush and spacious grounds and the very wide Michigan Avenue with its eight lanes and so many big cars coming and going. I didn't know much about the meeting and hardly understood the conversation, but I was able to pick up a few words here and there.

After the meeting, I asked Abdeen, "Did you ask them for a five-thousand-dollar donation to ACCESS?"

"Yes, we did."

"Wow… That's a lot of money. Do you think they can give you that much?"

Abdeen laughed. "Of course they can, that's chump change for them."

I didn't know what chump change meant and was embarrassed to ask. But I got the idea.

AS BUSY AS Abdeen was, he often took me with him to business lunches and meetings to introduce me to people he thought I might like. Not having much to do, I went along. Often, I was bored to death, especially if I couldn't get what people were talking about, or even worse, if I was unable to understand what was so funny when they laughed.

Among the many cultural shocks I had was during a meeting at some professor's home who was doing research about Iraqi Chaldeans in Metro Detroit. Before the meeting started, the professor asked if anyone would like some water. Everyone declined and that was it. The meeting lasted more than two hours and she never offered or asked again.

"What a cheap woman, this friend of yours," I told Abdeen as soon as we got in the car.

"Why are you calling her cheap? What did she do?"

"She offered us nothing. No coffee, no tea, no fruits. Not even a cookie!"

"It's a business meeting. She offered us her place to meet and we are grateful for that."

"Back home, not even the poorest in a refugee camp would do something like that."

"But this is not back home."

"I can't believe you say this. When people come to our home, you don't stop shoving food and drink down their throats."

I couldn't comprehend why Abdeen was defending her so strongly, but decided to let it go.

Around mid-November 1974, only a couple of weeks before our wedding date, I drove with my soon-to-be husband to the Arab American University Graduates (AAUG) conference in Cleveland, Ohio. Abdeen, along with other Arab American intellectuals and activists, had founded the organization in the aftermath of the 1967 Arab-Israeli war.

"You're going to like the AAUG people. We also have a great program," Abdeen assured me.

We arrived at the conference hotel around noon. The place was already packed with people, mostly Arab American university students and professors, coming from all around the country. I could hear a few speaking Arabic, which made me a bit more enthusiastic about being there. *Maybe I'll meet some interesting people, or at least understand what people are talking about,* I thought to myself. Once we settled in our room, Abdeen said, "I've got to go to a few meetings this afternoon. I'm sure you can manage."

With Abdeen busy running around from one meeting to another, and me not knowing but a couple of people from Detroit, I decided to attend as many lectures and panels as I could. While the conference program on paper sounded rather interesting, I had a hard time understanding much of what was being said. I kept moving from one panel to another, hoping I would have better luck, but didn't. On the second day of the convention, attracted by the sound of Arabic, I joined a large group of students gathered in the reception area. They had come from different parts of the country and were all excited about Edward Said, whom I didn't know at the time, giving a lecture that afternoon, so I decided to go. When Abdeen asked me if I liked Edward Said's talk, I said, "It's embarrassing to admit it. I was ready to leave after ten minutes, but unfortunately, I was sitting in the front row."

"Are you serious? Why did you want to do that?" he asked, irritated.

"Because I had no idea what he was talking about."

"Really. You know who Edward Said is? He is the most important Arab American intellectual, not only in the US, but possibly internationally."

Here I was, the once proud author, researcher, and freelance journalist, not only not knowing who Edward Said was, but unable to understand what seemed to be interesting lectures and discussions. How could my world be shifting so fast? And how, in less than a few months, had my identity became no more than Abdeen's girlfriend and future wife? As these thoughts invaded my brain, I massaged my throat to loosen the tightening grip. When Abdeen noticed my long face and repressed tears he said apologetically, "*Aini*, don't worry about it. By the next convention you'll be speaking English better than all of them."

During the three-day conference, however, I did encounter what I thought of as a pretentious welcome. Whether I was in the hallway, at the coffee shop, or in the restaurant, people, especially women, would introduce themselves saying, "I've heard so much about you," or "I've been eager to meet you." I was surprised by these friendly gestures wondering what they could have possibly heard about me.

My dear friend Elaine Hagopian, one of the founders of AAUG, later explained it to me: "Abdeen was the most eligible bachelor. Many women were seeking to win his heart. Everyone was curious to find out who was this woman he finally found and soon would marry."

Little did I know that I didn't only land a political celebrity but also a bachelor celebrity. Later, when frustrated by my marriage, I would call Elaine. "Where are all these women who wanted Abdeen? Send them over. They can have him. Or even better, you are single, you can have him."

"I appreciate the offer, but no thanks," she would say laughing.

ABDEEN'S ACTIVISM WAS not limited to AAUG. He played a leading role in the Chicago-based Palestine Human Rights Campaign, the National Lawyers Guild, and later, the American-Arab Anti-Discrimination Committee. Locally, in addition to ACCESS, he was involved in labor unions, civil rights, the anti-war movement, as well as Palestinian issues. All of the attorneys who shared his law office were radicals involved in one cause or another. Our home in Detroit was a hub for political activities, a place to have a meeting, a fundraiser, or heated political discussions over a drink or dinner. Abdeen's political colleagues would come for the evening, to spend the night, or to stay for the weekend. Arab hospitality was a tradition Abdeen learned from his family. He was at his best when people were at our home, drinking, eating, and discussing politics. While I enjoyed meeting and listening to the conversations and arguments of all the people who passed through our home, I was not that thrilled by all the cooking and cleaning that accompanied these gatherings. As I look back on those years, I'm not really sure how I ended up doing all the work while Abdeen hardly lifted a finger, short of serving drinks and piling food on guests' plates, whether they wanted it or not.

Unlike me, Abdeen grew up in a traditional household with a clear division of labor. He was also the youngest of seven, and his mother and his three sisters spoiled him. While I never envisioned myself to be a traditional wife, I often wonder if being financially dependent on Abdeen limited my ability to create a more equitable division of labor within our household.

I still vividly remember the time when a few male activists were in town for a meeting and ended up at our home. After dinner Abdeen said with his usual hospitality and enthusiasm, "It's a beautiful evening. Let's go sit in the backyard." While each carried his favorite drink and walked outside, I went to the kitchen and started to clean. There were dozens of dirty dishes, glasses, and pots. The deck was right behind the kitchen and I could hear the men talking and laughing. All of a sudden, I felt blood rushing to my neck and face. The more they laughed, the more furious I became. I wanted to smash all these dishes. Instead, I went to the front yard and sat on the doorstep, crying. I was amazed by the level of my resentment, and started telling myself, *you're being so silly crying over washing dishes,* but deep down I knew it was much more than that.

I had married Abdeen in the mid-1970s, a time when women were rebelling against male-dominated societies. But that rebellion had not yet penetrated most so-called progressive households, including ours. Although I was very much influenced by women's rights and feminism, somehow I had resentfully succumbed to the traditional role of women. I wonder why. Was it because that's what I saw among Abdeen's family and all of our friends? Or was it because Abdeen was the main breadwinner and my contribution was so small, even after I got my PhD since I opted to work for a nonprofit?

I grew up with a working mother who owned her own business and managed an all-male staff. Mom also hated housework and did very little of it. My father did none of it either. Although my parents were not rich, we always had live-in housekeepers, many of whom lived with us for a number of years. All of a sudden, I found myself doing all of the housework as well as cooking big dinners to accommodate my husband's guests. When I first arrived in the US, I didn't know a single soul and had lots of time on my hands. To busy myself, I would spend a few hours a day cleaning and rearranging furniture and artwork. Gradually I transformed Abdeen's bachelor flat into a warm home. And I cooked two and three course dinners on a daily basis. But within a couple of years, I became politically active and was enrolled in a PhD program, yet the division of labor within our home, which I contributed to create, stayed the same. And when I convinced Abdeen to get a housekeeper once a week, one of his sisters told me, "My brother really spoils you. I have raised my kids and worked all my life, but neither I nor anyone in our family ever had help." Abdeen was probably thinking the same, but to make me happy, he went along.

Nonetheless, Abdeen's activism and relationships helped me learn about progressive issues of the time and to meet many leaders within Arab and non-Arab communities.[8] Most of these people became personal friends who supported me throughout my career, including the two organizations I helped found: the Palestine Aid Society of America (PAS) in 1980, and the Arab American National Museum (AANM) in 2005. In fact, many became members of the boards of both organizations. So, while our marriage had its painful challenges, I will forever be grateful to Abdeen who supported me in getting my PhD, jump-starting my political activism and helping me forge lifelong relationships, all of which helped me chart my new independent life in the US.

ONE EVENING ABDEEN came home from work, announcing with much enthusiasm, *'Aini,* guess what! Today I had a new Kuwaiti client. He came to my office with his wife Nancy. I thought you might enjoy meeting them. I asked them to come for dinner tomorrow."

That did not impress me. My husband had told me the same thing every time he invited guests without consulting me, which happened rather frequently.

"I wish you'd asked me first. What if I have to study or don't feel like cooking or having guests?"

"*Aini,* you will like Shadi and his wife. He's involved in the Palestinian community in Detroit."

"Abdeen, this is not about whether I'm going to like them or not. It's about checking with me before inviting people over. Is that too much to ask?"

"I thought this would make you happy. You said you want to meet people."

"You know, Abdeen, I'm starting to resent all these people coming over for dinner tonight, tomorrow, or the day after. Yes, I'm lonely, and do want to meet people, but I don't particularly enjoy cooking big dinners and having a bunch of guests without even being asked."

"If it'll make you happy, I'll call and cancel," he said, sounding angry.

At that point, I wasn't sure if Abdeen could understand the source of my frustration, or if he could have said or done anything that would make me happy.

To keep up with Arab hospitality and to please my husband, I cooked an elaborate dinner and put on a big smile to welcome the guests. Although I hate to admit it, I did enjoy the evening and found Shadi to be rather engaging. We spent the night talking in Arabic, discussing politics, and telling jokes, something I missed tremendously. As a gift, he brought me the last few issues of *Al-Hurreyah,* an Arabic leftist political magazine published and shipped weekly from Beirut. After that evening, Shadi made a point of bringing me the latest issue of *Al-Hurreyah* the day it arrived. He would either bring it himself, or have one of his friends or "comrades," as he called them, deliver it.

After a couple months of sending me *Al-Hurreyah*, I was invited to join Shadi and his friends' weekly Sunday meetings, which were held in his home in the South End of Dearborn. It included eight men, but not a single woman. When I asked why they didn't have other women, I was told that it would be my responsibility to convince some to join. I found that worrisome, and wondered if these men would be telling me what I should be doing. Being the snobby city girl, I was also not sure I would be comfortable with a bunch of *fellaheen* males. Thanks to loneliness and the desire to be engaged in Palestinian politics, I decided to give it a try. Gradually, I started to like these men and enjoy their company. They were very kind, smart, and passionate, and they treated me with affection and respect, and as an equal member. I could hardly wait for our weekly meetings, just like a religious devotee eager to rush to Sunday services.

As we gathered at 10:00 in the morning, we read and discussed articles in *Al-Hurreyah*, especially the magazine's editorial article by Dawood Talhami, a friend and colleague from the Palestine Research Center where I worked before coming to the US. I've always liked Dawood, and had gone on a couple dates with him. Reading his article was kind of nostalgic, bringing back fond memories about my life in Beirut. The other part of the meeting was devoted to discussing and organizing political events such as the International Day of Solidarity with the Palestinian people, or commemorating May 15, the *Nakba* Day, or Palestinian Prisoners day. We also supported and attended every rally, lecture, fundraiser, and demonstration of other revolutionary support groups in Metro Detroit, all of whom we considered comrades and allies in the struggle. These included not only Arab leftist groups, but also other solidarity committees supporting liberation movements in Northern Ireland, Nicaragua, Guatemala, and South Africa. We also rallied in support of the poor and the unemployed. You name it, we were there.

Shadi and I became best friends. A few years later, he and his wife moved to LA to seek better job opportunities, but he continued his political activism. In 1988, soon after the first Palestinian Intifada, the Palestine Aid Society of America (PAS) decided to open a West Coast regional office and to hire a full-time community organizer. At the time PAS had its national office in Detroit, and I was working as the organization's executive director. Shadi quit his job as a high school student counselor to establish our West Coast office, taking a 50 percent cut in his salary. He and I worked together for many years to come. We were both underpaid and overworked, but we had dreams of a bright future. When I got tired or demoralized, Shadi would cheer me up promising a free oil pipeline from Democratic Kuwait to free Palestine. When he got frustrated or discouraged, I would assure him that the last Palestine Aid Society project would be a senior retirement home in free Palestine for all the supporters of our cause including him. I also promised him Palestinian citizenship.

CHAPTER 12
GOING HOME

BEIRUT, SPRING 1975

I t was already mid-March, but the cold winter of Detroit lingered, and the promise of spring seemed like a faraway dream. I had been home all day, moving back and forth from the couch to the bed, reading, studying English, and watching TV, while carrying along the colorful afghan my mother-in-law had knitted for me. This was my first winter in Detroit. I don't recall feeling warm no matter how many clothes I wore or how high I raised the thermostat. My body ached for the Mediterranean sun, and my soul yearned for company. By the end of the day, I started to feel slightly better. Abdeen would be home soon.

I got off the sofa, taking my time folding the small blanket. In the kitchen, I turned the radio on and started cooking.

"Hi, *Aini*. Guess what!" Abdeen said, almost yelling before he had a chance to close the entrance door.

"What?"

"I got an invitation to participate in a conference in Baghdad. All paid for. I'll be leaving in two weeks. On my way back, I plan to go to Amman and meet your parents."

A deep sadness engulfed me. *How about me?* I thought, feeling disappointed for not being asked to go along. I walked back to the kitchen. Abdeen followed.

"What's wrong, *Aini*?"

"Nothing."

"It's something. You seem upset. Are you not happy for me?"

"I thought we could go together once I got my green card. Now that I have it, you want to go by yourself? I want to be with you when you meet my family," I said, turning my face away, not wanting him to see my foggy eyes.

"Oh, *Aini*. Why the tears? Come here." He pulled me toward him and embraced me tightly. "I know how much you miss your family and friends. In the summer, we can go together. I promise. This time I'll be gone for only a few days."

That didn't make me feel any better. I wanted to go with him right then, but said no more. Without him offering, I was too proud to ask.

When Mymonie, the woman who never ceased to surprise me with her kindness or wisdom, found about Abdeen's trip, she told him, "You're not going to the old country to meet Anan's folks without her. If money is the issue, I'll pay for it."

"No, Mother, it's not the money. It's my work."

"Well, you either go together or don't go at all."

Knowing better than to ignore his mother, Abdeen suggested I meet him in Amman after the conference. "I can stay in Amman for two or three days. You can either come back with me or stay longer if you wish. Would you like that?"

"Are you kidding? I'd love to. But I'd like us to go to Syria and Lebanon also. I want you to meet the rest of my family in Damascus, and my friends in Beirut."

"Let me check my schedule. I need to find out if I can take that much time."

"You don't have to stay long. Two days in each city. I can't stay too long either. I promised Aliya I'd take the research job at ACCESS, and to be back in less than a month."

In early April, Abdeen and I took two separate flights. He went to Baghdad and I to Amman. It had been only nine months since I came to the US, but it felt like ages. I was longing to be with my family and friends, and was happy to spend some time with them alone, to be the center of their love and affection. I couldn't wait to wear my short sleeves and sit in my parents' yard soaking up the warm noon sun while inhaling the fresh air and the scent of lemon blossoms.

As planned, Abdeen joined me at my parents' home in Amman. My parents were glad to finally meet their son-in law, and they, especially my mother, fell in love with him. While my dad told me, "Good choice, Anan," he told Abdeen, "If I had a chance to meet you before you got married, I would've told you that she is a rebel. But it's too late now." At that time, as it was still early in our marriage, Abdeen had not yet seen my rebellious spirit. We spent a few days in Amman, introducing Abdeen to my friends and other family members, having huge dinners each night at someone's home. I also took Abdeen to various parts of the city showing him my old neighborhood, Mango Street, the Queen Zein High School, and the University of Jordan where I graduated. I was amazed how nostalgic I felt toward Amman, a city I never cared for that much and at one time couldn't wait to escape from.

After a few days, Abdeen and I headed to Damascus and then Beirut. Luckily my rich and snobbish Damascene family blessed my choice. While we were not able to spend more than three days there, I was delighted to have us stay with my two aunts at my grandfather's house where I was born. Like a child, Abdeen was fascinated by the 1737 house, and spent the time exploring its twenty-eight rooms, which occupied three floors. The large courtyard, with its colorful tiles, large fountain, cooing pigeons, and early spring-scented flowers, brought back many happy memories and reminded me how magical the place could be. The location of the house, in the Old City between the historic Umayyad Mosque and al-Hamidiyeh Souq, only added to its charm.

I was sad to say goodbye to my aunts and to my grandfather's home, not knowing when I would return. But Abdeen had only a few days before heading back to the States, and I wanted us to be in Beirut by April 12 to celebrate my sister Suad's birthday with her. Two days after we arrived Beirut, I sat with my friend Jawad, on a sunny afternoon, at the Roche Café reminiscing about the time we worked together, while watching the blue Mediterranean Sea and enjoying the spring breeze caressing our faces. In the distance, small fishing boats were gently rocking with the waves. Suddenly, distant shelling shattered my peaceful existence. I jumped out of my seat, saying, "What the hell was that?" Jawad laughed and said, "Come on, Anan. Relax. It looks like you've been in America for too long."

"What do you mean, relax? Did you not hear the shooting? I'm going home. I'll call you later."

I ran to my sister's apartment but no one was there. Abdeen was with one of his friends and Suad was at the university. Anxiously, I sat waiting, recalling the horror of the 1973 Israeli attack on Palestinians in Beirut when I was still living there. Three top PLO leaders were killed in their homes in front of their families. One leader's wife, along with scores of neighbors and guards, were also killed. Many PLO buildings were turned into piles of rubble.

I was startled when I heard a key in the door. I stood up, ready to run, but not sure to where. As Abdeen stepped in, I ran toward him. "Thank God you are here. I was so worried. Do you know where Suad is?"

"No. I thought she went to the university."

Soon Suad arrived. The three of us sat in the living room listening to the radio and television news but couldn't find out what had just happened. We called some friends, but they didn't know either. As darkness blanketed the city, the shelling became louder and more intense.

"This is getting scary. It sounds too close," I told Abdeen while clinging to him, unable to let go.

"You're right. This is scary. I hope it won't last."

The following morning, we learned that the fighting, which lasted throughout the night, was triggered by the Lebanese right-wing Phalange party attacking a civilian bus carrying Palestinian workers, killing twenty-seven and injuring nineteen. They were heading home to their Tel al-Zaatar refugee camp. As the news spread, an all-out confrontation erupted between various Palestinian groups and their Lebanese allies, against the Phalangists.

Abdeen, who in 1971 was shot in the shoulder by the Jordanian Army as they opened fire on the car he was sharing with other passengers, was not ready to take another chance. He decided to cut his trip short just in case the fighting continued or the airport closed. He tried to convince me to go back with him, but I decided to stay. I was hoping the fighting would stop so I could enjoy the rest of my trip. But as Abdeen predicted, the fighting did intensify, and I was pretty much confined to Suad's apartment.

"What kind of luck is this?" I told my sister. "I couldn't wait to come here, and now this?"

"Don't worry about it. It'll stop soon," she responded with her usual confidence.

The fighting did not stop, but I was glad to be with Suad in the same apartment we once shared. The university was closed, and so was most of the city. We both sat there listening to the news and remembering our days together. And as sisters do, we spent hours talking about love, sex, and lust, while inhaling leftover chocolate birthday cake. Although I was scared and worried, being "home" was comforting. I spent hours looking at my books and sorting out the ones I would ship to Detroit once the fighting subsided. But it never did.

Three days later I got a call from my mother in Amman telling me that my sister Arwa had had her baby girl.

"I thought she wasn't due for another two weeks."

"Well, she had an early delivery."

"What's her name? I can't wait to see her."

"You don't have to wait," my mother said. "Her name is Diala. I want you to come home as soon as you can. On your way, stop in Damascus and get me…"

Mother's list of what she wanted was endless. Part of it were the clothes my aunts had been buying for the baby. Then there was the long list of candies, sweets, nuts, and most importantly, the *carawyeh* pudding that accompanies the celebration of a baby's birth.

"Mama, I'm not ready to leave Beirut. With the fighting I haven't had a chance to spend time with my friends. I'll come for a few days, bring you what you want, meet my niece, then come back."

As delighted as I was to be in the area when my niece Diala was born, my highly anticipated trip to Beirut was not meant to be. The fighting escalated, and I was unable to go back as I had hoped. I was also not yet ready to return to Detroit. The warmth of people, my friends and family, the wonderful Mediterranean weather, and the vibrancy of the cities made me want to stay. Thanks to the promise of a job at ACCESS, it made leaving the area more tolerable.

The attack on the Tel al-Zaatar camp marked the beginning of the Lebanese Civil War that lasted until 1990. Like all civil wars, many atrocities were committed against civilians. Among them was the 1976 destruction of Tel al-Zaatar, along with the eviction of its 55,000 residents and killing of more than 2,000 men. Compounding this was the 1982 Israeli invasion of Lebanon and the Sabra and Shatila massacre. [9]

In the US, thousands of miles away, we watched with horror the unfolding events of the Lebanese Civil War—a war that left lasting imprints on Arab Americans, especially those with roots in Lebanon and Palestine, as well as many of their institutions for years to come. Many recent immigrants, including myself, lost close relatives and friends. Students were cut off from their families. The political conflict between parties in Lebanon found its way to the Arab American community. Some large and powerful organizations like the Organization of Arab students (OAS) saw their demise as members sided with different conflicting parties. As the war continued, the influx of new immigrants escalated and the demand on service organizations like ACCESS multiplied, as did the efforts to fundraise for victims of the ongoing war.

TO ME, BEIRUT was home. It was where I once went to college and where I lived and worked before coming to the US. It was where I taught kids in Palestinian refugee camps, including Sabra and Shatila. Beirut was the place where I met and worked with many great people, like Palestinian historian and intellectual Dr. Anis Sayegh and the Palestinian poet Mahmoud Darwish. It was where I met and fell in love with Abdeen.

When the war broke out, I was a newlywed, and trying to adjust to my new life in the US in order to pursue higher education and secure my future career, hopefully in academia. However, the unfolding tragedies of the war, coupled with the brutal Israeli occupation, consumed me intellectually and emotionally, and to a great extent influenced my future career choices. For hours on end I watched TV and listened to the Arabic news on shortwave radio. Sometimes I would cry, and other times I would yell at the TV or radio announcers, calling them names, as if the war was their doing. Sometimes I would turn the TV or radio off, cursing, only to get up a few minutes later to turn them on again.

"Oh my God," I would often cry out. "I can't believe this. They're destroying Beirut's old *souq*. They're bombing the camps. I wonder what has happened to my students and friends. They just attacked the Palestine Research Center…

There is fighting in the al-Hamra neighborhood. I wonder what happened to my sister, my brother, my cousins, and to all my friends."

"Stop watching the television. Stop listening to the radio. You're driving yourself crazy," Abdeen would beg. Despite the nightmarish visuals, I couldn't make myself stop. After all, these were my people—people I loved and cherished.

What saved me from totally losing it was meeting Shadi and his friends a few months after I came back from my trip to Lebanon. While getting up early on a Sunday, especially in the winter, was not that pleasant, I never missed a meeting. About ten of us would gather in Shadi's small living room, drinking sweet tea, while committing slow suicide inhaling cigarettes. Often all of us would be smoking at the same time. In winters, the room would get so foggy I had no idea how we could breathe. I'm so happy none of us, so far, have been diagnosed with lung cancer.

With the continuation of the war in Lebanon, our meeting evolved into endless political discussions and organizational hubs. We argued passionately about the war in Lebanon and the Israeli occupation, and we organized weekly demonstrations, lectures, and fundraising events. Most importantly we spent endless hours trying to figure out how to capture the energy of the thousands of people, Arab and non-Arab alike, who were sympathetic to the Palestinian struggle, and to transform it into long-term sustainable support.

CHAPTER 13

ROAD TRIP

DETROIT, SUMMER 1975

I sat in the Student Center at Wayne State University (WSU) having my lunch while trying to make sense of my urban sociology notes. Not only was I having a hard time understanding my professors, but I also had little knowledge of urban America. The prospect of failing terrified me. I needed to do well with the two prerequisite classes I was taking in order to start my PhD program in the fall, something I was eagerly looking forward to. It was hot and humid, and I felt rather lonely. Most of the students suddenly disappeared, including the Arab students, whose presence in large numbers attracted me to WSU.

"Hi, Anan. I am glad I saw you," said Ali, who seemed to appear from nowhere.

"Me too. It's kind of lonely here. Where is everyone?"

"Not many take summer classes, but you will see most of them at the Organization of Arab Students (OAS) annual convention in Berkeley. Are you going?"

"No. I wish I could."

"It's going to be a great one. Here's the program. You should come."

I would've loved to go, but didn't want to ask Abdeen as he was already paying for my education.

A few days before the convention, my dear Abdeen surprised me saying, "*Aini*, I know two students who are driving to the OAS conference. Would you like to go with them?"

"Are you kidding? I'd love to. When are they leaving?"

"Early Wednesday. They'll be back Tuesday night."

Sure enough, two young men were at our doorstep at the crack of dawn. It was hardly 5:00.

"Good morning," said one of them, extending his hand. "I'm Mohammad. This is my cousin, Ameer."

"Nice to meet you. I'm Anan. You want to come in for coffee?"

"No thanks. We have some in the car. We should get going. We have a long trip ahead of us."

Overjoyed by the prospect of attending the convention, I didn't give much attention to what Mohammad had just said. But what I did immediately notice was the difference in demeanor and looks between the two cousins. Mohammad was short and stocky with greasy hair, beat-up jeans, and an old, not so clean T-shirt. Ameer, on the other hand, was tall and slim with thick black hair, olive skin, and large bright eyes the color of fresh spring grass. He was nicely dressed and stunningly handsome. I was hoping that neither he nor my husband would notice the way I was staring at him.

I grabbed my bag, said goodbye to Abdeen, and left the house following the two young men. I was totally surprised when they walked to an old rusty VW Beetle parked across the street. I wondered how far this car could go before breaking down.

Mohammad gestured for me to sit in the back, which I did. By the time we reached the outskirts of Chicago, I was getting restless. "How far is Berkeley?" I asked.

"Almost 2,400 miles," said Ameer.

"Are you sure? That seems like a lot. How many kilometers is that?"

"About four thousand."

"That can't be true. I once traveled by car from Amman to Athens, through the length of Syria and the width of Turkey and that was only 1,300 kilometers. You mean to tell me we are going to drive three times as much in two days?"

"Welcome to America, my friend. This is a big country, and flying is not an option for most students," said Ameer.

"I didn't realize it was that far. How long will it take us to get there?"

"What do you mean you didn't realize it was that far?" said Mohammad, sounding like an elementary teacher scolding his student. I, on the other hand, felt stupid for not checking the distance, as well as many other details, before jumping in his car.

"If we drive nonstop we will be in Berkeley tomorrow before midnight, or Friday morning at the latest. Hopefully we won't encounter an accident or heavy traffic," said Ameer.

Four thousand kilometers in this car. Inshallah, *we'll make it,* I thought to myself.

"Where are we going to sleep tonight?" I asked. "I suppose it won't be that hard to find a hotel on the way."

"We're not staying in a hotel. We'll sleep in the car. Each one of us will drive a few hours while the others sleep," Mohammad said, sounding dead serious. I didn't particularly like his authoritarian tone, but said nothing.

"You might not want to sleep during the day. We will be driving through beautiful landscapes," Ameer said.

I dared not tell Mohammad about my limited driving skills especially with a stick shift. I was hoping he would be one of those men who didn't like women to drive them—so much for my feminism. I sat back examining the small car interior where we were to spend the next forty-eight hours. At least I had the back seat to myself. With a bit of luck, I was hoping it would stay that way until we reached our destination.

With three young Palestinians cramped in a small space, we spent the first few hours of the trip discussing or, more accurately, passionately arguing about politics. Only a year earlier, the PLO had adopted the two-state solution to the Palestinian-Israeli conflict, replacing its previous one-state resolution where Jews, Christians, and Muslims would live as equal citizens. This change was faced with severe opposition from various factions within the PLO, and intensified their competition to win the hearts and minds of Palestinians. The competition found its way not only to the US Palestinian community and the Organization of Arab Students, but also to our tiny VW soon after we started driving.

"You know, there will be an election of the OAS national executive committee. We want to be sure that none of the supporters of the two-state solution is elected. You'll vote for the right slate?" By then I had figured out that Mohammad was a bossy tight-ass.

"I don't understand. What do you mean by the right slate?" I asked, although I knew exactly what he was talking about.

"We want to be sure that the new members of the executive committee will be supporters of the one-state solution."

"But the PLO has already adopted the two-state solution, and it does have big support within Palestinian communities. Don't you think it is a more realistic and fair solution?" I said.

"Fair for whom? Definitely not for the Palestinians." Mohammad sounded angry. I was already regretting coming with him.

For long hours, my two travel companions tried to convince me to change my mind. I, on the other hand, was trying to convince them of my point of view. After a few hours of futile discussion, I was getting exhausted. Every time I managed to change the topic, one of them would get back to it. Realizing that neither of them was about to change his position, I said, "Listen, my friends. You are entitled to your opinion. But I've been advocating for the two-state solution since I was in Lebanon. I'm not about to change my mind, and obviously you're not either. So let's agree to disagree.

"That's too bad. We've brought you all the way to the conference and you're going to vote against us?" said Mohammad. Fumes were shooting out of his eyes as he looked at me through the mirror.

"I'm not voting against you. I'm simply voting for what I believe in," I said.

"I understand. To each his own," said Ameer, trying to reduce the tension that was building up between Mohammad and me.

"No one is asking your opinion," said Mohammad.

I tried my best not to get upset. Both men were at least ten years younger than me. But I did wonder how I got myself into this. And why did I not ask any questions before getting in a car with two men I'd never met before? And why, once again, do I find myself making rushed decisions without much thought?

I spent the rest of the trip quiet, looking at the beautiful and ever-changing terrain. I learned so much about the wealth of this country just being on the road. Although theoretically I knew how large the US was, it was still hard for me to actually comprehend its enormous size, its natural beauty, and its riches.

We drove through different states, some I had heard of before, others I had not. Each state had its own charm. The dense vegetation of good parts of Michigan and Illinois, along with the highly populated areas and heavy traffic, gradually disappeared as we moved into the more desolate states of Iowa, Nebraska, and Wyoming. While I had traveled a lot in the Arab world and Europe before, I'd never seen so many trees and bushes, enormous farms, or massive uninhabited areas. Even the deserts of Nevada and Utah were surprisingly stunning. With each beautiful view I told myself, *At least I had a chance to see this part of the country. I should come back with Abdeen.*

Luckily, Mohammad did not ask me to drive. He, in fact, drove most of the way except for a few hours when he slept in the front seat while Ameer took the wheel. After driving twenty nonstop hours except brief stops for gas, food, and the bathroom, Mohammad said, "I think we need to stop at the next rest area. I'm too tired to keep going."

"That would be great. I'm tired too," I said, trying to break the deadly silence.

I expected to see a hotel when we pulled off the highway, but there was none.

It was almost midnight. I was exhausted.

"I don't see a hotel here. Where are we going to sleep?" I asked.

"On park benches."

"I can't sleep on a bench out in the open."

"Suit yourself. You can stay in the car if you wish. We're going to sleep for a couple of hours only," said Mohammad.

It was past midnight. I could hardly see any of my surroundings, except for the big, bright stars, which I'd missed seeing since I came to the US. They reminded me of the stars of Petra in Jordan where I had spent multiple vacations. Suddenly, I felt homesick, not for Detroit, but for my "old country."

Mohammad and Ameer pulled a couple of sleeping bags from the car trunk and spread them out on two benches, while I stayed in the car unable to fall asleep. Every bone in my body was cursing me.

We resumed our trip at 4:00 a.m. After driving two hours, we stopped at a greasy spoon for breakfast—the food was bad, but at least I had a chance to brush my teeth and rinse my face. By then Mohammad was obviously pissed at me for not sharing his political views, and possibly pissed at himself for bringing an adversary to the convention who would vote against his agenda.

Thirty miles short of Salt Lake City, the car broke down. It was around three in the afternoon. The blinding sun and the sandy terrain looked like Saudi Arabia. It was hot, extremely hot, and cars passing by were few and far between. Finally, a truck stopped and Mohammad went with him while Ameer and I stayed with the car. Despite the oppressive heat, I was happy to get rid of Mohammad and have a chance to chat with his cousin who was not only more handsome, but also gentler and kinder. After almost two hours of waiting, alternating between sitting in the car and standing in the sun, Mohammad came back with a tow truck that took us to Salt Lake City. Sweat covered his already filthy T-shirt. "Let's go," was all he said. I wished I could find a way to go back to Detroit.

We sat in the small, hot, and dirty garage waiting for the mechanic's diagnosis. I was, nonetheless, happy to be inside and to have something cold to drink.

The mechanic, an older man in his late fifties with narrow, squinty eyes, a big nose, and greasy face, as well as greasy clothes and hands, came to the small room where the three of us were waiting. "I don't know how this car was running, or how you made it from Detroit. It needs serious repair." He started listing all the problems and the needed parts. I hardly understood what he was talking about.

"That cannot be true. It was running fine. And how much money are we talking about? And when can you have it ready?" Mohammad asked.

"At least three hundred dollars, and the earliest I can get it done is tomorrow."

Mohammad became really indignant. "We cannot wait until tomorrow. We have to get to Berkeley tonight. And what do you mean it'll cost three hundred dollars? That's too much money."

"Listen, son," said the mechanic in a gentle voice, "you're not going to make it to Berkeley tonight, and I am giving you a good price."

"Don't tell me you're giving me a good price. I'm not that stupid."

"If you don't like my price you can take your car someplace else."

I felt embarrassed by Mohammad's attitude and the way he was talking to the elderly man. *Asshole. Did your mother not teach you how to be respectful of elders?* I thought to myself. Instead I said with the friendliest voice I could muster, "Don't worry, Mohammad, we'll split the cost. If each one of us pays one hundred dollars it won't be too bad."

"Maybe you can afford it. I can't," he barked back.

"She is trying to help," said Ameer.

"I don't need her help," said Mohammad. Then he turned to the mechanic and asked, "How early can you get the car repaired?"

"Let me see. I'll work on it this evening and tomorrow morning. I open at 7:00 a.m., hopefully it'll be done by 9:00."

"That's too late. Can we get it earlier?"

The mechanic pulled a dirty cloth from his pocket and wiped his sweaty face. He squinted his small blue eyes and stared at Mohammad really hard. I was scared the two might get into a serious argument.

"Thank you," I said. "We've been traveling for the last two days. Mohammad is tired. We will pick up the car tomorrow by 9:00. Would you be kind enough to give us a ride to a nearby hotel?"

"For you, young lady, I will."

Mohammad looked at me but said nothing. He and his cousin were undergraduate students. The unexpected cost of the car repair and the hotel must have added to their frustration.

Like them, I wasn't that thrilled about the unexpected cost, but I was glad to spend the rest of the day and the night outside that car. After getting to a cheap hotel, not far from where we left the car, Ameer told me that he and Mohammad would be going to a restaurant later. "Would you like to join us?"

"Thank you, Ameer. I am tired and prefer to sleep. You go and enjoy yourself. There is a small restaurant in the hotel. I would rather eat there." Although the restaurant didn't look that appetizing, I was thrilled to take a break from Mohammad. All I wanted was to be left alone, to take a shower, and stretch my aching body. I had no idea how the two of them were going to find their way to a restaurant, and I didn't care.

"We'll be leaving the hotel no later than 8:30 tomorrow morning. Meet us in the lobby," ordered Mohammad.

Yes, commander in chief, I will.

We had to take a taxi to the garage. By the time we hit the road again it was almost 9:30 a.m. Mohammad was fuming, not only because we encountered unexpected expenses, but for missing the first day of the convention. He kept bitching about it while Ameer and I kept quiet. I focused my attention on the changing scenery, dozing off here and there. All I hoped for was to make it safely to our final destination.

We arrived in Berkeley after 9:00 p.m. The campus was still buzzing with hundreds of Arab students. Although I had lived in many Arab countries for thirty years and had attended universities in Beirut, Amman, and Cairo, I had never before encountered that many Arab students from different national backgrounds gathered in one place. It was at that conference where I met many delightful students, some of whom became close lifelong friends.

During the following two days, I listened to guest speakers and attended numerous workshops and panels. I was surprised by the extent to which Palestine and the Israeli occupation, as well as the Lebanese Civil War, dominated the conference. It felt like being in the Arab world. Regardless of the national background of students, being Egyptian, Iraqi, or from North Africa, Palestine was the cause that united all of us. Even when the discussion was about the Civil War, Palestine was at the heart of the discussion, since the presence of the PLO and Palestinians in Lebanon were central to that conflict. The debate over the Palestinian one-state or two-state solution that created such a rift in our small VW, dominated the conference as well. For three days, people passionately discussed and argued, danced and sang, and hardly slept. The energy of the conference was contagious. All the disappointment and exhaustion of the road trip evaporated soon after I arrived. Nonetheless, I had already made up my mind. I was taking a plane back to Detroit, no matter how much it cost.

CHAPTER 14
THE WEDDING GUEST

DETROIT, SUMMER 1976

"There is a wedding at Beit Hanina Club this Sunday. We should go," said my friend Shadi.

"Whose wedding?"

"Ahmed Othman. He's getting married to Leila Nassar."

"I haven't been invited. Besides, I don't know either one."

"Don't worry. You don't need to be invited. They'll be happy to see you."

"I can't just go to a wedding uninvited. And why would they be happy to have a stranger invade their wedding?"

"You're not a stranger. The groom's father is a comrade."

To my friend Shadi, everyone who supported the Palestinian struggle was a comrade.

As I became more acquainted with Detroit's Palestinian community, I realized that Shadi was correct. Invitations to most weddings, especially within the recent-immigrant communities of the West Bank villages of Beit Hanina and El-Bireh, were open. No invitation cards or RSVPs were necessary. Anyone could attend. Even when not invited, people felt hurt if you weren't there. An average wedding ranged from 350-400 people cramped in the small and gloomy Beit Hanina Hall. The number of the guests reflected the status of the families of the groom and bride. The more the merrier. News about weddings, as well as births and deaths, spread by word of mouth, and everyone from the immediate community, that is, immigrants from the same village, were expected to be there. This was a tradition brought over from the "old country," where most people in a village were related, and everyone came together on both happy and sad occasions.

My husband drove me to Beit Hanina Hall, where Ahmed and Leila's wedding was held. We could hear the live music blasting from a few blocks away. I was positive everyone else in the neighborhood could also hear it. The hall was on Wyoming Street in the South End of Dearborn, a working-class neighborhood and home to large Palestinian, Lebanese, and Yemeni immigrant communities. They all shared the same tradition of loud music well into the late hours of the night. But what struck me the most was the kind of music being played, which was hardly wedding music. The famous singer, Ali Harajleh, was singing Palestinian freedom songs. I was totally dumbfounded. I thought I went to the wrong place, or got the wedding date mixed up. But I was happy to hear these songs—they brought many fond memories of political rallies I'd attended in Jordan and Lebanon.

The parking lot, where Abdeen dropped me off, was filled with cars and people. Men and women were gathered in small groups talking and smoking. Groups of children were chasing each other. The women were in their traditional embroidered dresses and adorned with heavy gold: earrings, bracelets, necklaces, and even small fitted hats ornamented with shiny coins. I was wondering how they could move with so much gold. But this was the occasion to show their treasures, a symbol of their status and wealth. I had never seen so much gold, except in the gold markets found in most Arab cities. I, on the other hand, had a simple black dress and a single-strand pearl necklace.

Reluctantly I approached one of the women. "Is this Ahmed and Leila's wedding?" I asked.

"Of course it is. Whose wedding do you think it is?" Then she added, "And who are you?" I was taken aback by her questions and the tone of her voice.

"I'm Anan Ameri."

"Ameri! You're not from Beit Hanina, are you?"

"No, I'm not."

"Where are you from? *Inti bint meen?* Whose daughter are you?" asked another woman.

"My father is from Jaffa. I grew up in Amman," I said, already intimidated by their questions.

"*Hathi madanieyeh*. She is a city girl," said one woman.

"We have never seen you before. Do you live in the South End?" asked a third one.

"No, I don't."

Slowly, other women joined to form a circle around me, and started asking: "Where do you live? When did you come to *Ameerca*? Are you married? How long have you been married? Do you have any children? Why not? Why are you wearing a black dress for a wedding? This is not an *aza*." As their inquiries continued, which felt more like an interrogation, I was cursing my friend Shadi for convincing me to come to a wedding uninvited, and cursing myself for listening to him. I guess lonely people do crazy things, and I was lonely and eager to make friends, even if it meant going uninvited to weddings of people I didn't know. I regretted not stopping at Shadi's house, which was only a few blocks away, and coming with him. Maybe he could have saved me from all of the uncomfortable inquiries.

I felt so much like an outsider being the "*madanieyeh*" who was totally out of touch with Palestinian village culture. Realizing that I had no way out, I gathered all my courage, straightened my back, lifted my head, and with false confidence I walked into the hall in my black dress, which I thought was very elegant.

As I stepped inside, I became even more confused. Everything about the hall looked like a political rally. A large picture of the Palestinian leader Yasser Arafat, with his shabby beard and big smile, was facing the entrance. It was so huge you would think Arafat himself was about to jump out of the frame to greet you. A similarly large map of Palestine was hung next to him. The small dark Beit Hanina Hall was transformed into a colorful, festive space with hundreds of light bulbs and Palestinian flags hanging from the low ceiling. The tables were covered with plastic tablecloths of different colors: red, green, white, and black—the colors of the Palestinian flag. Vocalist Ali Harajleh was singing: "Palestine, you will soon be free... Palestine we will return to you." No wonder, among the uninvited guests, in addition to myself, there were some blond, blue-eyed, easily identifiable FBI agents. They probably thought a revolution was being organized right there and the wedding was just a cover!

The hall was packed. I started to panic wondering if I would be able to locate my friend Shadi, the only person I knew in the crowd. Had I had a way to get home, I would have just turned back and left. I walked slowly around searching for a pay phone to call my husband, assuming he could hear me, when two elderly women approached me. Soon, more women came to see this stranger coming to a wedding in a black dress. I was terrified by the prospect of facing another series of interrogation. But the music was so loud I could hardy hear what they were telling me. To my pleasant surprise the women started to hug and kiss me, which added to my confusion, but at the same time, made me feel more at ease. Whatever these women were saying didn't really matter. They acted like I was their lost cousin who'd finally come home.

The deafening live music, which I was never able to get used to no matter how many weddings or political rallies I attended, played all night long. The band continued to play freedom songs, which I found rather charming and fitting for the hall's decorations. Suddenly, and out of nowhere, a young man came running through the crowd, approaching the stage. As he whispered in Ali Harajleh's ear, all heads turned to one door. I was alarmed, not knowing what to expect. But within seconds I relaxed as the singer shifted to romantic songs about an everlasting love and a happy life together blessed by lots and lots of children. For dramatic effect, the iconic singer stopped mid-verse and after a few seconds of utter silence the loud music started again, and all the guests stood up. The singer started his introduction of the bride and groom and their parents as they stepped into the hall. "Ladies and gentlemen… Here come the parents of the groom, Abu Ahmed and Um Ahmed." The loud drums beat even louder. "And now, ladies and gentlemen, please help me welcome the parents of the bride, Abu Leila and Um Leila." But the loudest greetings were saved for the newlyweds. "Ladies and gentlemen…here they come…here they come… The bride and groom…Ahmed and Leila." The crowd started cheering and the hyper kids got even more excited. I often wonder how many of these children suffered hearing loss as they attended all of these weddings.

The first dance was saved for the newlyweds, then their parents would join, and soon almost the whole crowd was dancing. People danced all night long until their feet ached to the point that they could hardly stand. Men, who came with their pockets stacked with cash, were competing tossing dollars at the bride and groom. You would think the skies were raining green. This was another tradition brought from the village, where guests shower the bride and broom with cash as wedding gifts to help them start their new life. The money, which sometimes added up to thousands of dollars, would be collected by kids and later given to the newlyweds. But as I learned later, it was rather common that some or even all of the money would be later donated to Palestinian charities.

As I attended more weddings, mostly uninvited but expected to be there, I learned the wedding rituals. *Katib al Kitab*, the Muslim religious ceremony, took place days or possibly months before the public celebration. It was held at the bride's parents' home, and attended by the Imam and only a few family members and friends. Then came the public communal celebration shared by all. Women started making sweets and large buckets of yogurt in their homes a few days before. On the day of the wedding, the men went to wholesale markets early in the morning and brought boxes and boxes of food and delivered them to the Beit Hanina Club. The women went early to receive the goods. They spent the day cooking and decorating the hall while exchanging community gossip: who just had a kid, who is getting married next, who is getting a divorce, or who is buying a new house or a new business. Once done, the women rushed home, bathed, and put on their best traditional Palestinian embroidered dresses and gold galore. They came back accompanied by their husbands and children.

What I found most fascinating was the extent to which Palestinian weddings and political rallies were alike, almost identical, save the cake and the few romantic songs. In all of the ones I attended during the 1970s and 1980s—and trust me I attended a lot—one could count on the men delivering the food, and the women cooking the traditional *mansaf* made of lamb, yogurt, and rice. On both occasions, Beit Hanina Hall was transformed into a festive place with hundreds of light bulbs and Palestinian flags. People danced all night long to the music that blasted throughout the neighborhood, while vocalist Ali Harajleh sang about the lost land, the long years of yearning, and Palestinians who would soon return to their land and loved ones, *Inshallah*. People danced all night long while the men competitively tossed thousands of dollars at the dancers. On both occasions the money would later be collected and sent to Palestinian charities in the Occupied Territories or Lebanon. I often wondered if we, the Palestinians, were so bound to the cause, or simply lacked any imagination.

Before long, I started to join the women as they prepared the huge dinners and decorated the hall for political rallies or celebrations. While I wasn't much help when it came to cooking, I did take care of other chores, including serving the women coffee and tea, or going to the neighborhood bakery to bring them fresh *zaatar* bread and falafel sandwiches. What I really enjoyed the most was the company and the harmless gossip and dirty jokes. It was there where I learned that Nadia, the daughter of Um Mousa, was in love and about to get married to a Christian man. When a woman asked if her parents were upset, another woman said, "Not if he is willing to chop his penis," referencing the Islamic tradition of circumcision. I also enjoyed the camaraderie and bonding among these women, although I could detect the subtle competition, like who cooks the best, whose kids are doing better, and whose husbands are making more money.

With all the years I lived in the Arab world, I have never attended more weddings, ate more *mansaf*, saw more gold, or learned more about Palestinian village life than during my early years in Detroit. At these weddings, I also learned how to dance the *dabkeh* and started to wear the Palestinian embroidered dress I bought on my first trip back home. To them, however, I was still lovingly called "that *madanieyeh*."

Those were fun and hopeful times. I don't know if we were optimistic or naive, but we were convinced that the Palestinian State was about to happen, and many believed that going back to their villages and homes in Palestine was only around the corner.

CHAPTER 15
SHIFTING GROUNDS

DETROIT, FALL 1977

The phone rang, interrupting my peaceful existence. It was Sunday evening, and I had spent the weekend studying and writing a paper for one of my classes. It was my second year as a PhD student at Wayne State University, however I still found writing papers in English rather challenging. Although tired, I felt good about what I had accomplished in the previous two days. After dinner I took a warm bath and sat on the sofa with a light blanket, listening to Arabic music. I was enjoying my solitude while Abdeen was attending one of his out-of-town meetings. Annoyed by a persistent caller, I slowly walked toward the phone and picked up the receiver.

"Sorry, Anan. Did I wake you up? Is this a bad time to talk?"

"No. It's all right."

It was my friend Rami in New York. He wanted to introduce me to a woman who was visiting him from Lebanon.

"She's hoping to solicit our support for a worthy project helping Palestinian women."

"What kind of support is she looking for?" I asked.

"Here, you talk to her."

"Hi, this is Anita. Your friend Dawood Talhami at the Palestine Research Center and Liyana Hadi from the Union of Palestinian Women gave me your name. They said you might be able to support our work with Palestinian refugees in Lebanon."

"I'm happy to help. But I need to know more about your work and the kind of support you're looking for."

"I'm trying to raise money to help women who lost their husbands during the war and are now the main providers for their families. Most of them are from Tel al-Zaatar refugee camp. I would like to come to Michigan next week. I can tell you more when I see you." Then she added, "Would it be possible for you to have a gathering for me to tell people about our work?"

After talking to Anita, I called my friends, Dawood and Liyana, in Beirut.

"I just want to be sure she is genuine. With her non-Arab name and flawless American accent, I wasn't sure. Do you know her? Is she trustworthy?" I asked.

Liyana laughed. "Of course we know her. She is an American married to a Palestinian. She has been active with us for years."

With the help of my Sunday friends and Abdeen, who was strongly connected to most progressive communities in Metro Detroit, we managed to host a large gathering at our home. Anita shared slides with us that told heartbreaking stories of destruction, loss, and displacement. Her visit came only three years after I left Lebanon, and the horror of my 1975 visit to Beirut, when the first attack on Tel al-Zaatar took place, was still a vivid, painful memory. The minute we saw the grieving faces of the women and children, my friends and I knew that we had to help. Anita also shared with us her efforts, along with other women, to resettle Palestinian refugees who survived the Tel al-Zaatar massacre. They had recently established a new organization called Association Najdeh to train and help women find employment. Their first project was embroidery production.

"Who will buy embroidery in a war-torn country?" Khalid asked.

"There are large markets in most Arab countries, especially the Gulf States. We are also hoping to tap into potential markets in Europe and the US."

Anita had samples of embroidered pillowcases, table runners, and purses, which were stunningly beautiful. She left some with us to sell, but instead we bought them ourselves, and asked her to send us more. Forty years later, as I visit my friends in various cities across the US, I can find their homes filled with Association Najdeh embroidery that we have been importing and selling ever since.

During Anita's visit, a couple of my Sunday friends and I took her around to meet other Palestinians in Michigan and Ohio. We also connected her with progressive activists in other cities, many of whom we had met at the Organization of Arab Students conventions. After a three-week visit, she left with a few thousand dollars in donations and the promise that I would soon visit Association Najdeh in Lebanon.

Anita's visit came at a time when my friends and I were searching for a more effective way to galvanize the strong support for the Palestinians that existed within Arab and non-Arab communities. A few of us who had hosted Anita in our respective cities decided to get together in Youngstown, Ohio to coordinate our efforts. After a long day of discussion and weighing different options, we agreed to adopt one of Association Najdeh's projects and to import some of their embroidery to sell. We also agreed to form a coordinating committee with one member from each city, with myself representing Detroit.

I came home full of excitement, eager to tell Abdeen about our meeting in Youngstown, including our plans to raise funds for Association Najdeh.

"Anan, you ought to be careful. If you're going to send money abroad, you have to be registered as a nonprofit tax-exempt organization. Also, I'm concerned about the level of your involvement. It's going to interfere with your studies."

"You sound like my parents. Don't worry about my studies, I can manage. But tell me, why do we need to register as a nonprofit?"

"Because it's the law."

"I have no clue how to do that. Will you help us?"

"Of course I will. But you need to first draft the organization's bylaws and designate three officers."

Despite Abdeen's concerns about me spending more time organizing, his commitment to the Palestinian cause was just as strong. With his help, by the spring of 1978 the Palestine Aid Society of America (PAS) was registered as a nonprofit tax-exempt organization with its headquarters in Detroit, Michigan.

EAGER TO WITNESS firsthand the work of an organization we promised to support, and to visit my family and friends, I flew to Amman as soon as the school year ended. By then, I had been in the US for four years and was still trying to adjust. I had made a few friends, had become politically active, and was pursuing a PhD. However, I couldn't claim that I liked my new life or the city of Detroit, or that I could stop fantasizing about going "home," not only for a visit, but to actually move back. I wanted to take Abdeen and live permanently there, where I belonged.

To my distress, the home I'd been yearning for was slipping away. In Amman, where I landed first, many of my friends had moved on. Some got married and were consumed by raising their babies. Others sought employment in the more lucrative Arabian Gulf and Saudi Arabia. Aunt Naima, my father's sister whom I loved dearly, had moved to Cairo with five of her younger kids, where life was less expensive and universities were free. Only my parents' home was left intact, including their constant arguments. My mother was working at her print shop. My retired father, only six months short of his seventieth birthday, was planting flowers, exercising, and doing what he liked best: reading and writing. He was also enjoying his volunteer position as the president of the Jordanian Writers Union.

In Damascus where I went next, I was saddened to see my grandfather's home closed. My two aunts, Suad and Nahida, who were the last to live there, had moved to an apartment in Beirut. Age had caught up with them. They could no longer take care of the large aging mansion. But this was the home where deep-rooted traditions and rituals were passed from one generation to another. It was the home where my grandfather, his siblings, children, and most grandchildren, including myself, were born. It was where I, along with uncles, aunts, and dozens of cousins, spent our *eids* and summer vacations. This was the place that gave birth to my precious childhood memories. It was my haven, the place that gave me much needed stability during my early years when my parents were constantly moving after they became refugees in 1948. It was the one place I thought would always be there, at the end of the narrow timeless ally, *Zqaq al-Sawwaf,* with the same welcoming faces, noises, rituals, and scents. With a simple turn of a key, this treasure that held endless stories and secrets of generations became history.

Next came Beirut. My two aunts were cramped in a small apartment with my cousin Aida and her daughter. My sister Suad had left to attend graduate school at the University of Michigan in Ann Arbor. The once vibrant Palestine

Research Center, where I used to work before coming to the US, was almost deserted. Most of the staff were working from home, fearing an attack from the Phalangists, or the Israelis who had already attacked the center before. As the on-again, off-again Civil War continued with no political solution in sight, fear and apprehension dominated Palestinian communities, especially in refugee camps. The 1976 massacre and total destruction of Tel al-Zaatar camp were daily reminders of the atrocities this war could bring.

The only glimpse of hope or bright spot for me was visiting Association Najdeh. Anita took me on a tour of the two embroidery production sites and introduced me to the women working there. As we sat around having lunch, we talked, laughed, and cried. They shared with me not only the horror of death, destruction, and displacement, but also their hopes for a better future for their kids. I left feeling drained but motivated. And I promised to raise the needed funds so they could have what they wanted the most: a happy day care center where their children could find joy.

Uprooted. That's what I felt as I boarded the plane back to Detroit. The grounds beneath me were shifting. The scars from losing my childhood home to the Israelis in 1948 came back to haunt me. My wounds had deepened as my three anchor cities—Amman, Damascus, and Beirut—my triangle home, as I called it, was losing two of its legs. I wondered if it could still stand on only one.

In Detroit, which I couldn't call home yet, I buried myself in my studies, and PAS became my new refuge. I desperately tried to forget my losses, and to erase the image of my Baba's watery eyes as we said our farewells.

WHAT I WAS determined not to forget was the grief-stricken but hopeful women of Association Najdeh. Once settled, I contacted the five PAS committees. Together, we agreed to raise the needed funds to help Association Najdeh build the day care center. In Detroit we were the first to plan a fund-raising dinner at the Metta Hall in Dearborn. We decided to hold the event as a holiday celebration on the fifteenth of December 1978. The day of the event, men went early to the Eastern Market and bought food, women volunteered to cook, and students were assigned to set up and decorate. We even booked Ali Harajleh, the community's favorite singer.

Excited, I woke up early that morning. It was my first time being the lead person organizing such a large fundraising event. We had already sold over 200 tickets, a vote of confidence from our community and progressive allies to our new organization. While drinking my morning coffee I went over my checklist of every minute detail. By 9:00 a.m. I was in my car driving to Dearborn. I stopped by the bakery and bought breakfast for the volunteers. In the banquet hall kitchen, we sat enjoying the fresh *zaatar* bread and hot mint tea, while singing Palestinian freedom songs. Our joyful morning was interrupted when Mustafa, a student volunteer, came to tell me that a young man, who no one knew, was looking for me.

"Who is he? What does he want?" I asked.

"I'm not sure."

Adnan, Abdeen's nephew, who was staying with Abdeen and me, was standing by the hall entrance. His gloomy face carried bad news. Alarmed, I asked "What's up, Adnan? Why are you here?"

He put his arm on my shoulder and gently pulled me to the side. "I am sorry,

Anan, I hate to be the one to tell you, but…"

"Tell me what? Did something bad happen to Abdeen?"

"No. Abdeen is fine. He left the house an hour ago to have lunch with some friends. It's…it's your father."

"What do you mean it's my father? What about him?" I yelled.

"A friend of your mother called. Your dad passed away."

"My dad cannot be dead." I gripped his shoulder with my hands, shaking him violently and screaming. "Don't tell me my Baba is dead. You're lying. My Baba is in Prague. I just got a letter from him yesterday. He cannot be dead."

Women came running out of the kitchen not knowing what to say. They sat me down, brought me coffee and water, and kissed and hugged me. They told me *Allah Yerhamoh*. My brain went blank, my mouth was dry. I had no words or tears. Dizzy, I got up and dragged my feet to the parking lot. They held my hands and followed me. They took my car keys and asked Adnan to take me home.

I stood by the phone, wondering if I should first call my mother, or if I should call my sister Suad in Ann Arbor and give her the bad news. With shaky hands, I dialed our home number in Amman. Aunt Ne'mat, a close family friend, picked up the phone. "I'm sorry, Anan. He died yesterday... Yes, in Prague. In his sleep... No, he was not sick... Severe heart attack... He didn't suffer... Ayman and Arwa are coming tomorrow. Can you tell your sister Suad? Do you want to talk to your mother?"

"No. Not now. I can't. I'll call her later."

I hung up the phone feeling numb and disoriented and unable to talk to my mother or my sister. At the kitchen table, I spotted my dad's letter. I read it, and reread it. I marveled at his neat handwriting. How could this be? I just saw him six months ago. He was chasing my friend's three-year-old son around the yard. He was taking my niece Diala with him to the swimming pool. *How could he leave us? Leave me? I love you, Baba. Please don't go.*

Abdeen came home and called my mother. "Um Arwa, I am so sorry about your loss. Please accept my condolences. *Allah Yerhamoh.* He was a good man... Anan is shocked... Don't worry about her. She will be fine... Fine. Just a minute." Abdeen covered the phone receiver with his palm. "*Aini,* do you want to talk to your mother?"

"No. Not now."

"Anan will call you later."

Abdeen hung up the phone and hugged me. A loud cry escaped him. "I'm sorry, Anan. I know how much you loved your dad. I am sorry I didn't get to know him better. Please tell me, what can I do?"

The past tense of love did not escape me. A sharp knife stabbed my already broken being.

"Just call Ziad in Ann Arbor. He and Suad are coming together to the PAS dinner.

Have him bring her here instead."

Abdeen wanted to talk, to console me. I needed to be alone, to lie down, to be quiet, to envision my life without my dad. To figure out how to tell my sister. When Suad finally arrived, the only words I could utter were, "Baba is dead." Still, I had no words, no tears, only a big hole.

To avoid dealing with my new reality, I managed to convince Suad that we wait a few days before going to Amman. I wanted to get there after the funeral.

When we arrived, my parents' home was packed with people—many drove or flew from various cities. To my utter surprise, my father's body had not arrived yet. The Czechoslovakian government had made the necessary arrangements to send it, but the Jordanian government would not allow it. Their logic was that he left the country from Syria, and he had to come back, dead or alive, the same way.

My father went to Prague to attend a writer's conference of the non-allied countries in his capacity as the president of the Jordanian Writers Union. To the West, as well to its faithful allies, including the Jordanian government, non-allied was no more than a code word for anti-Western and pro-communist. My father got caught in the Cold War rhetoric. He was not allowed to leave for Prague from the Amman Airport, so he drove his car to Damascus and flew from there.

To honor my father, the Jordanian Writers Union planned to have a public memorial commemorating his *arba'een,* the fortieth day after his death. The day before the memorial, some unknown government entity put ads in all the local newspapers announcing that the Ameri family, for unforeseen reasons, had to cancel the memorial. Frantically, we tried to find out who placed the ads and to reach the people who came from various Arab cities. The day of the memorial, the police circled the auditorium, sending people away. We ended up cramped at my parents' home with my father's close relatives and friends, remembering him, telling stories and jokes about him, and cursing the Jordanian government, who would not allow us to honor the man known for his honesty and integrity—a man who served Jordan in various capacities, including holding the positions of Minister of Foreign Affairs, Minister of Education, and Ambassador to Egypt.

Alone and lonely, I flew back, stripped of my security blanket and of what was most dear to me. Suad decided to take the winter semester off and stay with our mother. At home, I dug out all the letters my dad had written to me since I came to the US. In his first one, before I got married, he wrote, "I was hoping you would stay here. I believe you have a lot to contribute to the Arab world, especially Palestine… I also hope that marriage will not stop you from pursuing your education." I felt guilty for not granting my dad his wish of staying "home," especially when my relationship with Abdeen, the man I left home to be with, was on a slippery slope of deterioration.

Finally, in 1988, during the PAS fifth national convention in Los Angeles, I was able to make peace with my father's departure as well as with my decision to come and live in the US. The convention, marking the tenth anniversary of PAS, was held during the Palestinian Intifada, which had galvanized unprecedented international support for Palestinian independence. We had a lot to celebrate, including having the renowned Palestinian-Israeli writer, Habibi, as the convention's keynote speaker.

As Habibi and I sat at the hotel bar enjoying a late-night drink, he casually told me, "I was so happy to spend time with your father in Prague. The night before he died, we had dinner together. We spent the night reminiscing about our days in Palestine."

"You had dinner with him the night before he died? Tell me about him. Was he sick? Was he in good spirits? Or was he depressed or sad?"

"Your dad died happy doing what he liked and being with people he loved. You should be happy for him. He seemed healthy and content. That's the best way to go."

"You said you knew my dad before 1948?"

"I knew your dad very well. He saved my life in 1947."

"What do you mean?" I asked.

"In 1947, due to my communist affiliations,[10] the Muslim Brothers[11] threatened to kill me. Your father was the director of the Arabic section of *Huna Al Quds,* the British-owned radio station in Jerusalem. Using the radio station car, he managed to smuggle me to Lebanon. After 1948 and the creation of Israel, I walked all the way back to my home in Haifa."

"Wow… That is amazing. My father never told me this," I said feeling proud of my father, as I always did.

"Your father never talked about his good deeds. He just did what he thought was right."

The following evening at the convention gala, Habibi started his keynote address:

"In the Palestine of our youth we, the young 'Decembrists'[12] of the time, used to look at the father of Anan Ameri, the late Mohammad Adib el Ameri, as our teacher and father. Here we come after forty years as guests to our baby sister who has grown

up and became a full pledge leader of her own people. Allow me to thank our sister Anan, and through her, all of you, for providing me with this opportunity of being with you at your tenth anniversary convention and giving a humble hand in promoting your efforts in providing substantial material and spiritual aid to your brothers and sisters in the persistent uprising. "[13]

CHAPTER 16
TAKE A BOAT AND GO TO CUBA

DETROIT, 1980-81

Wayne State University (WSU), where I was enrolled for my PhD between 1976 and 1981, helped me break away from my isolation, regain my independence, and chart my own future. In addition to receiving a good education, it was at Wayne where I became involved in the Arab Student Organization (OAS) and met other activists locally and nationally. Many of these students were instrumental in establishing the Palestine Aid Society of America. OAS was also my training ground for public speaking, and where my first publication in the US, a booklet entitled "The Civil War in Lebanon," was issued in Arabic and English.

At Wayne, I also learned about American progressive politics and the civil rights movement. There I met my lifelong friends, Diane Binson and Stuart Michael, who taught me about the complexity of American society, with its good, bad, and ugly. It was at WSU that Stuart and I partnered on a research project in the inner city of Detroit, where I learned about the cruelty, anguish, and harshness of poverty in segregated America. And it was at Wayne where I learned about class and race disparity, when my friend Diane took me on a drive along Jefferson Avenue, from desolate downtown Detroit to the adjacent affluent suburbs of Grosse Point. It was there where my extracurricular education included books like *A People's History of the United States* by Howard Zinn, *Who Rules America?* by G. William Domhoff, and *The Grapes of Wrath* by John Steinbeck. And it was at WSU where I was welcomed and embraced, but also learned firsthand about the popular misconceptions, stereotyping, and even discrimination against Arabs and Palestinians.

Among the very early classes I took was urban sociology. With my poor English, my textbooks looked like a dictionary, each page covered with Arabic on top of many English words. Without a family or friends and with a husband who worked long hours, studying compulsively was my refuge. Nevertheless, when the first exam approached, I was terrified that I might fail. I was shocked when my professor handed me my exam with an "A," while saying, "You write better than most students, except for your very long sentences. Your native language must be Arabic." While I did not quite believe him, I graciously accepted the compliment. Two years later, when I got my teaching assistant job, I realized that my professor's comment about students' writing skills were accurate. I almost incited a riot in my class when I gave an essay exam. For most of my students, it was the first time they were required to write down their answers as opposed to true or false or multiple-choice questions, which were formats I was never exposed to before coming to the US.

At WSU, I was lucky to have many supportive faculty and colleagues. But I wasn't so lucky to have a couple of professors who treated me as an outsider who didn't belong to the university or even to this country and, worse, as someone who lacked integrity. Once I was invited by an African American women's organization in Flint, Michigan, to speak about Palestinian life under Israeli occupation. The format of the event included another speaker representing the Israeli point of view. To my surprise, the speaker was my professor, Dr. Leon Warshay. Luckily, I had already finished my theory classes with him and passed my first set of qualification exams in his area. Dr. Warshay spoke first. His opening statement was about Palestinian culture, a culture that "encourages violence and does not value human life." Palestinian people, as he put it, "lie all the time. They have no respect for truth or honesty." I couldn't help but remember my father to whom no sin was as bad as lying.

I sat there listening to my professor talking about how horrible my people were. When it was my turn to speak, I said, "You have been listening to my professor for almost thirty minutes and have just learned how violent and uncivilized we Palestinians are. You also learned that the Palestinians are dishonest and unable to tell the truth. I'm wondering if you still want to hear from me since I will lie to you. And just in case you aren't aware, I am a Palestinian. Do you still want me to speak?"

Women started to clap. One older lady stood up and said, "Sister, of course we want to hear you. The same has been said about us for generations."

Dr. Warshay left as soon I was done. He apologized, saying, "I am sorry I have to run. I won't be able to participate in the Q and A. I have another engagement."

The second professor who was unkind to me, to say the least, was Dr. Wolf, or "the Wolf," as some students called her. Although she took pride in being a liberal, she became easily irritated when students did not agree with her or did not idealize American society the way she did. She had absolutely no tolerance for an alternative point of view, especially when it came from students of color.

One day while we were discussing Western democracy, I mustered the courage to ask, "Dr. Wolf, I'm curious if US democracy is an exclusively white privilege?"

"How dare you say this?"

"I noticed that when white people criticize American government or society, they are practicing their freedom of speech. But if people of color or immigrants do the same, they are told they are being ungrateful and unpatriotic."

"Who said that? And when did that happen?"

"It happens a lot." I fell short of saying it happens right here, in your class, but I think she guessed where I was going.

"Well, if that's what you think, you might as well drop my class."

I wished I could, but it was a required course, and she was the only one teaching it.

To study sociology and not explore societies' challenges and shortcomings was rather oxymoronic. Dr. Wolf was an advocate of the theory of Modernity, which claims that the US and the rest of the western world are more advanced because their people, meaning white people, are smart, hardworking, and democratic. On the other hand, the people of so-called underdeveloped countries, i.e., people of color, are lazy, authoritarian, and unable to plan for the future. They seek immediate gratification and that's why their societies are backward. It was not surprising that neither I, nor any of the not-so-white students, liked her. I'm not sure she liked us either.

One day, as we were discussing democracy and elections, the discussion became very heated as some of the students, including two African American women and myself, were questioning the extent to which the American electoral system was in fact democratic. I was totally stunned when Dr. Wolf responded to our argument by saying, "If you don't like it here, you can take a boat and go to Cuba." Being the smart aleck who could not keep her mouth shut, I said, "Dr. Wolf, what if most Americans don't like it? Shall we all leave and go to Cuba?" The students started to laugh. Dr. Wolf did not seem to appreciate my humor or the students' reaction, but said nothing. She had her revenge a couple of years later.

As PhD students, we had to take two sets of preliminary exams before we could start our dissertation. To my distress, the committee of my last exam was chaired by Dr. Wolf and included two other faculty members, Dr. Joseph and Dr. Newby, both of whom were up for tenure. The grading procedure was rather simple. Each student had to receive a passing grade from two of the three professors.

The day of my committee meeting, I went to my friend Diane's teaching assistant's office and anxiously waited for the result, usually announced as soon as the meeting was over.

Diane and I waited for a long time for the committee to emerge from the conference room. When they finally came out an hour and a half later with gloomy faces, my blood pressure hit the ceiling.

"You think I failed?" I asked Diane.

"Nah. You're not going to fail this one."

I waited a few minutes then went to Dr. Newby's office.

"Dr. Newby, did I pass or fail?"

"We didn't decide. We plan to meet again."

"Why not? And how come you met for so long?"

"I'm sorry, Anan, I can't discuss this with you."

"When are you going to meet again?"

"I'm not sure. I have to leave now."

Dr. Newby was the only African American in the Sociology Department. He was a civil rights activist, and I felt more at ease with him than with other faculty members.

I left his office perplexed, not comprehending what was happening.

I called my advisor, Dr. Nash. "They met for a long time but didn't reach a decision. I wonder what's going on."

"I'll try to find out and get back to you."

A week later, the committee met again. After another long meeting, the result came out.

I failed.

Everything about the process told me I should have passed. That was my strongest area, and except for statistics and the one class I took with Dr. Wolf, I was a straight A student. Naturally, I suspected Dr. Wolf was behind this.

I gave myself two days to cool off. I did not want to do or say anything I would regret, but my sense of injustice was too strong. I just couldn't accept their decision.

Two days later I walked into Dr. Newby's office and closed the door.

"Dr. Newby, I want to ask you one question. You need to trust me that this conversation will stay confidential."

Although I was positive he knew why I was there, he asked, "What's going on, Anan? What is this about?"

"I want to know how you graded me. Did you pass or fail me?"

"What difference does it make? It is a committee decision."

"It makes a lot of difference. I believe you have no reason to be prejudiced against me. If you have failed me, I will accept the committee's decision. But if you have passed me, I will challenge it."

"Look, Anan ..."

"Please, Dr. Newby. Just answer me, did you pass or fail me?"

"Well, I didn't fail you."

"Thank you. This is all I need to know."

I went to Dr. Joseph and asked him the same question, but I was unable to get a straight answer. He kept saying, "It doesn't matter how each professor graded you, it was the committee's decision."

"Dr. Joseph, can you at least tell me why I failed? I need to know where I went wrong. It would help me prepare for retaking the exam. You know if I fail again, I'll never have another chance to get my PhD."

"I'm busy right now. We can discuss your exam some other time."

That was during his office hours, and no one else was there, but he claimed he was expecting someone. Upon my insistence, he agreed to meet with me the following week. When I came back, Dr. Joseph sat in his chair for a long time, like he forgot why I was there.

"Dr. Joseph, I'm here to discuss my exam."

"I know."

Slowly he pulled my exam from his beaten-up leather briefcase and started to look at it while turning the pages. He then started to tell me the weakness of my answers, but his explanation was not that convincing. On the contrary, it reaffirmed my conviction that there was something not kosher about the whole process.

Then came my meeting with the Wolf.

"Dr. Wolf, I know I failed this exam, and I do plan to take it again. It would be helpful if you could point out where I went wrong. What is the weakness of my answers?"

"First, I would like to know what kind of universities you went to and what kind of education you got before coming to WSU."

Anan, count to ten. Think. Breathe. Do not say anything you might regret.

"I got my BA from the University of Jordan and my MA from Cairo University."

"I don't know much about their standards or what kind of educational institutions they are, but obviously they did not prepare you to be a PhD student at an American university."

Fuck you and fuck your universities.

"But I did submit my grades and diplomas with my application, and I have kept an A average here at Wayne. How much more prepared could I be?"

"You didn't have an A in my class."

"You are right, not in your class, but I am here to discuss my exam. WSU must have checked my education background and qualifications before I was accepted."

My temperature was rising, and cold sweat trickled down my spine. I had to grab the chair's arms to stop my hands from shaking.

Anan, calm down. She is trying to provoke you. Don't let her.

"Dr. Wolf, I'm here to discuss my exam," I said again, while trying to stabilize my voice. "Can we please do that?"

She totally ignored my question. Instead she asked, "Do you subscribe to the American Journal of Sociology?"

"No, I don't. I thought that's why universities have it in their libraries."

"Maybe you need to check your attitude first because with such an attitude you are not allowing yourself to learn."

"Thank you, Dr. Wolf."

I couldn't stop my salty tears from stinging my face as I drove home.

"I need your help suing the University," I told my husband, who had already sued many corporations and government agencies, including the FBI.

"Sue them for what? You have no proof she unfairly failed you. Besides she couldn't have done it unless the other two professors agreed with her."

"I know she put pressure on them. They are up for tenure and they cannot piss her off."

"You can't afford to piss her off either. Not if you want to get your PhD."

Since I promised Dr. Newby to keep our conversation confidential, I did not tell Abdeen that he passed me.

I spent the following days with my friend Diane, plotting what to do next. I was not going to have my fate decided by the vicious Wolf.

With the help of Diane, I wrote a letter to the chair of my department stating that I was not treated fairly. I demanded that the university bring three professors of their choice from outside Wayne to review my exam. Otherwise I planned to sue the university.

"Abdeen, I want you to review this letter. I plan to turn it in tomorrow to the department chair."

"Anan, why are you making your life difficult? Just take the exam again. It won't kill you."

"I wasn't treated fairly. That's why."

"*Aini*, listen to me. They are not going to bring an outside committee because that would be an admission of not trusting their own faculty. Remember that Dr. Wolf will be grading your exam when you take it again. If she knows about the letter, and trust me she will, she will never pass you. You know what that means, don't you?"

"You know, Abdeen, for me this is a matter of principle. Even if I end up not getting my PhD, I'm not going to allow her to push me around or dictate my future."

"*Aini*, you have to learn when to push and when to back off. As they say, 'God help me change what I can, accept what I can't, and give me the wisdom to know the difference.'"

"Sorry to disappoint you, Abdeen. I'm going to take the letter to the Department Chair tomorrow." By then I had been in the US for six years, and was gradually regaining my rebellious spirit and self-confidence. I was willing to take a chance and fight back, even when Abdeen advised me otherwise.

"Suit yourself, but I think you're making a big mistake," Abdeen said, clearly unhappy with my decision.

I submitted the letter first thing in the morning. Then came the anxiety of waiting.

A week later, I was called to the Chairman's office.

"What if they kick me out of the university?" I asked Diane.

"I don't think they will. If that happens, you'll have a better reason to sue them."

I knocked at the Chairman's door and walked in with all the confidence I could muster.

"Have a seat," he said while pushing back on his swivel seat.

I sat facing him. My heart was jumping out of my chest and my throat closing on me.

"We reviewed your letter. First, I am glad you decided to write to me. You know I'm very happy you chose our university for your PhD."

Why don't you cut the bullshit and get to the point?

"Thank you."

"You have been an excellent student, and an excellent teaching assistant. I predict a bright future for you."

For God's sake, stop patronizing me.

"Thank you. But I thought this meeting was about my letter."

"I am coming to that."

"And…"

"Well…I'm happy to tell you that the committee reversed its decision."

Unable to believe what I heard I said, "Excuse me, I didn't hear you. Can you say this again?"

"The committee reversed its decision."

"What does that mean?"

"Well, you passed. But I want you to promise that this will remain confidential."

Confidential, my ass.

"Thank you. Of course it will. But I need to have something in writing."

"It's already done."

He picked up the phone. "Elizabeth, can you please bring Ms. Ameri's letter?"

My mind drifted to Abdeen's advice to know when to back off and I was glad I did not listen to him. I couldn't wait to tell him.

Elizabeth walked in, handed an envelope to the Chair, and left. He handed it to me without saying a word. With shaky hands I looked at the letter. It had one sentence indicating that I passed, written on WSU stationery, signed by the Chair.

I wanted to ask him what happened but decided not to. Instead I carefully put the letter back in the envelope and tried to steady myself by walking slowly out of his office through the adjacent secretaries' office, and then started jumping up and down as soon as I hit the hallway heading to my friend Diane, who was waiting in her office. I carefully closed the door behind me.

"They changed my grade. I passed. I passed. Thanks for your help. I'm so happy I didn't listen to Abdeen." I was dancing and shaking the letter in my hand.

"You're kidding me. Let me see it."

"Keep your voice down, I promised him I would keep it confidential."

"Yeah, right. Nothing is confidential around here," she said as she hugged me.

"We won. Let me call Abdeen and give him the good news."

"But I thought he wasn't that supportive of you challenging the university."

"I know, but he's supportive most of the time. I'm sure he will be happy for me."

"Hi, Abdeen, guess what, the committee reversed their decision. I passed."

"Seriously? Congratulations. I guess I was wrong on this one. I'm so glad you didn't listen to me."

"Diane and I are going out to celebrate. You want to join us?"

"I wish I could. I have a client coming in a few minutes. Go ahead and enjoy yourself. You and I will celebrate tonight."

I hung up the phone and turned to Diane. "Let's go celebrate. This warrants a big drink."

"Maybe two," said Diane, laughing as we walked out the door.

The second day I went to Dr. Newby's office.

"Thank you, Dr. Newby."

"Thank me for what?"

"For your support."

"I just did what I was supposed to do."

"You did more and you know it. I will forever be grateful to you."

When I thanked Dr. Joseph, he said, "Each year I do one good deed. This year it happened to be your turn."

As Diane said, nothing was confidential in the department. Later, I found out that both Dr. Newby and Dr. Joseph initially passed me, but they were pressured by Dr. Wolf to change their grades. Dr. Joseph did, but Dr. Newby did not.

In protest, Dr. Wolf resigned her position as chair of the PhD prelim exam committee and refused to ever grade another exam again.

CHAPTER 17
THE BIRTH OF THE PALESTINE AID SOCIETY

DETROIT, 1980-82

Toward the end of graduate school, I was becoming more politically active, and slowly but surely regaining my confidence and independence. True, I would have favored living in a more cosmopolitan city like New York or Washington, DC, but in many ways Detroit was the perfect place for me to start my life in the US. During the first decade of my arrival (mid-1970s through the mid-1980s), Detroit, with its large concentration of Arab immigrants, was emerging as the capitol of Arab America. Newly established cultural, political, and charitable organizations were being built to serve the needs of our communities and to support causes that were close to our hearts. With the continuous influx of newly arriving immigrants, including Palestinians from the Occupied Territories, it was no coincidence that Detroit was also the birthplace of the Palestine Aid Society of America.

Detroit was also where PAS held its first national convention in the summer of 1980, only two years after its inception. By then, we had already established six committees in various cities, with memberships ranging from fifteen to fifty. The goal of the convention was to unite the loosely affiliated committees (later named chapters) under the umbrella of one organization with a shared vision, mission, and bylaws; to set the organization's future direction; and to elect its first national executive committee. As one of the most involved in creating the organization, I was elected its first president.

While the vote of confidence boosted my ego, I was rather apprehensive about the responsibilities such a position would entail, especially because I was in my last year of graduate school.

The convention, attended by around 150 people, was highly spirited. Members traveled from various cities at their own expense. There was harmony and camaraderie among the attendees, who were mostly young Palestinian Americans, with a smaller number of Arab Americans and fewer non-Arabs. There were also a couple of FBI agents. When asked at the registration table if they were members, they admitted they were not, but insisted they were there to support the Palestinians and to learn more about PAS. Since we had an open convention and had nothing to hide, we let them be.

With much enthusiasm, each agenda item was discussed and debated passionately. The most controversial issue, however, was whether PAS membership should be limited to Palestinian Americans, Arab Americans, or open to all regardless of their background.

"We can't have open membership," Steve, a white Anglo member, said, who came all the way from California.

Many people started to talk at the same time: "You're right. Membership should be for Palestinians only." Another shouted, "Why should we have open membership?"

"How about Arabs?"

"And how about Americans who support us?"

"No, we don't want Americans."

I was chairing the meeting but had no experience managing such a large, rowdy crowd. After many unsuccessful attempts to bring the meeting to order, I stood up and started pounding on the table, yelling as loud as I could, "Please, let's talk one at a time... Please raise your hand before talking... Can I have your attention?" As I repeated my plea over and over without success, I started to contemplate pounding the table with my shoe, as did Khrushchev, the Soviet Union leader, at the United Nations in 1960. But luckily a couple of people on the floor managed to help bring order to the meeting.

I sat down, had some water, and disguised my frustration with a forced smile. Then I turned to Steve and asked, "Steve, can you please explain to us why you are against open membership?"

"Because it'll make it easier to spot FBI agents when they penetrate our meetings…like those who are here uninvited," said Steve pointing at the two agents. They were the same agents with the same cheap suits who had been previously spotted at large Palestinian gatherings, including weddings.

The room got very quiet. All eyes turned to the suspects, who sat there talking to each other pretending not to pay attention to what was going on. Mazen broke the silence. "Don't worry about them. These are our friends who sneak into all of our events." People who had seen these agents before started to whisper and laugh, then the whole room broke into hysterical loud laughter, including the two agents, who disappeared soon after the session was over.

Once the laughing subsided, Fuad, who came from California and knew Steve, said, "Steve, you've been one of our most committed members. You took the time and incurred the cost to be at this convention. You bring good organizational skills. So why should we not have you, or people like you, in our organization?"

"I'm just concerned that open membership would make it easy for unwelcomed individuals to penetrate the organization."

Those who were against open membership were citing examples of FBI infiltration of the civil rights movement, and other progressive groups. After a very long and heated discussion, we decided to take a vote. The overwhelming majority was for PAS membership being open to all.

The conference lasted two and a half days. It included training workshops ranging from recruiting members and raising money to holding cultural and political events and building coalitions. One of the convention's resolutions was to write a how-to handbook to help people strengthen existing chapters and establish new ones. The handbook, typed on a typewriter, was one of the earliest PAS publications. I still have a copy in my basement.

Among the guest speakers who attended the convention were three iconic civil rights leaders: Congressman George Crockett, Congressman John Conyers, and the convention's keynote speaker, Detroit City Councilwoman Maryann Mahaffey. After congratulating us on our success and expressing her solidarity with the Palestinian people, Mahaffey started to talk about poverty and racism in Detroit. She went on and on, to the point that Muna, a member from New York, whispered in my ear, "She makes it sound as if people in Detroit are poorer than Palestinians in the refugee camps. I'm afraid people might feel compelled to donate to her rather than to PAS."

"I live in Detroit, and trust me, some neighborhoods are worse than the camps."

The Detroit conference set the tone for what kind of an organization PAS would be—an inclusive organization with membership open to all, it would build both local and national coalitions with other progressive groups in the US, and it would politically and financially support Palestinians in the Occupied Territories and Lebanon with a special focus on empowering women.

ONCE THE CONVENTION was over, I started to wonder about the wisdom of taking on the responsibility of the PAS presidency. Not only had I no experience in managing a nonprofit organization, but I was in my last stretch of finalizing and defending my dissertation, which was set for the first of May, 1981. I wasn't sure what was more intimidating—writing a 350-page dissertation in English, or leading a newly founded organization in a country as huge as the US, with an ambitious plan but hardly any resources.

During the seven months between the convention and my graduation, I hardly did much for PAS other than feel guilty. But once school was behind me, I decided to focus on my new responsibilities, and to postpone looking for a full-time job until the organization could stand on its feet. In the meantime, I settled for a part-time teaching position at Wayne State University for the academic year 1981-82.

Among the convention's resolutions that needed my immediate attention was opening an office and hiring a part-time community organizer. With all the vacant office spaces in downtown Detroit, we were able to locate a spacious one-room office at the Woodward Tower building on the same floor of the Lawyers Guild and the American-Arab Anti-Discrimination Committee. The rent was only eighty dollars a month, provided we were willing to take the room "as is." With the generosity of a Palestinian store owner who donated one year's rent and the enthusiasm of our members, we cleared the office of a massive amount of junk, painted the walls, fixed broken windows, collected donated

furniture, installed a new carpet and a telephone, and printed our first station-
ary. Our open house was attended by a large number of community members,
activists, local politicians, and the media. What we were unable to find, however,
was a community organizer who would manage the office and accept our skimpy
compensation.

With no job until the fall, I started going to the office almost daily. Gradually the two hours became three, then four, and ultimately a full day. Soon,
other PAS members and students started to volunteer. Before we knew it, we
were getting calls from the media seeking information about Palestinian issues,
including the war in Lebanon, and the situation in the Occupied Territories,
among others.

By the fall, I had started my part-time teaching at WSU, and had to cut
down on the time I could spend at the PAS office without being able to hire a
community organizer. The executive committee offered me a meager part-time
salary of $4,800 a year. As one board member put it, "You're already spending
all these hours at the office, you might as well forget about hiring a community
organizer and get paid for some of your time."

Reluctantly, I accepted the offer. On one hand, I enjoyed PAS work much
more that my teaching job, but on the other hand, I was eager to get my financial independence, which was not possible with such a small salary. It was especially painful when Abdeen said, "That's four hundred dollars a month. You
might as well work for free."

"It's a temporary job. I'll do it until we find someone."

"With this salary, you're not going to find anyone."

AS I REFLECT on my decision thirty-five years later, I have to admit
that what I got out of my work at PAS was much more than what I gave. No
university, PhD, or any other job could have provided me with the wealth of
knowledge, skills, relationships, or lifelong friendships. These were the skills and
relationships that made it possible for me to successfully lead and manage the
Arab American National Museum. PAS also provided me with a platform to
meet many progressive American organizations and individuals, and allowed me

to gain a better understanding about other struggles. One of my early lessons of solidarity, which has left its impact on me until today, came from Congressman John Conyers, who unexpectedly called me at my home during the 1980 presidential elections.

"Hello, Dr. Ameri. I want to ask you for a personal favor. I need your help in the upcoming presidential elections."

My help? What do I know about American elections? And how could I possibly help an American Congressman?

"Of course. I'll be happy to help," I said, hoping he wouldn't detect my reluctance.

"As you know, I've always been supportive of the Arab American community and of the Palestinian struggle."

"I know. We are very appreciative of your support."

"I want you and your friends to help us mobilize the Arab American community for the upcoming elections. We have to support Carter, and we need your votes."

At the time, the Arab American community, especially Palestinians, were very upset by the Camp David Accords between Egypt and Israel, which Carter helped negotiate. The treaty did not address the Israeli occupation of the West Bank, Gaza Strip, or East Jerusalem. It also stripped Palestinians of their strongest ally, Egypt, and left them alone to deal with the much more powerful Israel. So I had to tell him the truth.

"I'm sorry, Congressman, I wish I could help you. But Carter betrayed us. People in our community are very angry. No one trusts him."

"I know exactly what you mean. You have every right to be angry. But please hear me out. It would be absolutely horrible for us as African Americans, as well as other minorities, to have Reagan in the White House. Many of the victories of the civil rights movement would be erased," said Conyers.

These few words had so much impact on me, and made a significant shift in the way I think about American politics. Until then, I, like many members of our community as well as our progressive allies, did not see much difference between the Democrats and Republicans. Both were viewed as responsible for US aggression against liberation movements and the exploitation of third world countries. After I hung up the phone, I gave a lot of thought to what Conyers had said. For the first time, I was able to look at the elections beyond the lens of US foreign policy or what it would do for "us," as Palestinians.

BY OUR SECOND national convention, held in San Francisco in May 1982, PAS had already established ten chapters, implemented most of its first convention resolutions, and established itself as a reputable grassroots progressive organization. The convention was very well attended and had an impressive list of guest speakers including two Palestinian leaders, Tawfiq Zayyad, the Mayor of Nazareth, and Abdel Jawad Saleh, the Mayor of El-Bireh in the West Bank. While the two and a half days were packed with panels, workshops, and serious discussions, the evenings turned into big celebrations. Most of us stayed up until the early hours of the morning talking, telling jokes, and singing and dancing.

As if it's not meant for Palestinians to ever be happy, only a few days after the convention came the June 6 Israeli invasion of Lebanon. Our excitement and euphoria were suddenly replaced with anxiety, fear, and despair. From thousands of miles away, we watched the images of deliberate destruction of a country that had already been devastated by long years of civil war. In response, the PAS executive committee had an emergency meeting and developed an action plan. In the Detroit office we coordinated a national tour for Palestinian convention guest speakers, and helped chapters organize various activities demanding an end to the Israeli aggression. Meanwhile, the phone at the office never stopped, nor did the unsolicited donations.

Throughout the summer, we continued to watch the Israeli land and sea attacks on Beirut and other Lebanese cities, including the bombardment and siege of Palestinian camps. Then came September 1982: the horrifying Sabra and Shatila massacre, which killed thousands of Palestinians, mostly women and children. Initially I was glued to the television, wanting to learn more. But the images of the lined-up bodies wrapped with sheets were more than I could bear. No words can describe my pain, rage, and the hate I felt toward the Israelis and their Lebanese Phalangist allies.

Breath, Anan, breath, I kept telling myself as I often felt ready to pass out or vomit, or actually lose my mind. For days I could not eat or stop the flood of tears. The fact that my relationship with Abdeen was not at its best did not help. Neither he nor any of my friends could calm me down. "I was there," I would scream when anyone tried to console me. "These were the camps I once volunteered in to teach. I knew my students on a first-name basis. I knew their families and was welcomed into their homes. I shared their bread and tea. I have no way to find out what happened to them, or if they are still alive. Why can't you understand?"

Taking rides on Lake Shore Drive in Grosse Pointe was often my refuge when I felt stressed or depressed. It had always had a calming effect on me until I caught myself, a few days after the massacre, contemplating driving my car into Lake St. Clair and putting an end to my pain. I was so terrified by my own thoughts I didn't dare take that drive for a long time to come.

Not knowing what else to do, I buried myself in PAS work. We took to the streets protesting, we called the media and had press conferences, we wrote our representatives and occupied their offices in all the cities we had PAS chapters. In Detroit, we demonstrated in front of the federal building. Hundreds of us, including elders, parents, and children, occupied the offices of Senator Carl Levin and Donald Riegle, refusing to leave and demanding a public condemnation. While initially Levin's staff threatened to call the police to evict us, Senator Riegle said, "These are my constituents and they have the right to stay." Levin followed suit. By 5:00 p.m., the senators and their staff took off, leaving us under the watch of their African American security guards who were much more sympathetic. At first, they were careful about what to say, but as the night progressed they started asking questions about why we were there. They even made us coffee and let us order pizza. In the morning we left without being able to get what we wanted.

Only two weeks after the Sabra and Shatila massacre, the Israelis stormed the Palestine Research Center, where I once worked. They ransacked its interior and stole its entire library, consisting of over twenty-five thousand works. The Center's archive about Palestinian history was one of the largest in the world. On February 5, 1983, an Israeli car bomb totally destroyed the Palestine Research Center, killing eighteen and injuring 115. Many of them were my colleagues.

My part-time teaching job at Wayne State University was becoming more and more irrelevant. I decided to quit and accept the offer of becoming PAS's full-time founding director—a job I agreed to do for a year or two until we found someone to replace me, without realizing where my decision would take me.

On the home front, my husband wasn't happy with my decision. He couldn't understand why I would spend five years getting a PhD only to end up working for a small nonprofit making a meager salary. Though I did understand his point of view, which was shared by many friends, in my heart I knew what I wanted to do. I had to remind Abdeen that when we first met in Beirut I was working for a meager salary at the Palestine Research Center. Reluctantly, Abdeen accepted my choice. However, my long working hours, evening meetings, and constant travel did not help our already strained relationship. While living the tragedies of the Lebanese and Palestinians from thousands of miles away, I was also living the tragedy of watching my relationship with Abdeen crumble, and the distance between us became wider by the day.

CHAPTER 18
BELLY DANCING IN SAN DIEGO

NEW MEXICO AND SAN DIEGO, WINTER 1983

The ongoing conflict in Lebanon, coupled with my troubled marriage and the lingering cold, gloomy, short days of early December, only added to my depression. To keep my sanity, I decided to go on a fundraising tour to help those who survived the horrible ordeal of Sabra and Shatila.

Among the first cities I visited was Gallup, New Mexico, where my friend Asaad had promised to help me. The Palestinian community there was small, but affluent, and pretty much controlled the wholesale of the Native Americans' arts and crafts. Most, including Asaad, had beautiful, expensive stores selling indigenous jewelry, pottery, and rugs. All I had to do was go with Asaad from one store to another. He would introduce me, saying, "This is my friend, Dr. Anan Ameri, the founding director of the Palestine Aid Society. She is trying to raise funds to send to the survivors of Sabra and Shatila. When she lived in Lebanon a few years ago, she used to volunteer teaching at these camps."

"*Ahlan wa Sahlan*, welcome. Happy to meet you. Can we offer you coffee or tea, or do you prefer something cold?"

"Thank you, I'm good."

"You can't come into our store and have nothing."

"Coffee will be fine."

Worried my visits would become social, the minute the coffee was served, I would start talking about the situation of Palestinians in Lebanon and their

~ 138 ~

desperate need for our support. Luckily most of the store owners had adequate help—usually a brother, a sister, or a cousin, which made it possible for them to take the time to listen to what I had to say.

The visits to each store lasted no more than thirty minutes. After my presentation, people would ask a few questions, then give me a check. Not only did they give generously, but they also insisted on giving me, as a personal gift, a piece of jewelry from their store. At the first couple of stores I tried to kindly turn down the offer, but Asaad told me, "You should take it. They will feel hurt if you don't." Asaad also drove me to Albuquerque, where we did the same—visiting stores, raising more money, and acquiring more bracelets, necklaces, and rings. Thirty-five years later, I still have most of these gifts. They bring both happy and sad memories.

One morning Asaad was going to a reservation to check on some orders he had placed. "Can I come with you? I've never been to one," I asked.

"It's not such a nice place to visit. It's like a Palestinian refugee camp. Possibly worse."

"If you don't mind, I'd love to come."

Although I have been to many Palestinian refugee camps, nothing had prepared me for the level of poverty and despair of Native Americans. The similarity between the fate of both people, who lost their lands and independence to outside settlers, did not escape me. Nor did the irony of Palestinian merchants, who were refugees themselves, getting rich off Native Americans.

As we drove back, I told Assad, "I find it a little unsettling that we Palestinians end up making money off Native Americans. How do you feel about that?"

"There're happy to sell their crafts. As long as we give them a fair price."

I gave a lot of thought to what Assad said, trying to give him and other Palestinians the benefit of the doubt. But I also wondered if I was their partner in crime by accepting their donations. I was able to justify it by telling myself, "It's a gift from one oppressed group of people to another."

A COUPLE OF days before I was about to return to Detroit, Asaad said, "I have a close friend in San Diego who can help you raise money. The Palestinian community there is small, but most are well-to-do. There is also a well-established Iraqi community. I'm sure they will contribute. You can fly from here; it's not that far."

"Who's your friend, and what does he do?"

"His name is Jaber Abdoun. He is a good man and has a couple of successful businesses. He is also well connected. I'm sure he'll be happy to organize a fundraiser at his home or at one of his restaurants."

"It's short notice. We need to give him more time."

"Let me call him and see what he has to say."

Sure enough, Asaad called his friend.

"Send her," said Jaber. "Of course I can organize a gathering by this Saturday."

"But it is already Thursday afternoon," I told Asaad.

"I know he can do it. Just go. You're not going to lose anything by trying."

Asaad insisted on paying for my plane ticket and drove me to the airport. "You are going to love Jaber and his wife Nadia. They are really good people."

I called Abdeen to tell him about my last-minute plan to go to San Diego. "As you like. Be careful and have a safe trip," was all he said. His voice was cold and distant. My gut muscles tightened as I slowly hung up the phone, yearning for the passionate love we once had.

I landed in the San Diego airport on a Friday afternoon in a sour mood. My short phone call with Abdeen was playing over and over in my head. I wondered if I should have stuck to my initial plan and just gone home.

Jaber Abdoun and his wife Nadia met me at the airport. Like most Arabs, they welcomed me as if I were a close relative or a friend they hadn't seen in a long time. Jaber's welcoming was with a warm handshake, while Nadia gave me a warm embrace and kissed me on both cheeks. Throughout the half hour drive from the airport to their home, they kept telling me how happy and excited they were that I decided to visit them. They kept saying *Sharaftina, sharaftina.*

"I would have been very disappointed if I found out that you visited my friends in Gallup and Albuquerque, but not us," said Jaber.

"Thank you. You are very kind."

I have to admit I found his extra warm welcome disingenuous. To give him the benefit of the doubt, I thought to myself that maybe he wanted to be part of the fundraising efforts.

Jaber is a Palestinian immigrant from the West Bank town of Hebron. His wife, Nadia, also a Palestinian, was born and raised in Cairo, where her parents settled after 1948. The new shiny black Cadillac Jaber drove, the Mercedes and BMW parked in their driveway, their huge home, and what seemed to be an in-law suite on the other side of the yard, all told the story of immigrants realizing the American dream. After all, Hebronites are known to be shrewd businessmen, and Jaber's success was an affirmation of that.

As soon as we entered the house, Jaber said, "Nadia, why don't you take Anan to her room. Let her rest."

"I'm not really tired. I'd rather learn about tomorrow's event."

"You don't need to worry. I'm taking care of everything."

"Thank you, I know you are. But I still need to know some of the logistics."

"Like what?" Jaber asked, looking surprised.

"Like, what time is the event? What kind of audience will we have? And how long should I speak?"

Jaber had a puzzled look. It seemed to me he had never organized anything like this before.

"Let's talk about this later. You go rest now. I have to go back to work," he said.

I did not particularly like his dismissive attitude, but being his guest, I decided to let it go. I was already feeling irritated and anxious, not knowing exactly what I was getting myself into.

As soon as Jaber left, his wife Nadia said, "Why don't I take you to your room. You get refreshed while I brew us some fresh coffee."

I assumed Nadia was going to take me to the in-law suite, but I was taken to a very large room inside the main house, which had its own living area and very fancy bathroom. After rinsing my face and hanging up my dress, the one I was to wear for the Saturday event, I sat on the bed thinking about Jaber. Recalling Asaad telling me that he was a nice man, I decided not to be too quick to judge him. After a few minutes I went back to the family room.

Nadia had a big spread. In addition to the coffee, she had various teas, all kinds of soft drinks, cheeses, crackers, fruit, and much more. I was not particularly hungry, but I felt obliged to eat, especially after she troubled herself setting out all this food.

"Nadia, this is a lot of food. I thought we were just having coffee."

"We won't be eating dinner until after 7:00 when Jaber comes home. You should have some food now, otherwise you're going to be very hungry."

Nadia and I sat around the table eating and drinking coffee for more than an hour enjoying each other's company. She was a very attractive woman, had a great sense of humor, and spoke Arabic with a beautiful Egyptian dialect. I couldn't help but think about the contrast of what seemed to be an unpolished, harsh husband and a very gentle wife. But I had seen many couples like this before. I didn't let it consume me.

"I need to pick up the kids from school. Would you like to come with me? If you don't mind leaving now, I can take you for a ride to see a bit of the city."

"I'd love that," I said, and off we went.

The dinner spread was enough for twenty people. We didn't eat till past 8:00 waiting for Jaber. I was happy I ate earlier.

"Your husband owes me at least ten thousand dollars, if not more," Jaber said as soon as we were seated to eat.

"Jaber..." said Nadia. He waved his hand in a gesture suggesting she stay quiet.

"Excuse me, I'm not sure I understand. What did you say?" I asked.

"You're married to Abdeen Jabara, aren't you?"

"Yes, I am. Do you know him?"

"No, I never met him. But he does owe me at least ten thousand dollars. Probably more." I was confused, not sure if the man was serious or just kidding.

Nadia looked as puzzled as I was. She stared at her husband, but he acted like he did not notice her.

As it turned out, a couple of years earlier, Jaber, Nadia, and their two children went to Egypt to visit Nadia's family. Jaber was planning to stay for a couple of weeks, while Nadia and the kids would spend the summer. At the Cairo airport, Jaber was arrested and sent to jail. The Egyptian security mistook him for my husband, Abdeen Jabara. They accused him of signing a petition condemning the arrests of Egyptian journalists who had criticized the Camp David Accords between Egypt and Israel and demanding Sadat's resignation—something my husband in fact did. Nadia and the children were sent back to the US without being allowed to visit Nadia's parents, not even for a couple of days.

Upon her return, Nadia hired an attorney, and with the help of the US embassy in Cairo, she managed to get her husband out of jail and back to San Diego.

"Your husband is a successful attorney. He should compensate me not only for all the money I spent, including attorney fees and four overseas plane tickets, but also for my time in jail. That is much more than ten thousand dollars."

Jaber's face and tone of voice were stern, but I was still not sure if he was serious or kidding, "I'm so sorry to hear about what happened, but Abdeen had nothing to do with it. The Egyptian government should compensate you."

"You know they won't," said Jaber.

"Jaber, *habibi*, you know she or her husband had nothing to do with what happened," Nadia said, noticing my discomfort, and obviously not liking what her husband had to say.

He looked at her disapprovingly, but said nothing. She said no more but looked at me with knitted eyebrows while shaking her head in an apologetic gesture. I was not sure how to respond, or how the rest of my short trip was going to go. I also started to wonder if his warm welcome was genuine or if he had just wanted the opportunity to tell me about his unfortunate experience, hoping I would convince my husband to compensate him. Regardless, the butterflies in my stomach were rioting harder by the minute. I couldn't wait to get this dinner ordeal over with.

The following morning Nadia apologized to me. "My husband has a good heart, though he is sometimes crude." After I assured her that I was fine, she asked me if I would like to see her dance studio.

"You have a dance studio?"

"Wait till you see it; you'll love it."

I was getting more confused and intrigued by what this trip had in store for me. I followed Nadia, crossing the front yard toward what I had assumed to be an in-law suite. The studio was quite spacious with wood floors and large windows. It had an elaborate sound system and dozens of Arabic records, as well as a large closet full of dance outfits.

"Tell me again, whose studio is this?" I asked.

"It's mine. I teach women belly dancing. They just love it."

This was hard to believe. Nadia and I spent hours the previous day talking, but nothing about her indicated that she was a dancer, let alone a dance teacher.

"You know, Nadia, I did live in Cairo, but I've never seen anything like this."

"Wait until you see the dancers. They should be here any minute."

Four young women soon arrived. I sat there watching. To be honest, neither the instructor nor the students were that good. It felt like being at a scene from *One Thousand and One Nights*.

"Do you like teaching this?" I asked.

"I do. It gives my something to do. I also like making an extra few dollars." Then she added, "I pick the best of my students to dance at my husband's nightclubs."

By then I had had enough surprises, and I was not sure what to think or expect.

"Your husband has two restaurants or two nightclubs?" I asked anxiously, since the fundraiser was supposed to be at one of them.

"Well, they are kind of both."

Damn you, Asaad, where did you send me, and what the hell have I gotten myself into?

Saturday evening, I got dressed to go to what I had hoped would be a restaurant. To my surprise, Nadia was not going.

"You are not coming with us?" I asked.

"No. I wish I could. Jaber doesn't like me to go to his restaurants."

"Why not?"

"Because there is dancing and drinking."

"But you teach dancing."

"Well, you know how it is," she whispered.

Sure, I did. But all I told her was, "Wish me good luck."

Here I was, alone with this man whom I just met a day earlier. We were going to a nightclub he didn't think was respectable enough for his wife. I was ready to tell him to forget it, but the promise of raising money to send to the survivors of Sabra and Shatila was too tempting. On our way, I tried to ask him about the evening's plan, but he kept telling me, "You worry too much, everything will be fine."

"I'm not worried, I just want to know what time and how long I am supposed to speak. It's already close to 9:00," I said, then added, "I usually give a short presentation about Palestine Aid Society, the political situation in Lebanon, then I ask for donations."

"The club is not the place for a woman to give political speeches. People will be drinking and watching the dancer. They won't give you any attention."

"But didn't Asaad tell you why I'm here?"

"He did. You just tell me what you want to say, and I will say it."

Again, I wasn't sure if he was teasing or serious. Regardless, my anger was building, and my blood pressure was rising rapidly.

"You know, Jaber, this is not what I expected. Maybe we should cancel. Just take me back to the house. Obviously there is a big misunderstanding."

"No, no. Trust me. Everything will be fine." He kept driving.

It took me a few minutes to adjust my eyes and ears to the dark and loud nightclub packed with small tables and chairs facing a corner stage. Four musicians with their *oud,* drum, *nye,* and *qanoon,* along with a vocalist, were playing. A not very good belly dancer was swiveling her body on the stage. Most of the tables had Arab-looking men, and only a few had their wives or girlfriends with them.

I stood there wishing there was a way for me to escape. Jaber must have seen the pained look on my face, "Come on, let me take you to your table," he said, while placing his hand on my shoulder and gently leading me to the one closest to the stage, which had a "Reserved" sign on it.

"Sit here. I had the manager reserve this table for you."

"Thank you, Jaber, but I'd rather sit farther from the speakers. The music is too loud for me."

"What's wrong? You don't like the music? This is the best Arabic band in California, even in all of *Ameerca.*"

"I like the music, but I'd rather sit a bit farther away."

"No…no. This is the best table."

He asked the waitress to bring me a coke and lots of food. I sat there not knowing what to expect.

"When do you think we should start the program?" I asked.

"We have to wait until they've had a few drinks. They give more when they're drunk."

Wait until they got drunk? How could Asaad send me here? How could he be a close friend of this strange man? I got so indignant, ready to kill Asaad for talking me into coming here.

"But I don't want to speak to a bunch of drunks," I told Jaber, almost yelling. Thanks to the loud music, no one else could hear me.

"Relax, Anan, relax. Stop worrying. As I already told you, you don't have to speak. I will."

I was dumbfounded by his insistence to speak on my behalf, but didn't know what else to do or say. I just sat there questioning myself: *How did I end up here, sitting alone in a nightclub in California raising funds for Palestinian children and women? What would they say if they could see me?* I needed a stiff drink, but dared not ask. Once in a while Jaber would come and sit with me for a few minutes ordering more coke and more food, then he would disappear. The music was too loud, and the dancing was too vulgar. I was no longer interested in giving any presentation or asking for donations. I felt like a hostage.

It was almost midnight when Jaber got to the stage. He took me by surprise when he announced, "Ladies and gentlemen. I am so proud to announce to you that we have with us tonight Dr. Anan Ameri. She came all the way from Michigan…" As I moved in my chair getting ready to go to the stage, Jaber gestured for me to stay seated, and continued, "She has come to ask you for donations to help Palestinian women and children in Lebanon. I'm also here to let you know that all the money I'll make tonight, in this and my other club, will be given to Anan to be sent to Lebanon. So please give generously. Evelyn"—referring to the waitress—"will be coming to your tables with a basket. You can give her cash or a check. Enjoy your evening and thank you."

They clapped. Jaber returned to my table.

"How did I do?" He asked.

"Great. Just great. Thank you. Can we go home now?"

"In a little bit," he said and waved to the waitress to get us more coke and food.

When we got into his Cadillac it was past 2:00 in the morning. He handed me a brown bag with cash and checks. The whole evening seemed so surreal. It was just like the action movie *Mission Impossible*, with two thieves running away with money in a grocery bag.

"I haven't had the time to count the money," Jaber said.

"We'll count it as soon as we get home," I replied.

"It's too late. Don't worry about it. Thank you for coming."

"I need to know who gave and how much. I want to send them thank-you notes and receipts."

"They don't care for getting receipts. By the time they wake up, they probably won't even remember how much they gave."

The following morning, Jaber went to his other nightclub and brought me another brown bag with money.

"Nadia and I counted the money from last night. We have $3,950 dollars. Nadia added $50 to make it $4,000 even. Thank you both. How much money is in this bag?" I asked.

"I don't know. The manager gave it to me."

"Let us count it now so you know how much you're giving me."

"We need to get you to the airport. You can count the money later."

On our way to the airport, Jaber kept thanking me again and again for coming and giving him a chance to do something for the victims of Sabra and Shatila. He didn't say another word about his trip to Egypt.

As we said our farewells, Jaber shook my hand warmly and said, "Come back. Nadia and I enjoyed your visit. Please give our regards to your husband."

I never had a chance to count the rest of the money until I got to Detroit. To my pleasant surprise I had another $3,625, and an additional $1,000 check from Jaber and Nadia. As soon as I finished counting the money, I called.

"Thank you, Nadia, for your hospitality and generous donation. Please thank Jaber on my behalf and tell him there was $3,625 dollars from the second restaurant, not including your check. I can't believe it, we raised $8,625 dollars in such a short trip."

"Well, you should come back soon, give us a longer notice and we will help you raise more."

"Thank you. You are very kind. *Inshallah*, I will come back soon."

A couple of days later I sent Jaber and Nadia receipts with the total amount collected, as well as thank-you notes to all who donated by check. Although my last-minute trip to San Diego did not go as anticipated, Jaber came through in the end, and my agony was not in vain.

CHAPTER 19
WHERE IS HOME?

TEL AVIV BEN GURION AIRPORT, ISRAEL, 1983

If I tell you I had been waiting for this journey all my life, you might think I'm exaggerating. But I'm not.

It was the summer of 1983. I was leading a US delegation to participate in Nazareth's International Work Camp. I felt my heart beating as we approached the final landing of this long trip all the way from Detroit. It was my first visit to this part of my country, Palestine. They gave it a new name. But whatever they named it, to me, it was my homeland. The one I had been yearning for all my life.

I'd been dreaming about this moment for too long. True, my dream had changed over the years. I used to dream about a grand reunion with my family and all my people coming home. Gradually, my fantasy was replaced by the simple prospect of a personal visit.

When my country disappeared in 1948, my nationality became obsolete. Although I later acquired a Jordanian passport, like many Palestinians, I was not allowed to go to Palestine, not even for a visit. Now that I was a US citizen, I could visit the country of my ancestors, the country where my father, grandparents, and many generations before them were born. I knew I couldn't stay beyond my visitor visa limit, nor could I reclaim my father's home in Jaffa. But at least I could finally see it.

I stood in the long line at Passport Control remembering my father and how much he loved and missed this land. He sure talked enough about it. I wondered if I would remember any part of Jaffa from the many stories my father had told me about his childhood there. And I wondered if I would recognize my own childhood home in Jerusalem, where I lived until I was six years old.

My dad used to drive us back to Jerusalem on Fridays, only a one-hour drive from Amman where my family finally settled in 1951. I do remember the Old City, its elaborate *souq* and the ancient Zalatemo bakery where we used to go for breakfast. Then came 1967. The seventy-two-kilometer drive became impossible. We could no longer go there.

"Your passport." Her harsh voice startled me, interrupting my nostalgic reflection.

She looked at my passport and then looked at me. She actually stared at me, then back to the passport, to my face again, then to her computer. After doing this a few times, she said in a nasty voice, almost yelling, "You wait right here," and left. The few minutes she was gone felt like hours. Cold sweat started to slide down my spine, and the beads forming on my forehead and upper lip were about to give me away.

What if she knows I am here with a solidarity delegation to participate in the Nazareth Work Camp? Will she send me back to the US or take me to jail?

Before boarding the plane in New York, I told members of the delegation to pretend they were coming on their own, as individuals or as friends, and to never mention my name or PAS. And in the event I was held at the airport, I asked them to call Tawfiq Zayyad, the Mayor of Nazareth, who was also a member of the Israeli Knesset. He would come to my rescue.

The Passport Control woman returned with a male security officer. They both stared at my face, at my passport, and then at their computer. Finally, with my passport in the hand of the male officer, he ordered, "Come with me." I followed him to the luggage area. He asked me to identify my bag once it arrived.

As eager as I was to visit, I was also scared. My friend Paul, who along with his wife Jojo owned a restaurant in downtown Detroit, hosted an annual fundraiser to send the US delegation to the Nazareth Work Camp. Paul was from Nazareth, and had personally experienced the Israeli oppression, including being jailed due to his activism. He, as well as other friends including Abdeen, had advised me not to take this trip, but I had been waiting for this return for too long. I knew I was taking a risk, but I had to come.

While standing in line, I recalled Paul's advice, but kept telling myself, *I am an American citizen now. My government will protect me. They can't mess with me.* My thoughts drifted down memory lane recalling my earliest activities against the state of Israel. I remembered 1966 when I was kicked out of the university for organizing a demonstration protesting the Israeli destruction of al-Sammoa, a Palestinian village in the West Bank, which was under Jordanian control and had not yet been occupied by Israel. I didn't understand why the Jordanian government was offended, but it was. I had been kicked out twice before while in high school for similar activities, and my father had warned me that he would not tolerate my behavior any longer. Once he learned about the university's action against me, he kicked me out of the house. My mother got mad at me, not only for being kicked out of the university, but also for upsetting my father, who when upset was not that pleasant to deal with.

I also remembered how my activities against Israel intensified after the 1967 War and the Israeli occupation of the rest of Palestine. I started volunteering in refugee camps in Jordan and Lebanon. What could be even more upsetting to the Israelis was that in 1972, I joined the Palestine Research Center in Beirut, the same one they bombed twice and ultimately ransacked and destroyed. As I stood in Ben Gurion Airport awaiting my fate, I wondered if the Israelis had any record of all of this. I didn't think so, as it had happened many years ago.

But my activity against Israel had continued even after coming to the US. With the help of many friends, we established the Palestine Aid Society of America to politically and financially support Palestinians. And we established the Friends of Nazareth Committee to send delegations to participate in the Nazareth Work Camp. We even hosted Tawfiq Zayyad, the Mayor of Nazareth, a respected Palestinian-Israeli leader, and a strong advocate for the Palestinian right to independence and self-determination. Zayyad was also a popular poet whose poetry reflected the tragic history of his people. Neither his nonviolent resistance nor his election to the Israeli Knesset protected him. The Israeli government jailed and tried to assassinate him more than once. His youngest daughter, Oboor, was shot in the face during one of the failed assassination attempts against his life.

When it comes to the Palestinian-Israeli conflict, things can get very complicated. For example, when Tawfiq Zayyad ran for the Mayor of Nazareth in 1975, the Israeli government warned the city residents not to vote for him. But they did. Since Israeli democracy was not intended to include its Palestinian citizens, the Israeli government retaliated by drastically reducing the budget of Nazareth. In defiance, the victorious Mayor Zayyad initiated the Nazareth Work Camp. And we, at PAS, formed the Friends of Nazareth in solidarity with our Palestinian brothers and sisters.

Every summer, thousands of Palestinians from Israel and the Occupied Territories, along with solidarity delegations from countries around the globe, including the US, would descend upon the city. During the day, they paved roads, painted schools, and repaired and cleaned parks. At night, they danced and sang. Their voices could be heard by the surrounding villages who would join in the singing. Freedom songs would echo throughout Galilee while the intimidating Israeli soldiers circled Nazareth.

As far as PAS, we did not only send delegations to be part of the Nazareth Work Camp, but we also sent delegations of union leaders, civil rights activists, attorneys, and journalists to witness the brutality of the Israeli occupation and its daily violation of international law. We tried to influence American public opinion, hoping that would ultimately change the US government's unconditional support to Israel. In addition, thanks to our two Congressmen, Conyers and Crockett, I was invited, along with other Palestinian leaders from the Occupied Territories, to testify in US Congress about the Israeli treatment of Palestinians. I have to admit, that was serious!

As I recalled all of these subversive activities I had committed against the "only democracy in the Middle East," I could hear my heart pounding against my chest, ready to escape my body. Many of my friends, including my husband, were convinced that our US government exchanged information with Israel. I liked to think of myself as someone who had committed heroic acts against the state of Israel, and was important enough for the US government to waste time or money on collecting information about. But was I?

"Bring your suitcase and follow me," ordered the male officer, interrupting my scary thoughts, as soon as my small bag arrived.

I followed him to a large room filled with other passengers and their luggage. He asked me to sit there and wait. Before I had a chance to ask him what was going on, he took off.

All I needed was to look around at the faces in the room to realize what was going on. This was the room where Palestinians were brought. We were coming home with our Australian, French, British, American, and even Israeli passports. We came from different parts of the world and had acquired many nationalities, but we were gathered in this room because we were all Palestinians. However, we didn't say much beyond the simple greetings. Somehow, we knew they were listening.

Before long, two new security officers came and asked me to bring my bag and follow them. They took me to a small room. After thoroughly searching and x-raying my bag and my shoes, they started their endless questioning: *Why was I there? Where I was going to stay? Whom did I know in Israel or the West Bank? What messages was I bringing and to whom?* It was obvious that my American passport was not helping me. What made things worse was the fact that I was born in Damascus, Syria. For these guys, that was not a good thing. My mother should have known better. But to be fair to her, I was born before Hafez al-Assad came to power, whom the Israelis hated. Also, when I was born, Syria was not at war with Israel, simply because Israel did not exist then. But as I tried to tell my interrogators all of these facts, I was making things worse.

The two police officers kept asking me the same questions over and over again. To their distress, I was giving them the same answers, which made them even more upset. Suddenly I realized that I was not scared anymore. I was rather fascinated. They were actually angry because of the simple realities of my existence—my name, original nationality, and place of birth.

Finally, they left and asked me to stay there. After a long wait, a young female officer came to the room. She had a small body and soft face, with large pale blue eyes.

"Take off your shoes."

I did.

"Take off your clothes."

"What clothes?" I asked.

"Everything."

"Why?"

"I need to search you."

"Search me for what? What could I hide under these clothes?" It was summer and all I had on was a T-shirt and lightweight pants.

"I've already been through your security gates. You have used your electronic wand on me. You have frisked my body with your hands. You have felt my arm pits, my breasts, and between my thighs, what more do you want?"

"I said take off your clothes."

I looked at her. She was young, hardly twenty years old. She could have been my daughter. Her cheeks were getting bloody red. Somehow, I felt sorry for her.

"Why are you doing this to me?" I asked in a very gentle voice.

"I'm not doing this to you. This is a routine procedure."

"Can I ask you a question?"

"What?" she said.

"If at any airport in the world, you were singled out and treated this way because you were Jewish, would you call it a routine procedure?"

"I am just doing my job." She paused for a few seconds, and then said, "Pick up your stuff and just go."

For a split second I felt victorious for not being stripped. Then came the grief attack. How pathetic! Was I feeling good for making her reexamine her attitude, or was it because I was not humiliated all the way?

CHAPTER 20
RAISING MONEY FOR JESSE

DETROIT; WASHINGTON, DC; AND CLEVELAND, 1984

Finally, our community saw a light at the end of the tunnel. A US presidential candidate who was supportive of the Palestinian right for independence and statehood. Who else, but the African American civil rights activist, Reverend Jesse Jackson!

With all the enthusiasm his run for presidency generated among Arab Americans, we decided to hold the third national convention of the Palestine Aid Society (PAS) in Washington, DC, and to invite Jesse Jackson as our keynote speaker.

"You must be crazy to expect him to come," said executive committee member Awad.

"Doesn't hurt to try," I said.

"If he supports us, that would be the end of his presidency. He is not about to sacrifice that."

"He's already publicly supported the PLO," interjected Zahra.

"I think you're being naive to expect him to accept our invitation," Awad said again.

Despite the skepticism of a couple of PAS executive committee members, we went ahead and sent Jackson an invitation. Then came the waiting. We waited and waited. We called and left messages, but there was no response.

Two months before the convention, we were still waiting. We started to wonder if we should invite someone else to be our keynote.

"Give it up," said Awad. "I told you he won't come. It's too risky for him."

"That's not why he didn't get back to us," Samia, who lived in Chicago, argued. "I heard from a very dependable source that his speaking fee is ten thousand dollars. He won't even respond unless he's guaranteed the full amount. Did we offer to pay him?"

"How do you know?" I asked. "And who is your dependable source anyway?"

"This is what I heard."

"No, we didn't offer him any speaking fees," I said. "We never pay any of our speakers, and we've had many great ones like Edward Said, Tawfiq Zayyad, Ramsey Clark, and June Jordan."

"None of them were presidential candidates," Samia said.

Samia's proposal to offer Jesse Jackson ten thousand dollars triggered another round of heated discussions within PAS's executive committee.

"This would set a precedent. Besides, where are we going to get ten thousand dollars? It's not in our convention budget," I insisted.

"Why don't we try to contact the Arab Embassies in Washington? They might give us the ten thousand dollars. That's nothing for them. They give regularly to other Arab American organizations," suggested Awad.

"Jackson is too progressive for them, and so is PAS. They won't give us a penny, and we don't need their money," I said. "I will contact my friend Jack O'Dell. He will help us get Jackson."

Jack O'Dell, a longtime civil rights activist, was living with his wife Jane in Washington, DC. Both were members of PAS. Jack was also the head of Jackson's Rainbow Coalition International Affairs.

"If you think he can help, how come you never contacted him before?" Awad asked.

"I tried, but he travels a lot. I haven't been able to reach him."

Despite the objections by some, the motion to seek Arab embassies for funding passed by one vote. Since I was the only paid PAS staff member, the burden fell on my shoulders. Not only did I have to make the appointments, but I had to go to Washington, DC and make the actual asks.

Reluctantly, I made calls to a few embassies requesting meetings with the ambassadors. I was happy not to hear back and ignored making follow-up calls. Only the embassies of Kuwait and the League of Arab States responded positively. To make the best of my trip, I also made appointments with Dr. Hisham Sharabi, founder of the Jerusalem Fund, and Jane Power, the wife of Jack O'Dell.

Noel, a PAS Board member from Detroit, and I took an early flight to DC. Pierre, a Lebanese graduate student and PAS active member, met us at the airport and drove us to our meetings. We headed directly to our first appointment at the Embassy of the League of Arab States. Ambassador Clovis Maksoud, an avid supporter of Palestinians, came to the reception area to greet us. I had met Dr. Maksoud and his wife Hala, a feminist activist, several times before. Dr. Maksoud also knew my father, which made our meeting relaxed and friendly. He walked us to his large, sunny office, which had so many books and artwork from various Arab countries. A large picture of his beautiful wife, Hala, sat on a low bookshelf next to his desk. Dr. Maksoud, an advocate for women's rights, loved and supported his independent, professional wife. Once we settled in his office, and after ordering coffee, he said, "I've been following your new organization. I have to admit, I'm very impressed by your work and the progress you've made in such a short time."

Before we left, Dr. Maksoud promised to send us three thousand dollars. He walked us all the way to the embassy entrance, wishing us good luck.

"That's not bad. You've been here for only one hour and raised 30 percent of your goal," Pierre said with much enthusiasm.

"That's why we started with Dr. Maksoud," I said.

After lunch, we were ready for our second meeting with the Kuwaiti Ambassador.

"I'm not that optimistic," Noel said, "but I'm going to put a big smile on my face and do it."

"I'm not either. But since they called back and set the appointment with the ambassador, they could be interested in supporting us. Let's keep our figures crossed. Who knows, maybe this is our lucky day," said Pierre.

Hopeful that our job would be easier than we thought, we got in Pierre's old beaten-up Fiat car and headed to the Kuwaiti Embassy.

"I wonder what the people at the embassy will say if they see your car," I told Pierre.

"Don't worry about it. I'm planning to park a few blocks away."

We parked on a side street next to a small park, and headed to the embassy arriving exactly at 1:30 p.m. A friendly receptionist welcomed us and offered us coffee in real china cups on a silver tray, then said, "His Excellency will be with you shortly."

After a full hour of waiting, the receptionist led us to a large bright office. An expensively dressed, handsome young man came from behind his shiny desk to greet us.

"Ibrahim Hammad," he said as he shook our hands. "Please have a seat. Would you like coffee or tea? Or maybe something cold?"

"Thank you. We already had coffee while waiting."

"I'm sorry His Excellency is tied up. He asked me to meet with you."

I gave my short presentation, which included an introduction to PAS, the convention's program, and our invitation to Jesse Jackson.

"It sounds like you do impressive work. I'd love to support you, but the decision is not mine. I'll definitely convey your message to His Excellency and encourage him to support you."

"Do you have any idea when he might get back to us?" I asked.

"*Inshallah*, soon."

I knew exactly what that meant. A polite no. I had learned that from my mother at a very young age. Nonetheless, we thanked him for taking the time to meet with us.

We walked to the car discussing the meeting, predicting that we wouldn't see a penny from these guys. Noel and I were engaged in our conversation when we heard Pierre, who was ahead of us, yelling, "Oh my God, they broke into my car."

Our two small suitcases were gone. Pierre had left the car unlocked. Luckily no damage was done to the vehicle, which was already on its last leg.

"A thief wouldn't dare walk through this area with two suitcases," said Pierre,

"Let's search the park."

Pierre got into the park and we followed him. He was searching behind the bushes. Sure enough the bags were there, wide open, with most of our clothes on the ground.

"How did you guess?" I asked.

"It's common sense."

We started to pick up our belongings. They were spread out all over the place, including my underpants and bras. "What would we tell people in the refugee camps if they could see us? This is raising money American-style?" I said.

"They would see how far we are willing to go to support them," said Noel, laughing.

"I know it's early, but after this, I could use a drink," I said.

"Me too," said both of my companions.

"Pierre, take us to a nice bar. My treat."

The next day, our first meeting was with Georgetown University professor and founder of the Jerusalem Fund, Dr. Hisham Sharabi. We arrived at his Jerusalem Fund office five minutes before 10:00 a.m. A young receptionist led us to a conference room dominated by a very long, highly polished table.

"Dr. Sharabi will be with you shortly," the young woman said as she left the room, closing the door behind her.

The three of us sat at one end of the table, leaving the head seat between us for Dr. Sharabi. He walked in fifteen minutes later. He was dressed in a nicely fitted, elegant three-piece suit and a matching tie, and expensive worry beads nested in his hand. The three of us stood up to greet him, but to our surprise he just sat at the far head of the table.

After we introduced ourselves and exchanged a few pleasantries, Dr. Sharabi leaned backward, tilting his chair on its back two legs. He raised his head, as if looking down at us, then said in a very slow and controlled voice, "And what can I do for you?"

At that very moment, he lost control of his seat. The chair fell backward hitting the bookshelf behind him. A few books fell on the floor. The three of us jumped out of our seat to rescue him, but luckily he managed to control his chair. I had a hard time not laughing. The scene reminded me of al-Jahez, a legendary Arab scholar who lived in the ninth century in Iraq. Al-Jahez died instantly in his private library after one of his many large piles of books fell on him!

Dr. Sharabi sat straight and readjusted his eyeglasses, acting like nothing had happened. But his deep red face and neck told a different story. A few minutes later he looked at his watch and abruptly stood up. "Sorry, I have another appointment. I have to go now. Please leave your contact information with the secretary. We'll get back to you soon." He walked out of the room leaving us behind. We looked at each other and burst out laughing. The minute we left the building, Pierre started imitating him. I was laughing so hard, begging Pierre, "Please stop. I'm about to pee in my pants."

After our Jerusalem Fund meeting, we had lunch with Jane Power at a small restaurant near Dupont Circle. We wanted her to help us reach out to her husband Jack O'Dell, who would hopefully get us an answer from Jesse Jackson. As always, Jane was welcoming and gracious. Before leaving, we handed her a copy of our invitation to Jackson and asked her to pass it on to her husband.

"Don't worry about it. Jack will be home in two days. I'll have him call you," she assured us.

After we thanked Jane and said our goodbyes, Pierre asked me, "Do you think he will call you soon?"

"I'm positive he will. Jane and Jack are good friends and very supportive."

"I KNOW HOW to raise the ten thousand dollars," I said as Pierre drove Noel and I to the DC National Airport.

"How?" they both asked at the same time.

"You wait and see."

Soon after our DC trip, I called my friend, al-Taher, who had moved from Dearborn to Cleveland, Ohio, a couple of years earlier. With Michigan's bad economy in the 1970s and stagnant car industry where many recent Arab immigrants worked, some of the Beit Hanina community had moved to Cleveland as well. Al-Taher, a highly respected elder, was considered the godfather of his community. He had immigrated earlier than most, and was supportive of those who came after, helping them adjust and start their new lives. He was also extremely supportive of the work of the Palestine Aid Society.

"I need your help. I'm raising money for the PAS convention. Would you be willing to take me to your friends' stores to ask for donations?"

"Of course, I will."

I called my friend Silvia, and we headed to Cleveland early. We arrived at al- Taher supermarket at 10:30 in the morning.

"You must be hungry. Let us have breakfast first."

"Thank you, we're not hungry," we both said.

"You'll do better with a full stomach. Leave your car here and let's go."

Al-Taher enjoyed good food. He was short and stocky with a very pleasant demeanor. He was loved and respected by everyone who knew him.

He took us to a nice restaurant. After we ate, he handed me a one-thousand-dollar check and said, "Let's go."

For the next few hours al-Taher took us from one grocery store to the next. As soon as we entered a store, the owner would come to greet us, saying. "*Ahlan wa Sahlan,* you honor us with your presence."

"Thank you. These are my friends, Anan and Silvia. They drove from Detroit this morning to raise money for the Palestine Aid Society convention. They invited Jesse Jackson to speak as the keynote speaker. It's Palestine tax time. Get your checkbook out and give them a donation."

"I am happy to help. But, please, have a seat, let me first get you something to drink."

By 4:00 in the afternoon, we had visited nine stores, drank nine cans of soda, and received nine checks, ranging from five hundred to one thousand dollars. Al-Taher insisted on feeding us again before we left.

Before dark we were back in Detroit with seven thousand dollars in hand. Then came two checks, three thousand from Clovis Maksoud, and one thousand from Dr. Sharabi. First, I called Pierre, then Noel. "Guess what? I have not only ten thousand dollars but eleven thousand!"

"You're bullshitting me," said Pierre.

A week or so later, I got a call from Jack O'Dell. "Anan, I'm so sorry it took me so long to get back to you. I was traveling overseas."

"Thank you for calling. I need your help. As Jane told you, we've invited Reverend Jackson to speak at our convention, but we haven't heard from him.

We're told that he didn't get back to us because we didn't offer him a ten-thousand-dollar speaking fee. I want you to know we'll be happy to pay it."

"I personally don't think the money is the issue. He is very busy campaigning. I'll talk to him and get back to you. I promise."

"I would greatly appreciate it. Our convention is only a month away."

In less than a week, Jack called to tell me that Jackson accepted our invitation. "You can count on him to be there. Jane and I will also be there."

"How about his fees? How much should we offer him?"

"Nothing. I told you, money isn't an issue."

"Are you sure?"

"Of course I'm sure. I specifically asked him, and his exact words were 'I can't take money from PAS. It's like taking it away from Palestinians in the refugee camps.'"

"Thank you, Jack, you made my day. Please thank the Reverend on our behalf and tell him we are sending not only ten, but eleven thousand dollars in his honor to the Palestine Red Crescent in Gaza."[14]

I called all the donors and told them that Jackson waived his fees and we would send their donations to Gaza. Everyone was happy about the news.

Once we announced Jackson's attendance, registration for the convention skyrocketed. We were sold out. Jackson arrived twenty minutes late with Jack O'Dell and four security guards. People lined up to greet him as his car entered the H4 Conference Center.

I had the honor of introducing him. As he addressed the crowd, people kept interrupting, clapping and cheering, especially when he talked about his support for Palestinians.

Our Washington, DC third national convention was best attended to date. Abdeen also attended the convention and was extremely supportive and attentive to my needs. While I was very happy about the outcome of the convention and appreciative of Abdeen's support, I was not looking forward to returning to Detroit. Working on such a large project had occupied my time and my mind for several months. It made it possible for me not to think about much else. Now that it was over I had to deal with my relationship with Abdeen, which was, despite our sincere efforts, not at its best, to say the least.

CHAPTER 21
I ALMOST KILLED MY HUSBAND

DETROIT, 1984

As the Arabic proverb goes, *Sharru al balliete ma yudheck* (It's so bad, it's funny). Thirty some years later I still remember this Thanksgiving and laugh, I hope you can laugh with me.

I still have a vivid memory of the night I almost killed my husband. It was on my fortieth birthday. After dinner, the men sat in the dining room playing cards. We, the women, went into the kitchen to clean. And believe me, there was plenty to clean after feeding thirty-five people. Had I complained about the unfair division of labor or about being tired, my mother-in-law and sisters-in-law would have said, "Oh, honey, if you're tired, why don't you go sit down. We will cook, or clean, or wash dishes." Had I said, "That's not the point," they would have asked, "What is the point?"

Once the kitchen looked like an advertisement in a home magazine, we made a fresh pot of coffee and sat in the living room. The aroma of the coffee could be smelled in the adjacent dining room where the men were getting loud and excited.

I was happy to finally sit down, to give my aching body a break. The minute my butt hit the sofa cushion, my husband called, "*Aini*, can we have coffee too? Please."

"Sure," I replied.

I got up, started the coffee, and sat at the kitchen table waiting for it to brew. I took the fresh pot, placed it on the dining room table, and went back to the living room. By then my coffee was lukewarm, but I had no energy to get a fresh cup. I sat down, put my feet up, only to hear my dear husband calling, "*Aini*, can we have some cream and sugar?"

I got up, took him what he wanted, and went back to my seat.

"*Aini*, can we have some of that pumpkin pie?"

Why can't you get off your butt and get it? I thought.

"Of course you can."

This time I was sure to take not only the pie, but also plates, napkins, and forks, hoping he would not ask me for one more thing.

"*Aini*, can we have some whipped cream?"

Damn it…I'm not your servant.

I got up, and took the whipped cream to him. At that moment, I had a hot flash that had absolutely nothing to do with menopause.

"*Aini*? can we have more coffee? Please."

Although I am a strong woman, violence is not one of my attributes. I hate violence, especially the domestic kind. And my relationship with my husband didn't have a trace of it. Nonetheless, at that moment a flood of anger washed over me. My relatively calm demeanor turned into uncontrollable aggression. I was ready to smash the coffeepot over his head. I was ready to kill.

As I look back on that Thanksgiving Day, I am still unable to understand where all that hostility came from. But thanks to *Allah,* he survived my rage. Not only because he didn't deserve to die, but also because I would have had to spend the rest of my life in jail. Even if I could afford to hire the best attorneys like Robert Shapiro to represent me, they wouldn't be able to come up with a good defense.

My husband was the youngest of seven, and everyone adored him. I have to admit, he was a charming fellow and I, at one point, adored him too.

My in-laws were very kind and decent people. They wouldn't have been dishonest had they testified. *Everything seemed to be going just fine, and everyone was having a great time. We, the women, had just finished cleaning and were sitting in the living room by the fireplace relaxing. The men were in the dining room playing cards. We could hear them laughing and enjoying themselves. They did that every time we got together. All of a sudden, she*—meaning me—*went berserk and murdered him. She smashed the coffeepot on his head, killing him instantly. He wasn't even paying attention. Nothing unusual seemed to have happened. We don't think she was upset or drunk, she only had one drink, a gin and tonic, her favorite. She also seemed to appreciate all the gifts we and Abdeen gave her for her birthday. They were still piling up by the fireplace. We just don't understand why she suddenly went crazy.*

Had I murdered my husband, my in-laws would have resented me for the rest of their lives. But they would have also felt sorry for me. It is most likely that they would have believed I killed him due to temporary insanity. The truth is, it wasn't temporary or permanent insanity. It was simply repressed anger.

Had he died, there would be close to thirty-five witnesses, all of them my husband's relatives—his mother, two uncles, one aunt, six brothers and sisters, their spouses, and their children. And if I remember correctly, a couple of the nephews also had their girlfriends with them.

I guess it was my fault to insist on getting married on my thirtieth birthday, which happens to be November twenty-third. For the last eight years I have had my in-laws for every Thanksgiving dinner—it was not an ideal way to spend my birthday and wedding anniversaries.

Truth be told, I was the one who suggested hosting the family Thanksgiving dinners at our home. It happened on the third year of our marriage after his sister Salma hosted the previous two. I told my husband, "You know, Abdeen, I don't think it's fair to have Salma host the family dinner three years in a row. Why don't we have it this year?"

Abdeen, who was so proud of his wife's cooking, and was at his best when we had people over, couldn't pass up the opportunity. My in-laws loved having Thanksgiving dinner at our home and enjoyed my infusion of Arabic cuisine with the traditional American feast. Abdeen loved it even more, so we kept hosting it every year.

I loved my in-laws, or most of them, to be exact. They loved me too. And while they were Arab Americans like myself, we were very different. As I explained earlier, we had what you might call a cultural gap.

I grew up between Amman and Damascus during the 1950s and '60s, a period when we were struggling to change our male-dominated society. The newly independent Arab countries were taking pride in their free public educa-tion. Women, especially from the urban middle class, were attending universi-ties in relatively large numbers. My in-laws, on the other hand, except for their mother, were born and raised in the small town of Mancelona. In their struggle to preserve their culture, like most immigrants, they overkept some of it. They kept intact the part that made me almost kill my husband. I have kept part of the culture too. Never in the presence of guests would one mention being tired, or get in an argument with a spouse. Such behavior is not compatible with Arab hospitality.

Being young and enamored by my Abdeen, I ignored my mother's upbringing.

Instead, I worked very hard to meet my husband's expectations, to be what he envisioned me to be—a modern woman who would also adhere to a woman's traditional role. Since we got married, ten years earlier, every night I would cook elaborate dinners, and I kept the house spotlessly clean. I accommodated his generosity of inviting people over for drinks, brunches, dinners, or to stay with us, although he often forgot to check if it was OK with me. I even smiled and looked pretty when the guests arrived. I also accompanied him to his numer-ous political and social events. Meanwhile, I was pursuing my higher education, becoming politically active, and aspiring to establish my own career. Without being aware of it, I became, or more accurately, tried tirelessly, to become the superwoman I was not. Sooner or later I was bound to have a nervous break-down, kill my husband, or both. It was only a matter of time.

Unlike O. J. Simpson, I had many witnesses. They would all testify that I killed my husband for no apparent reason. As they witnessed it, I killed him after he asked me to get him and his relatives some coffee. He asked in a very gentle voice, saying, "*Aini*, can we have more coffee." He even said "Please." They would further testify that Abdeen was a good husband, a good provider, and was madly in love with me. They also thought I was madly in love with him as well, which I was.

All I remember from that evening is that I got up after he asked for more coffee. I slowly walked to the dining room, picked up the empty pot, and smashed it on my husband's head. I was so happy he was killed instantly. One strike. I didn't want to hear the word "Aini" one more time.

My heart was pounding hard and my legs and arms were trembling. I walked into the kitchen and held the counter to steady myself. Fearful I was about to pass out, I reached for a chair and sat down. It was only then that I realized that the coffeepot, which was still in my hand, was not broken. I closed my eyes and reopened them, stared at the coffeepot, and moved my palm around its smooth surface—it didn't even have a scratch. I slowly got up and looked into the dining room. My husband was sitting there, unharmed, still playing cards. I touched my face and my eyes and I looked again at my hands. Was I dreaming? Or worse, was I losing it? Whatever the case might have been, I was frightened by my own state of mind.

Later that night, as we retreated to our bedroom, my husband snuggled up to me and said as he was trying to kiss me, "Happy Birthday, *Aini*." Not getting any response, he asked, "Are you tired, *Aini*?"

"Are you kidding? Me, tired? I'm ready to run a marathon."

"What is wrong, *Aini*? You sound upset."

"Nothing." I gave him my back, pretending to go to sleep.

CHAPTER 22
JUST EXERCISE!

DETROIT, 1984-1987

The image of smashing the coffeepot on my husband's head haunted me all night long. True, I was tired and frustrated. I didn't particularly appreciate having us, the women, do all the work, while the men were visiting and playing cards. But did that warrant my uncontrollable desire to kill him? I knew it was much deeper than that. In many ways it was a reflection of my own fear and the realization that Abdeen and I were drifting apart, and I didn't know how to stop it.

As soon as my mother-in-law, who came a few days earlier to help me, went back to Mancelona, I called Dr. Joseph, a therapist friend of my husband's.

"I need to see you as soon as possible. This is an emergency. I need your professional help."

"Are you OK? Is Abdeen OK?"

"Yes, yes, we are. I just need someone to talk to. Someone who can help me."

I sat in Dr. Joseph's office, recalling Thanksgiving dinner. I spent more time crying than talking.

"I don't understand why I got so mad. I just wanted to kill him. My life seems to be just fine. I already got my PhD, I have a full-time job as the director of the Palestine Aid Society, and I have made a few close friends. It seems like I have everything I've hoped for. Yet I'm not happy. I feel like a big weight is sitting on my chest. I cry a lot. I just cannot understand why I'm so miserable or why my relationship with Abdeen is deteriorating. I often wish I never got married. Maybe marriage is not for me."

"Abdeen is a close friend. I don't think I'm the best person to discuss your marriage. However, it's clear to me that you are experiencing depression caused by repressed anger. I can send you to another therapist."

"But I don't want to see another therapist. Can you just give me some anti-depressant pills?"

"Sorry, Anan, as a psychologist I cannot prescribe medication. What might be better for you than pills is some good vigorous exercise. It won't only save your marriage, but it will also save your life."

"I'll do anything to save my marriage. I left my country, my family, and my friends for him. I have invested ten years of my life, my prime youth, in this marriage. I am starting to resent him for that. Please help me," I pleaded, sobbing.

"Why don't you join a health club and try to exercise regularly? It's good for your health and will reduce your frustration and anger."

"Ok, I'll try exercise. But I don't want to see another therapist. Can I come back and see you?"

"You should try exercise first. I'm sure you'll feel much better soon."

I was once given the same advice by my father but for a different reason, or to be more exact, to deal with a different aspect of my love life. I was in my early twenties living at home in Amman and had found my first love. My parents were not that crazy about the man, to say the least. He was eight years older, divorced, had three children and had no college education or a steady job.

My dad, who used to call me a rebel, was worried I would marry the guy regardless of what he or my mother thought. But being the wise man he was, he kept his worries to himself. He did not scream, yell, or say "How dare you?" Instead he told me in a very calm voice, "You're still young. You shouldn't think of marriage, not until you get your university degree. In the meanwhile, I want you to exercise."

I was so happy my dad did not get mad at me for loving the man, so I didn't ask him what he meant, or try to figure out why he advised me to exercise.

Later I recognized that my father's understanding of the benefit of exercise did not differ drastically from that of Dr. Joseph's. My father, who was a health freak and exercised regularly, probably thought that exercise would reduce my sexual desire. Dr. Joseph was prescribing exercise to reduce my depression and anger caused by, among other things, my deteriorating relationship with my husband.

I don't remember if I took my father's advice about exercise seriously, but by the time I finished college, I was no longer in love, nor was I interested in getting married.

This time I was already married, and I was still in love with my husband. I wanted to save my marriage by any means necessary. Therefore, I decided to take Dr. Joseph's advice about exercising seriously. My husband, not aware of my visit to his friend the therapist, couldn't understand my urgent desire to join the health club, which had recently opened not far from where we lived.

"It is too expensive. I'm afraid you'll pay the money, go once or twice, and then drop it."

"You don't understand. I need to exercise." Despite myself, I started to cry and ran upstairs to the bedroom.

A couple of weeks later my loving Abdeen handed me an envelope and said, "Guess what I got you?"

"What?"

"A lifetime membership at the health club."

That was much more money than I was planning to spend. I tried to sound appreciative and excited but failed miserably. All I could utter was "Thank you."

At the health club I signed up for aerobics, hoping that such vigorous exercise would ease my depression and get rid of my anger. Every single day before going to work I would head to the health club. I tried to exercise with all the energy I had, to get a good workout, "to sweat it out," as they say. But my depression persisted, and I was losing weight fast, something I did not intend or need to do. So I begged Dr. Joseph for his professional help.

"I'm taking your advice seriously. I am exercising every day, but I don't feel any better. Nothing seems to lift this heavy weight off my chest. Sometimes I just want to hide and cry, or even run away. My heart is still aching. The only difference is that my whole body is aching now."

"Your body aches will go away soon, and so will your depression. Keep exercising. Give it time."

"For how long?" I pleaded.

"You have been exercising for only two months. Be patient."

"But my relationship with my husband is deteriorating even further. I cannot put my finger on why we lost the passion we once had, or why we don't seem to have much in common anymore. I just yearn to be single again. Do you think a temporary separation would help us?"

"Abdeen is my friend, and as I told you before, it's better for you to see a different therapist—one that doesn't know you or your husband. Here is Dr. Williams's card. He is a bit pricey, but very good. He specializes in marriage counseling."

"But…"

"Trust me, you are better off seeing him. In the meantime, keep exercising."

With me sinking into a deeper depression, I decided to go see Dr. Williams, who, like Dr. Joseph, affirmed that I was depressed. In addition to prescribing an antidepressant, he advised me to keep exercising.

"How much exercise do I have to do? And for how long? I'm almost living in the health club. When am I going to feel better?"

I spent most of my time at Dr. Williams's office crying, trying to have an answer to why I was so unhappy. "He's a great guy. I love him and he loves me too, so why am I so miserable?" I kept asking, while the doctor continued to hand me more tissues.

"Can you stop crying, so we can talk?" he said in a very firm voice. Then asked, "Do you have a tennis racket?"

I was taken by his question. "No, I don't. But what's that have to do with my depression?"

"I suggest you buy one. I want you to spend time hitting an old mattress as hard as you can. Or if you prefer, take boxing and hit a punching bag. You can imagine you are hitting your husband. Get rid of your anger that way."

"How dare you? I find your suggestion disgusting. I would never want to hit my husband. I love him and I hate violence."

"Well…you did fantasize about killing him with a coffeepot. Did you not?" He sounded angry and hostile, as if giving up on me.

"Have you never been so upset by your wife or children you wished you could strangle them? Am I the only one on this earth who for a short moment wished that?" By then I started to regret telling my therapist about the coffeepot incident and probably regretting going to therapy as well.

"This is about you, not about me," he said, sounding like he was ready to strangle me.

"YOU SEEM TO be miserable. What's going on?" asked my friend Diane.

"My therapist wants me to buy a tennis racket or take boxing and imagine I'm hitting Abdeen. What kind of bullshit therapy is that? I got so angry I was ready to hit him. I don't want to ever see his ugly face again."

"Well maybe he knows what he is talking about. Why don't you give it a try?"

"I can't. How is that going to help me understand why I'm so depressed or save my marriage? How will that help me rekindle my relationship with Abdeen, who's neither physically or verbally abusive? On the contrary, he is very sweet and loving to the point that it's impossible to even have an argument with him. No matter how furious I might be, he always manages to diffuse any anger by buying me flowers, apologizing, or admitting guilt, even if he hasn't done anything wrong."

"Maybe that's one of the reasons you are always upset. It seems like you never get a chance to deal with what bothers you."

"Or maybe Abdeen is correct, and therapy is a waste of time and money."

"Anan, just listen to me. Abdeen is a good person, and so are you, but that doesn't necessarily mean you are compatible as husband and wife."

"Of course we are. We are both highly educated, progressive, and politically active, and we love each other. What more do we need to have a successful marriage?"

At that stage, I hadn't shared my marriage troubles with any of my other friends, other than Diane and Dick. All my friends loved Abdeen. Everyone kept telling me how lucky I was to be married to him. But I don't recall anyone saying how lucky he was to be married to me, which I took to mean if I'm not happy married to him, then there is something seriously wrong with me. Only my mother-in-law thought differently. When Abdeen told her about our troubled marriage she said, "Find out what she wants and do it. You'll never find a woman like her. They don't make them like this anymore."

After eight months of strenuous aerobic classes, I recognized that exercise was not the answer to my failing marriage. When I finally mustered my courage and told Abdeen that I needed to temporarily have my own place, he was totally devastated.

"But we're happy together, aren't we?"

"I'm really sorry, Abdeen. I'm not."

He couldn't understand why, and I couldn't explain it either. All I wanted was a break from it all.

I rented a one-bedroom apartment in downtown Detroit. It was a beautiful penthouse on the roof of the historic Garden Court Apartments. It had a huge terrace overlooking downtown Detroit, the river, and Windsor, Canada. I biked to my Palestine Aid Society office, and took long bike rides to Belle Isle Park. My friend Dick was also going through a divorce and had moved to an apartment in downtown Detroit not far from where I lived. He and I would spend time together crying on each other's shoulders. But my heartache and depression persisted.

My friend Hisham, who was working at Ford Motor Company, suggested introducing me to his engineer friend, a divorced man, who was "just great," as my friend put it.

"I'm not ready for a relationship. I still love my husband."

"Give it a try. It won't kill you."

By then I was still hopeful that I could save my marriage. For the next two years, Abdeen and I continued to see each other, and we visited a marriage counselor a few times. In spite of our best intentions, our relationship did not get any better, and as time passed we were seeing each other less and less. Then, in 1986, Abdeen accepted the offer to be president of the American-Arab Anti-Discrimination Committee (ADC). He closed his Detroit law office, and moved to Washington, DC.

Although we had not talked about divorce yet, we both knew that was the end of our relationship. As I reflect back on it, I realize that that was the most painful experience I ever had. Although our separation and later divorce was as civil as a divorce can be, it broke my heart to see the end of my marriage to a man who loved me like no one ever did before, and whom I loved dearly and never stopped caring for until this day.

* * * *

DEPRESSED AND LONELY, I asked Hisham if his friend was still available.

"I think so. Let me talk to him."

I decided to give dating a try. I convinced myself that maybe a relationship would heal my ailments. *Men do it all the time, why shouldn't I?*

John was very handsome, the kind of a man that makes women swoon. He was smart, highly educated, liked movies and concerts, owned a large boat, and belonged to the fancy Detroit Yacht Club. He was also snobby, but I convinced myself that no one is perfect. But as I got to know him better I realized that the man, though an African American, was to my utter surprise a bigot. He would often say, "I grew up poor too, so if I can make it, why can't they?" And when I finally began to protest by telling him, "That's a racist statement," he would become indignant and say, "How dare you tell me this?" or "Have you not noticed I'm black?"

By the time I met John, I had quit therapy, but thanks to Abdeen's gift of a lifetime membership, I kept going to the health club and doing my aerobics every single morning.

"Punch harder. Put more power into it," our instructor would enthusiastically yell. Suddenly it dawned on me that my favorite part was actually punching the air, alternating my right and left fists. I would just close my eyes and imagine I was hitting John.

I was wondering if Dr. Joseph or Dr. Williams were thinking the same when they asked me to exercise. When I ran into Dr. Joseph at a friend's son's graduation, he said, "How are you feeling? You look better. How is Dr. Williams? I hope he was able to help?"

"I am feeling a bit better, but I stopped seeing Dr. Williams a while back."

"Why? Wasn't he helpful?"

"He couldn't be that helpful. Abdeen and I are getting a divorce."

"I know. Abdeen told me. I'm sorry to hear it."

"Can I ask you a question?"

"Of course."

"I've been dating this man for a few months, but I'm ready to dump him soon. While doing my aerobics, I imagine I'm hitting him. The more I do it, the better I feel. Sometimes I wish this part of the exercise would never end. I wonder if this is what you had in mind when you advised me to exercise? Did you want me to imagine hitting Abdeen?" I said kiddingly.

Dr. Joseph did not appreciate my humor. He ignored my question and ended our conversation. He even walked away, making it clear that he did not want to talk about it anymore.

As the actual court day of my divorce approached, deep grief came back to haunt me. It was like watching the death of a loved one without being able to help. A few days before the court date, I felt severely anxious. I also felt angry at Abdeen, although I was the one who filed for divorce. At the health club I would do the aerobics, the punching, the deep breathing, the screaming, but nothing seemed to work. One day I was at it so hard, by the time I was done I felt like my head was about to explode. I went to the whirlpool and put my head under the water, hoping to get some relief.

On the other side of the small pool sat a man staring at me. Though irritated, I pretended not to notice him. Slowly, he started to inch his way toward me. As he came closer he said in a soft voice, "It looks like you have a headache."

"No, I don't," I said in a rather nasty tone, but that did not deter him from getting even closer or from pursuing the conversation.

"You know what you need?" he went on.

Somehow, I knew exactly what he was going to say. I just admire men for having such self-confidence. They truly believe that they are the solution to almost any problem a woman might have.

"Please don't tell me I need a man."

"You guessed it. That is exactly what you need." He was smiling, so proud of himself.

I looked him right in the eye and said, "I have two. Do you want one?"

The expression on his face seemed to take care of my physical and emotional pain, at least for that moment.

CHAPTER 23
THERAPY IN BLACK AND WHITE

DETROIT; WASHINGTON, DC; AND AMMAN, 1988-89

All the exercise, aerobics and punching, and all the hours I spent in the health club and in therapy didn't help me that much. I was unable to save my marriage. After the divorce I continued to drown in sadness, anxiety, and depression.

"Therapy and pills. That's what will cure all your ailments," said Joyce, my friend's wife. Joyce was always upbeat and she had a solution for every problem. I could not figure out if she was so upbeat because of her name, or because she had been in therapy and on antidepressants since her teens.

"I tried therapy. It didn't work for me. And I hate pills," I said.

"But you are in a different place now. You need to get over your divorce. You need to move on."

"I'll think about it," or "That won't work," I said to Joyce every time she brought it up.

"Maybe you don't believe in therapy because in your country you don't have good medical or mental care. This is America. Take advantage of what it has to offer."

I didn't want to disappoint Joyce, or challenge her expertise about my culture or my country, so I didn't bother telling her that my sister Arwa, who lives and works in my country, Jordan, is in fact a therapist. Meanwhile, I was contemplating her suggestion, and wondering if I needed more therapy.

I sat in Dr. Peterson's[15] office waiting. The reception area was beautiful enough to lift one's spirit. It was a much fancier place than my two previous therapists. I wondered if there was a relationship between the expensive furniture and artwork and the quality of therapy I might get. I recalled how a visitor to my Detroit Palestine Aid Society office advised me to get better furniture. When I said, "I don't feel right about spending the money we raise to help Palestinian refugees on furniture," his answer was, "It's all about image. If you have a nicer place, people will think you're worthy of larger donations." That didn't make much sense to me at the time, but maybe he was right.

My thoughts were interrupted when a door opened. A middle-aged man with large, bulging blue eyes said, "Hello. Please come in."

His office was even fancier than the waiting area. He had a large, shiny desk and expensive leather chairs—I have to admit they were very comfortable—and a chaise lounge that looked almost like a bed. I assumed it was for his patients to lie down and to really let go. I was wondering if he was going to ask me to do that. Expensive artwork filled three walls. Behind his desk were many framed degrees, as well as shelves filled with books of all sizes. A large family photo of Dr. Peterson with a nice-looking wife, two kids, and a dog was at the center of the bookshelves. You couldn't possibly miss it. The perfect American family!

"Our first meeting is to get acquainted with each other and to learn about you and what brings you here."

It took me a while to be able to say why I was there. Partly because I was not sure where to start, and partly because I couldn't stop crying. Thank God he had a big tissue box and a trash can right next to me. Between the tears, runny nose, and my immigrant accent, he could hardly understand what I was saying. He kept asking me, "Can you say that again? Can you help me understand?" When I finally stopped sobbing and began to talk in comprehensible English, he interrupted me midsentence, "We have to stop now. Your time is up. I'll see you next week."

I did come the next week, the one after, and each of the following weeks. On my way out, his assistant would be waiting for my hefty payment, a respectable portion of my salary. I had to cut down on eating out and forget about going to movies and concerts. I stopped buying clothes and shoes, and avoided weddings and graduations. All in order to pay my therapy bills.

"I've been coming here for a while, but I don't feel much better."

"Your depression and sense of failure is not totally due to your divorce. It's much deeper than that."

"What do you mean?"

Instead of answering me, he looked at his watch, and said, "Your time is up. We can explore this next time."

The following week, after asking me his routine question as to whether I felt better since my last visit, and after getting the usual "No, I don't," he said, "Do you play any musical instruments?"

"No. But what does this have to do with my depression?"

"You mean to tell me your parents didn't have you learn?"

"No, they didn't."

In the following weeks, my therapist explored all the skills and talents I lacked. He wanted to know if my parents truly loved me.

"Do you play tennis? Do you play golf? Do you swim? Do you have any other hobbies to fill your time?"

My answers to all that were no, no, and no.

"Did you grow up poor?"

"No."

"Why do you feel ashamed about growing up poor?"

"But we weren't poor."

I didn't want to elaborate. I was not about to complicate the situation by entering my parents and the Palestinian question into the picture. I was not about to tell him that my parents became refugees in 1948 and had to send my sister and I—their only two children at the time—to Damascus, fearing for our safety as the war between the Israelis and Palestinians escalated. I was only three-and-a-half years old, and the scars of the one-year separation continue to haunt me. And I was not about to tell him when I was growing up, Amman was a rather small town with only one swimming pool, or that my sister Arwa had to share her bike with me, my sister, and brother, and with lots of other kids because it was the only bike in the neighborhood.

Dr. Peterson had tried his best to convince me that I had terrible parents, I was raised as a deprived child, I was born depressed, I lacked talent, and of course, I was totally uncultured. When I told him I wanted to stop seeing him, he got really upset. His neck and face got bloodred and his large bulging eyes were about to depart his face.

"Why do you want to stop now? You're making real progress."

I used money as an excuse. "I'm sorry, I can't afford therapy anymore."

"Why do you work for a nonprofit? You have a PhD. Why can't you get a real job that pays you real money?"

At that stage, I was not ready to explain myself anymore.

"You don't know what you're doing. There will be horrifying consequences to your actions." He breathed deep and tried again in a quieter tone. "It's my professional responsibility to tell you that you need to continue coming here possibly for many years to come. You might also need to be on antidepressants and anxiety medication for the rest of your life."

"I will think about it," I said, as I left.

I took my chances and quit. But overcoming my depression and grief over my failed marriage was a long, painful process. It took me a few years to make peace with the fact that although Abdeen and I loved each other, we weren't suited to be husband and wife. Maybe Abdeen was correct when he said that the gap between our upbringings was too big. While we both tried very hard to shed some of the culture and values we grew up with to accommodate each other, we were unable to save our marriage.

IN EARLY 1989, the Palestine Aid Society's board decided to move the organization's national office from Detroit to Washington, DC. As president and executive director, they expected me to move. It was during the first Palestinian Intifada. We believed opening an office in the nation's capital would advance our agenda of supporting the Palestinian struggle and hopefully influence public opinion, in turn creating a more balanced US-Middle East policy.

As much as I wanted to get out of Detroit and its sad memories, and to live in one of my favorite cities, I was reluctant to move because Abdeen was already living there.

"Give me some time to think about it," I told the board.

As I was sharing my dilemma with my friend Diane, she said, "Washington is a big city, and you don't have to see Abdeen unless you want to. You've been divorced for two years and you parted on good terms. So what if he lives there? You love the city. You should go."

By July of that year, I packed my few belongings and moved to DC, ready for a new adventure. I found an inexpensive office in the George Washington University area. Michael Moore, the radical film director, had an office in the same building and donated some of his furniture. Bally Health Club was only two blocks from the PAS office, and thanks to Abdeen's gift, I was able to use my lifetime membership. I found a nice apartment in Adams Morgan, a wonderful diverse neighborhood, which was walking distance from my office. It took me no time to meet people and make new friends. Gladly, I didn't listen to my friend Dick's advice when he told me, "DC might not be a good choice. There are two women for each man."

"I don't care about statistics," I said, "I only need one man." Sure enough, I did find a man not long after I arrived. Life was getting better, but my grief and sense of failure lingered.

My dear friend, Lubna, swore by Dr. Payton at Howard University's Counseling Department. "She's great. She is the best therapist you will ever find. I'm sure she can help you."

"No thanks, I'm done with therapy."

"Just try her. Go once and see if you like her."

"But there is a great cultural gap between us and the Americans. We have a different perspective on love, money, and sex. I'm not sure an American therapist will understand. Also therapists are expensive and I can't afford one right now."

"Trust me. Dr. Payton has traveled the world. She helped me a lot. She also does not have a set price. She uses a sliding scale and leaves it to her patients to decide how much they can afford. You pay her what you can."

"What do you mean I pay her what I can? That reminds me of my socialist father who used to say, 'From each according to his ability.' But who would do this in America?"

My blues persisted. I finally succumbed to Lubna's advice, telling myself, *If Dr. Payton was able to help her, maybe be she can help me too.* Lubna was a Palestinian American who grew up in Beirut. She lived through the long Lebanese Civil War and the Israeli invasion of Lebanon, and had seen much death and destruction before coming to the US.

I knocked at the partially open door and walked in. An elegant African American woman in her early seventies came from behind her desk to welcome me. She was small with dark brown eyes, rosy cheeks, and short gray hair. As the Director of Counseling Services at Howard, I was surprised by the simplicity of her office, which wasn't much fancier than my Palestine Aid Society office. She had a couple of chairs and lots of books. No degrees nor fancy art were hanging on the walls.

When our first session ended, I told her I wanted to come back.

"That's fine. I have some homework for you."

"What?" I asked, curious.

"I want you to sit down in a quiet place and make two lists—one about what is good in your life, and one about what's not as good. Take your time doing it, and bring it with you next week."

I was puzzled by her request. Reluctantly, I said, "I will."

Noticing my hesitation, she said, "Don't come back without it."

I drove home thinking about Dr. Payton. I liked her, but I wasn't sure about those lists. It sounded a bit strange. But before going to my second appointment, I did write down what she had asked for.

Dr. Payton held the sheet of paper in her hand and looked at it for a few minutes, then she asked me for some clarification. "What do you mean by this?" and "What do you mean by that?" And then she started her endless questions, which I found intimidating:

"Have you ever been hungry?"

"No," I said, bewildered by her inquiry.

"Have you ever been physically or emotionally abused?"

"No. But in 1948, my parents lost their West Jerusalem home to the Israelis. I was separated from them for almost one year. I still have a vivid memory of sitting on my grandfather's doorstep waiting for them."

"That must have been hard. Did your family end up in a refugee camp?"

I was amazed that she knew about Palestinian camps. Later I found she also knew a lot about the Palestinian's tragic history and was rather sympathetic.

"No. My parents managed to rent a flat in East Jerusalem."

"Do you remember it? Was it a nice place?"

"Yes, it was. We always had a nice place to live."

"How about school? You are highly educated; did your parents encourage you to go to university? Did they support you?"

"Yes. To them, education was like their calling. They were determined that their kids, especially their three daughters, get the best education possible."

"Do you have any student loans?"

"No."

"Do you like your job?"

"Yes, I like it a lot."

"Have you made any friends in DC?"

"Yes, I have. Actually I had a few even before I moved here."

"You don't say much about your health. Are you suffering from any illness?"

"No, Dr. Payton, I'm very healthy."

With each new question, I was getting more frustrated. *Where are you going with this? When are you going to stop? This is an interrogation, not therapy. Damn you, Lubna, why did I listen to you?*

As if she read my mind, she asked her final question. "Why didn't you write all of these things down on your good list?"

"I didn't think about them."

"Why not?"

"I don't know."

"I know why." She said, "Because you took them for granted."

I was taken aback, but said nothing. The few seconds we were both silent felt like forever. I was wondering if she had sensed my indignation.

"When we feel down, and I mean you and I and most people, we tend to see everything dark, like nothing is really good in our lives. But I learned that writing down the good things in our lives helps us keep things in perspective," she said. Her voice was amazingly gentle. I could feel her warmth wash over my tense body.

For the next few days I couldn't stop thinking about Dr. Payton and her unconventional therapy. She reminded me of my mother insisting that I eat the food on my plate because of all the hungry Palestinians in refugee camps and the starving children in India. Despite my cynicism, I decided to give it a try. Her not-so-sympathetic approach was not unkind, and in fact there was something comforting and validating about her. As I got to know her, I learned that she spent many years with the Peace Corps and had lived in many countries initially as a volunteer, and later as a high-ranking officer. In fact, she was the first female and first African American director of the US Peace Corps during President Carter's administration. With her impressive background, and being a woman of color who dedicated her life to public service, Payton was rather inspiring. She was also able to understand me. I didn't have to explain a lot.

After seeing Dr. Payton for about six months she said, "You seem to be doing well. I don't think you need to see me anymore."

Payton was right. I was feeling much better. I also got in the habit of focusing on what was good in my life, which has stayed with me until this day. I was enjoying Washington, DC and what the city had to offer. I had made a few new friends, and had a boyfriend whom I liked a lot. I hardly cried anymore and was sleeping much more peacefully. True, I never stopped thinking about my failed marriage, but the pain associated with that seemed to ease. The few times I ran into Abdeen at political gatherings, we were both warm and friendly toward each other. Nonetheless, I was scared of ending my therapy with Dr. Payton.

"Are you sure I'm going to stay feeling good if I stop seeing you?" I asked.

"Yes, I am. And remember you can always come back if you need to talk. Even if you don't need me as a therapist, please stop by just to say hello and let me know how you are doing."

MY MOTHER, KNOWN as Um Arwa, or the mother of Arwa (named after her firstborn), wasn't that excited about my decision to marry Abdeen or to live in the US. She, however, became very fond of my husband. I dreaded telling her I wanted to get a divorce, especially since my sister Arwa had done that a couple of years earlier. I thought this would totally devastate her.

Before the divorce was final, I flew to Amman. I needed a break and wanted to tell my mother. My father was no longer living. Not knowing how to bring her the news, I kept avoiding the conversation. Every day I would tell myself, *This can wait, I will tell her tomorrow.* My mother, as mothers do, sensed my unhappiness and kept asking if everything was all right. After a few days I gathered my courage and rehearsed what I was going to tell her over and over again. I anticipated all the questions she would be asking me and prepared the answers.

Despite all my preparation, as soon as I started telling her about my decision, I started crying. She looked me in the eye and said, "Why are you crying? No man is worth these tears. Go wash your face and make us some coffee. Then we can talk."

As we settled down with our Arabic coffee, she said, "*Ya binti, ya habibti*, listen carefully to what I have to tell you. Your dad and I did not have a happy marriage or lots of money, but we both worked hard so you and your sisters could have a good education. We wanted you to be independent so you would never ever get stuck in an unhappy marriage."

"But you love Abdeen."

"I do love him, but you are my daughter and I love you more. Abdeen is a good man, but that doesn't mean you have to stay with him if you're not happy." Then she added, "Your father was a good man too, but if it wasn't *eib* to get a divorce in my time, I would have left him a long time ago."

Although my mother and I did not see eye to eye on many issues, she never ceased to surprise me with her wisdom and support, even when I least expected it. This was therapy, Um Arwa-style.

CHAPTER 24
A SHEKEL FOR PALESTINE

TEL AVIV AIRPORT, JANUARY 1990

My friend Diane and I arrived at Tel Aviv Airport before dawn. We had been in Palestine for two weeks and it was time for us to go back home. We were taking the same flight to New York, then would go our separate ways, she to San Francisco, and I to Washington, DC. Our plane was not leaving until 8:00 a.m. You'd think two hours would be sufficient time to arrive before an international flight. Not if you are a Palestinian trying to leave Israel, even with an American passport.

The drive from East Jerusalem to Tel Aviv Airport is about one hour. To be at the airport four hours in advance, we had to leave our Jerusalem hotel at 3:00 in the morning.

When I visit Palestine, I usually stay with my sister Suad, who lives in Ramallah. She has a car and would have been more than willing to drive my friend Diane and I to the airport. But things are much more complicated in that part of the world. Let me try to explain.

My sister, a Palestinian living in the occupied West Bank, has a car with a blue license plate. Israelis, even those living in West Bank settlements, have a yellow license plate. It's really not a discriminatory system, it just makes it easier for the Israeli soldiers to spot Palestinians when they go to places they're not supposed to, or if they dare to drive on the Jewish-only freeways.

Diane decided to join the Palestine Aid Society (PAS) delegation I was leading to participate in the December 1989 Hands Around Jerusalem Peace March, which was organized by Israeli and Palestinian activists. More than 160 Americans joined, a rather impressive number, but not as impressive as the 800 Italians. Sadly, peace was shattered as the Israeli soldiers attacked the rally. An Italian woman lost her eye. My heart ached for her. She came all the way from Rome chanting for peace and she left with one eye.

The peace march was in solidarity with the 1987 Palestinian Intifada that had been going on for a couple of years. The nonviolent uprising that took the world by surprise had energized the Israeli peace movement, and generated unprecedented international support for the Palestinians. It was a time of optimism. Many believed that the end of the Israeli occupation was around the corner. In the US, we moved the PAS national office from Detroit to Washington, DC, hoping to be more effective in rallying support for our cause, and in convincing our government to join the international community in supporting the Palestinians' aspiration for independence and statehood.

That was before the infamous, but hugely celebrated, Oslo "peace" agreement, which in fact brought an end to Israeli and Palestinian peace activism. That was before the siege of the Gaza Strip and the construction of the West Bank separation wall, and before the confinement of the Palestinians to South Africa-like Bantustan.

At the time of the 1989 Hands Around Jerusalem Peace March, Palestinians from the Occupied Territories, like my sister, could work in Israel during the day, but were not allowed to spend the night. During the day, Palestinians provided cheap labor—that was a matter of economy. But if they were to spend the night, that would become a matter of politics. They might be reclaiming their country, or negating the Jewishness of the State of Israel. Not a nice thing to do, to say the least.

Had my sister driven me to the airport, she would be easily spotted with her blue license plate. And since we would be traveling before dawn, she would be violating the Israeli sleeping law. Being older and wiser, I wouldn't allow my sister to commit such a ridiculous crime. Instead I chose the safer, and more importantly, *legal* way to depart Israel. I decided to spend the night at the Mount of Olives Hotel in East Jerusalem rather than worry about the color of license plates. Since East Jerusalem had been occupied and illegally annexed to Israel, all cars in Jerusalem had yellow plates. I justified the inconvenience and the extra expense by telling myself, "After all, we lost our country. I can't cry over spending a few extra dollars." In fact, I say this every time I encounter unexpected expenses or I lose something valuable. Maybe I ought to be thankful to the Israelis for helping me keep things in perspective.

The night before our departure, I said farewell to my sister, her husband, and other friends, and headed to Jerusalem, along with my friend Diane. At the hotel, we slept only a few hours. At 3:00 in the morning we were in the lobby ready to be picked up by a taxi that Abu Ibrahim, the hotel owner, had ordered for us.

Anticipating that I would be questioned by Israeli security at the airport, I told Diane, "In case they question you as well, don't mention the PAS delegation or participating in the peace march. Just say that we came to spend the Christmas and New Year holiday with my sister. And in case they keep me too long, you don't have to wait or miss your flight; go ahead and leave. I'll be all right."

Diane is not a Palestinian or an Arab like me; she is a "real" American. She was born in Detroit and is white. I was confident that the Israelis had no reason to mess with her, not that they ever needed a reason to mess with Palestinians and those who sympathize with them.

Well, I was wrong. The security agents were waiting for both us. They knew that Diane and I were picked up from the Mount of Olives Hotel and shared a taxi to the airport. I had to admit their ability to spy on us was rather impressive. As soon as we stepped into the airport, two male security guards met us at the entrance, took our passports, and ordered us to bring our luggage and follow them.

They took us to two separate rooms away from other departing passengers and closed the doors. Then they started their interrogation, asking the same questions over and over again. "Where did the two of you meet? Why are you traveling together? Where did you stay? Whom did you see? Who paid for your trip? What did you bring with you?" Since we were telling the truth, short of mentioning the peace march, we gave them the same answers no matter how many times they asked. They even asked each one of us why we stayed in Jerusalem last night, and why my sister did not drive us to the airport. I guess they either did not hear about the Israeli sleeping law, or the law didn't make sense to them either. After questioning us for a while, they would leave the rooms, probably to compare notes, then come back again to ask us the same questions. Later Diane told me that they had asked her if I, or any other Palestinian, had given her anything to carry. They also told her, "We're very concerned about your safety. You should know better than trusting these people."

It was a long and tedious investigation, which we both proudly passed. Then came the body and luggage search. Security agents emptied our suitcases and x-rayed them along with our shoes—I still don't know what I could have hidden in them, even if I had wanted to. All of our belongings were spread on a filthy table. My sisters, who accuse me of being obsessed with cleanliness, would have loved seeing this. I did not.

The agents carefully examined every piece of clothing, including our underwear. I felt violated but said nothing. I just stood there watching them as they looked at every cosmetic and toiletry item we had, and unwrapped all of our gifts. I lost my cool when one officer opened a sealed bottle of *arak*, a colorless liquor in a clear bottle, and stuck his nose in it. I couldn't restrain myself from asking, "Why do you have to open this? What could I possibly hide in it?"

"I'm just concerned about your safety," he said with a mocking smile.

Not in my wildest dreams did I ever think the day would come when I would regret not traveling with filthy, smelly clothes. At that moment, I did. To be more honest, I actually wished I had a can full of shit—I would have loved seeing him open that and stick his nose in there.

Time was running out and I resigned myself to the possibility of missing my flight. But I felt sorry for Diane. She had to report to work only a couple days after our expected arrival in the US. Personally, I didn't care if I missed my flight. I could always spend more time with my sister, and at that moment, getting back to work on time seemed irrelevant.

It was almost 8:00 when one of the officers said, "You can pack your luggage now," then added, "Hurry up if you don't want to miss your flight." We tried to pack as quickly as we could while his watching eyes were staring at us. We had a hard time fitting the clothes and the unwrapped gifts in our suitcases. At that moment, a female security officer came and asked for our passports and plane tickets.

"Why?" I asked. I was worried I might never see my passport again.

"Get your luggage and meet me at the departure gate. I'll get your boarding passes."

Reluctantly we handed her our passports and tickets, then finished shoving our belongings in our suitcases and rushed to the gate. Sure enough, the agent was there with our boarding passes and our passports. She also handed me an Israeli shekel, a coin worth about fifty cents.

"What's this for?" I asked.

"It is yours. I found it in the jacket of your plane ticket." This was before e-tickets were invented.

I looked at her with the shekel in my outstretched hand. I couldn't help but laugh.

"What is so funny?" she snapped.

"How honest," I said. "Why don't you keep the shekel and give me back my country?"

I rushed as fast as I could to the plane, fearing she would stop me. She did not.

CHAPTER 25
FREEWAYS

WEST BANK, DETROIT, AND
JOHANNESBURG, SUMMER 1990

In spite of the hassle I often encountered at Tel Aviv Airport, one of my favorite PAS programs was taking fact-finding delegations to Israel and Palestine. My colleagues and I were convinced that once people visited, they would come back with a better understanding of the plight of the Palestinian people. Upon their return, these delegates would work with us to raise funds for humanitarian projects in Lebanon and the Palestinian Occupied Territories, as well as create greater support for the Palestinian struggle for national independence. Each year we would take three or four delegations, which included journalists, educators, union leaders, women, and church groups. After a few years of taking so many delegations, we came to the conclusion that America is too big and has too many people—it would take thousands of delegates before we could make a dent. We simply didn't have the money, the human resources, or the know-how to operate efficiently in such a complicated and money-driven political system.

Among the many delegations I personally took to Israel and Palestine was a delegation of fifteen civil rights activists. It was 1990, a few months after the Hands Around Jerusalem Peace March. The Palestinian Intifada as well as the Israeli peace movement were still at their peak. The promise of a peaceful resolution for the Palestinian–Israeli conflict prevailed on both sides. During these hopeful times, we coordinated our visits with the Israeli organization Peace Now,

ANAN AMERI

which organized the itinerary on the Israeli side, while the Palestinians took care of our itinerary in the Occupied Territories.

Our delegation's visits, as organized by our Israeli partners, included a settlement on the outskirts of Jerusalem, built, like all settlements, on confiscated Palestinian land.

"I don't feel like going to a settlement. It will be too painful for me," I told David, the organizer from Peace Now.

"But this is important. It will clearly demonstrate the cruelty of the occupation."

Although I had already experienced that cruelty more than once, I decided to be respectful of our partners. By then the Israeli government had already expanded the borders of the illegally annexed East Jerusalem to include a few nearby villages. Newly constructed settlements circled the expanded city. To protect the settlers from angry Palestinians whose land was confiscated to build these settlements, more land "had" to be confiscated to build the Jewish-only freeways. Settlers would go in and out of their homes without ever having to see their Palestinian neighbors who were robbed of their lands, the main source of their livelihood, and were living in poverty and despair.

We arrived to the settlement in the early afternoon. The lush green elaborate playground and the swimming pool told the story of separate but definitely not equal living arrangements. Rachel, a middle-aged woman with a heavy Brooklyn accent, and two younger men, one with a machine gun, greeted us as we descended from the bus. Rachel led us to a spacious conference room in the settlement's community center. After exchanging routine welcoming remarks and introductions, Rachel started her lengthy presentation about the history of the settlement, which couldn't have much of a history to begin with, because it hadn't been built that long ago. The more she talked, the angrier I became. When she was done, a delegation member asked her, "How do you feel living in such an affluent place while your Palestinian neighbors suffer from high unemployment and poverty?"

"They're not poor, they're lazy. They don't want to work. They want things to be handed to them."

I remembered hearing this in America, and I wondered who learned from whom.

After a few questions, I checked my emotions, swallowed my pride, then asked, "Excuse me, Rachel, doesn't the land on which your settlement is built belong to the Palestinian villagers of Shu'fat?"

"This is Jewish land, and we have the right to be here."

"But not so long ago, this land belonged to Palestinians from Shu'fat. Did you buy it or just take it?"

"This is Judea and Samaria. It's *Eretz*, Israel. It is our promised land."

By then I was too drained to argue and couldn't wait to get out of there.

As we left, a deep sadness washed over me. My soul ached and burning tears soaked my face. I felt powerless and defeated. Our small bus drove back on the Jewish-only freeway that freed them from encountering Palestinians, and from confronting the ugly reality of their own creation.

BACK IN WASHINGTON, DC, my mind kept drifting to my last trip, and to Detroit where I once met two Palestinian store owners from the village of Shu'fat. I wondered if the settlement we just visited or the Jewish-only freeways were built on land their family or friends once owned. And I recalled my early years in Detroit where I learned how to drive and was advised to stick to the freeway, and I couldn't help but see the resemblance, and the many faces of racism.

Detroit is the city where I lived more than any other place. I lived on the West side, I lived on the East side, and I lived downtown. From any of these locations, I could always count on the freeways to take me quickly to my destination. I would drive three or four blocks and then get on the freeway. I did that when I went to university, work, visited friends, went shopping, or drove out of the city. The Detroit freeways were always there for me, not only to get me to my destination quickly, but to shield me from seeing the inner city's harsh poverty and decay.

Despite the freeway advantages, I never liked driving on them. The speed of the cars scared me and I was intimidated by huge trucks, especially those that transported cars. I would never drive behind one, just in case the chain would get loose. I didn't want to be crushed in my used car by brand-new ones.

My husband kept telling me, "Don't drive on side streets. It's just not a good idea. Besides it'll take you forever to get any place. Just keep using the freeways. In no time, you'll overcome your fear."

My husband might have thought I was a paranoid immigrant who was not used to American modernity, as owning a car and driving on the freeways were important aspects of life. I was so thrilled when I learned that my statistics professor at Wayne State University, born and raised in Motown, was also scared of big trucks, and would never drive on the freeway.

ON A WARM spring day, I left Wayne State University early wanting to enjoy the rest of the day while it was still warm and bright. Once I got in my car I thought to myself, *I'm not in a hurry so why take the freeway?* I wanted to see the city and what lay between the university and my home. I drove south on Woodward Avenue, then east on Harper. That should have taken me home. But to my surprise I was totally lost. Not a big deal, I told myself, as the Egyptian proverb goes, "Those who ask don't get lost." So I stopped by the first grocery store I found. The store had bars on the windows. Two hairy brown men stood behind a thick plastic wall. They were chatting in Arabic.

"*Marhaba.* How are you?" I said.

"I'm fine," said one of them with a surprised look on his face. Then he asked, "What country are you from?"

"My father is Palestinian from Jaffa. I grew up in Jordan."

"I am from Shu'fat, a village near Jerusalem."

"I know Shu'fat," I said.

"I thought you were Arab as soon as you entered the store, but I wasn't sure because Arabs don't live or come to this side of town," said one of the men.

"I'm embarrassed to admit it, but I'm totally lost. I need directions to Harper and Cadieux. I usually take I-94, but it is such a nice day I decided to take side streets."

"You're lucky to come to our store. You should never ever come to this neighborhood. This is not a place for a *muhtaramah* woman."

"What's wrong with this neighborhood?" I asked.

"Can't you tell? They're all Blacks here."

Shocked by his answer I said, "If it's so bad being among Blacks, why don't you move?"

"I have to make a living. I make good money here. That's why."

"You can make…"

Before I had a chance to finish my sentence, the man interrupted me, saying, "Listen, young woman. I know what I'm talking about. Just go home and don't get on these roads. Just stick to the freeway."

"You think you're better than Blacks? Try telling a few white people you're Palestinian and see what they think," I said, as I walked out of the store fuming. *You sons of bitches, after all the oppression you experienced? How dare you?*

IN DECEMBER OF 1991, almost one year after Nelson Mandela was released, I went to South Africa as a member of a US solidarity delegation. We wanted to celebrate the end of apartheid and the miraculous transformation of the country. During our two-week visit, we had a chance to travel throughout the country. The contrast between the life of white Europeans and that of indigenous Africans was striking. No matter how much I thought I knew about South Africa, nothing prepared me for the cruelty and horror I saw.

Our delegation itinerary included attending an African National Congress (ANC) rally at one of the universities. The day before, I decided to spend the night with a friend who was doing her PhD research in Johannesburg. We spent the night talking and discussing politics. The next morning, I woke up late. Not knowing my way around, and not wanting to miss the rally where I was to meet our delegation, I decided to take a cab. A few minutes after I got in the cab, the traffic came to a complete halt. We just sat there. The cab driver, a white man in his sixties, kept getting out of the car and looking down the freeway trying to figure out what the problem was. As time went by, he was getting more restless and frustrated. I was getting more anxious.

"Do you think we'll make it to the university by 11:00?" I asked.

"How would I know?" I could hear anger in his voice.

"Does it usually get congested at this time of day?"

"It didn't used to. This was a beautiful city. We used to cruise this freeway without having to see any of these people. Not now. Not anymore. Now there are too many Blacks in the city. Just too many Blacks."

Trying to hide my smile, I said, "But, sir, this is Africa."

He gave me a look that oozed hatred and anger, a look that got me really scared. "You're right, sir. I know exactly what you mean. Just like in Palestine... excuse me, I mean Israel. There are too many Palestinians there. Just too many."

CHAPTER 26
A NEW LOVE

WASHINGTON, DC, 1993-94

I sat in my Washington, DC apartment reading the thirtieth draft of my resignation letter. It was past midnight and I was tired. *This is it. No letter will be good enough. Just do it,* I told myself. It had been fifteen years since establishing the Palestine Aid Society of America (PAS) and thirteen years of working as its executive director. I wanted so badly to quit my job and take a one-year sabbatical. I was totally exhausted and demoralized. No matter how hard my colleagues and I worked, we were unable to make any progress—not even a dent—in bringing a just and peaceful solution to the Palestinian-Israeli conflict. The widely celebrated Oslo "Peace" Accord was the last straw. Like many Palestinians in the Occupied Territories and the Diaspora, I believed Oslo would only strengthen the Israeli occupation. The promise of an independent Palestinian state, a cause to which I had dedicated most of my adult life, was slowly slipping away.

While my body and soul were begging to have mercy on them, taking a one-year sabbatical, without knowing what was to come next, was a scary venture. Not only because it was an admission of defeat, but also because I couldn't afford a year without pay. Luckily, during my years of activism, I had the privilege of working with many young men and women who had graduated from college with hefty student loans, and they seemed to be cool about it. So I kept telling myself, *I should be able to do this. It is OK to be in debt. I can take a year off to figure out the next chapter of my life.*

Before submitting my resignation, I decided to talk to my therapist, Dr. Payton, whom I hadn't seen as a patient for a few years. I wanted to consult with her, or more accurately, to have her assure me that I was making the right decision. After all I wasn't as young as these recent graduates, nor was I able to live like a student at this age.

Dr. Payton and I spent a good amount of time talking. In her magical way, she was able to make me explore all the good things that could possibly happen if I did take a sabbatical. After almost two hours, she said, "Congratulations, Anan. This is a courageous step. A one-year sabbatical will rejuvenate you. It will also provide you with opportunities you haven't even considered."

"Thank you, Dr. Payton, I needed your assurance and your blessing."

"Trust me, Anan, you're going to be just fine."

"I hope so." As I stood up and extended a hand to say goodbye, Dr. Payton got out of her chair, walked around her desk and gave me a warm embrace. Then she looked at me and said, "I want you to promise you'll come back any time you need to talk. You pay what you can or not pay at all. Don't you ever hesitate to come because of the money."

"I won't. I promise. And thank you Dr. Payton for your love and support, and for your annual donation to PAS."

I did continue to visit Dr. Payton even after I moved from DC. When she retired from Howard University, I would visit her in her home, which was as elegant and warm as she was. Dr. Payton died peacefully in her bed in 2001, but her love, warmth, and wisdom continue to keep me company.

The minute I told my mother that I quit my job, she started nagging me about moving to Amman. "You're not married anymore, and you don't have a job, so why don't you come back? You have family and friends here. What do you have there?"

"I have lots of friends. They're like my own family."

"Nothing is like your own blood."

"Mama, I am happy here. You know I never cared to live in Amman."

"Why don't you come for a long visit and see how you like it. I'm not going to be around forever. I'd love to have you live here before I die."

Knowing my mother and the guilt trips she was capable of, I decided to sublease my DC apartment and go to Amman. I convinced myself that three months there couldn't be that bad. After all it's the city where I grew up, my sister Arwa and her two daughters were living there, and I had a few close friends. Within a month, however, I was getting restless, and wanted to go back to my own place in Washington, DC. I missed the city, my own space, and my friends. With my apartment leased for three months, I decided to stay and make the best out of it. I broke the monotony with a couple of short visits to my sister Suad and her husband Salim in the West Bank, a place I felt more at home in than Amman. But my mother kept calling and asking, "When are you coming back? I thought you came here to see me... I miss you."

It was during these three months that I realized how much I had changed. True, most of my close friends in the US were Arab Americans and my activism centered around Palestine, however in many ways I was more Americanized than I cared to admit. While I enjoyed the hospitality and the outpouring of love, I missed living alone. I missed my privacy and solitude.

In the fall of 1994, a few months after I came back from Amman, the Palestine Aid Society was getting ready for its eighth national convention in Philadelphia. For the first time since 1980, I wasn't in charge. I felt both sad and relieved. I was sad for leaving the organization I had played a major role in creating and managing, but relieved not to be worrying about taking care of the conference guests and all the logistics that came with organizing a national gathering. Unlike all of the previous conventions, I had the time to listen to speakers, spend time with friends and comrades, and stay up late, eating, drinking, and laughing. It was at that convention that I reconnected with my Detroit friend, Noel Saleh.

At the time, I was dating Kwame, an interesting fellow whom I had met through my friend Ethelbert. It was the kind of non-committal relationship I was comfortable with. During our two-year relationship, Kwame had met many of my friends, including Faris who lived in Chicago, and often came to DC for PAS Board meetings or just to visit me. Faris and I had been close for many years. He was the kind of person who would give the shirt off of his back for his friends. Faris was also big on matchmaking. He felt comfortable telling people what they should or should not do in all aspects of their lives, including dating, love, and marriage.

"This so-called boyfriend of yours, what's his name?" Faris asked, during one of his visits.

"His name is Kwame. What about him?" I asked, knowing from his tone that he was ready to give me unsolicited advice.

"He's a nice guy, but honestly, Anan, would you marry him?"

"No," I said. "I'm not planning to get married to him or to anyone else."

"You shouldn't be wasting your time with a relationship that has no future."

"Thank you, Faris, but no one is asking your opinion."

"But…"

Before he had a chance to say more, I interrupted him, saying, "I know you love me, but I really don't want to talk about it right now."

As soon as Faris went back to Chicago, he called to ask if I was planning to go to the PAS convention in Philadelphia.

"Of course I am. Why wouldn't I?"

"I just talked to Noel; he is coming too. He is a nice man. He's single, and not involved in a relationship. You should forget about this Kwame of yours, and start dating Noel."

"You don't need to tell me about Noel as if I don't know him. I agree with you, he is a nice guy. But I'm not going to date every nice man I know."

"I bet he'd love to date you. Why don't you give it a try?"

"No thanks. I'm not interested in a long-distance relationship or in dating someone from Detroit. I've already been there and done that. Besides, how do you know Noel would be interested in having a relationship with me?"

"Why wouldn't he?"

Later Faris admitted that he did talk to Noel, and asked him if he was dating anyone. When Noel said no, he had the same conversation with him about me.

Although I told Faris I wasn't interested, I didn't completely dismiss the idea. I often caught myself thinking about it. Noel was no stranger. I had known him since the early 1980s when he joined PAS and later served on the organization's board of directors. Noel also acted as the organization's pro bono legal advisor, and was always very generous with his time, and never complained no matter how much we asked of him. In 1991, after the Iraqi invasion of Kuwait and the US war against Iraq, Noel lead a PAS delegation of lawyers to investigate the systematic violation of Palestinian human rights by the Kuwaiti government.[16]

The son of a Lebanese father and Irish mother, Noel had a fair complexion, small light brown eyes, and a very gentle demeanor. Single, young, and handsome, many women, Arab and non-Arab, were seeking his attention. I have to admit, I liked him too, and even had a crush on him when I was living in Detroit. But I hadn't seen him much since I moved to DC in 1989. The thought of a relationship with Noel both intrigued and terrified me. I kept telling myself, *I am enjoying my single life and my sabbatical, so why do I want to stir things up? And why do I need the heartache of real love?*

In Philadelphia, Noel and I spent lots of time catching up. We talked and covered all kinds of topics about family, friends, work, and travel, but never mentioned dating, or getting together in the future. After he went back to Detroit, and I to DC, we managed to find excuses to call each other regularly. Every time we talked, I wondered if Noel was going to mention getting together again. Although I was still fearful of where this might lead me, I wanted to see him again, to be with him. A few weeks passed, and we were still dancing around the idea of dating, not admitting that we were interested in pursuing a relationship.

My nosy friend, Faris, who also kept calling, wanted to know what was going on between Noel and me.

"Not much," I insisted.

"You're lying. Aren't you?"

"Well, we talk on the phone once in a while, but that's about it."

"Listen, why don't you come spend a weekend with me in Chicago?" Before I had a chance to respond he said, "Do you mind if I invite Noel at the same time? This way you can spend time with each other, and then you can take it from there."

Knowing Faris, I asked, "You've already talked to Noel, haven't you?"

"Yes, and he likes the idea."

We got to Chicago early November on a cold rainy weekend. Despite the bad weather, Faris kept leaving the house claiming he needed to buy one thing or another. He also insisted on cooking us gourmet meals, while Noel helped clean and wash the dishes. I did not object when they refused my help. It was wonderful being pampered by two men. Faris also kept the fireplace going, lit candles, and had all kinds of snacks and liquor. Even in the morning, he would offer us

Kahlua or Baileys, saying, "Here, have some with your coffee. It will warm you up." Then he would go out to get more wood, saying, "Let me put one more log in the fireplace," or "How about some candles?" He was trying so hard to create a romantic setting, it was rather comical.

"You're acting like a teenager. Stop it," I said.

"Don't listen to her. I like your style," Noel said laughing.

With the continuous rain and wind, we spent most of our time at home, enjoying our host hospitality and each other's company. When we got to the airport, Noel gave me a hug and a passionate kiss, then said, "I love being with you. Do you mind if I come to see you in DC?"

"Of course not. When would you come?"

"I'll let you know soon."

In less than two weeks, Noel came to DC for my birthday, which coincided with Thanksgiving. The following month I went to Detroit for his birthday, which happens to be on Christmas day. For the following three years, Noel and I would regularly get together in Detroit, in DC, or wherever my new nomadic life would take me.

During these years I got to not only feel comfortable around Noel, but to also admire him and what he stood for. Because Noel tends to say very little about himself, it took me a while to learn about his long years of involvement in the civil rights movement and other social justice issues. As an immigration attorney, Noel was always helping his mostly working-class clients. His caring for the poor and powerless fascinated me. As he once said to me, "I have promised myself to always remember the privilege I have just because I am a white male, and to never ever take advantage of that."

MY ONE-YEAR SABBATICAL was turning into eighteen months, and still, I had no clue where I was heading. Then, without warning, I received a call from my friend Hilda Silverman, which changed the trajectory of my plan, or lack thereof, to be more exact. Hilda was an active member of PAS and a close friend. In 1991, she and I established the Act On Consciousness Committee, advocating an end to US military aid to Israel, as long as it continued to occupy Palestinian land.

"I want to tell you about the Peace Fellowship at the Bunting Institute of Radcliff College at Harvard. With all the work you've done, I think you should apply."

"Thank you, Hilda. I'll look into it, though I doubt I'll get it."

"You won't get it if you don't apply," Hilda said.

As promised, I did look into it. That year the Bunting Institute granted thirty to thirty-five fellowships to women, mostly scholars, doing work in a variety of fields. The Peace Fellowship was given to only one woman engaged in making our world a more peaceful place. It was a long shot, but upon the encouragement of my friends, and strong recommendation letters, including one from Dr. Edward Said, I did apply. To my surprise, out of hundreds of applicants, I was the one selected.

CHAPTER 27
THE WANDERING PALESTINIAN

CAMBRIDGE, MA; THE WEST BANK; AND DETROIT, 1994-96

My one-year fully funded fellowship allowed me to rent a nice first-floor flat in a small house in Cambridge, which was only a ten-minute walk from the Bunting Institute. I was given a spacious office and two undergraduate research assistants. My cohort was comprised of thirty-three women. The fellows were all scholars with the exception of five—a physician from Doctors Without Borders, three female artists, and myself.

Within the first two months, the three fellow artists decided to have a joint art exhibit at the Bunting Institute's gallery. One woman exhibited her photographs focusing on horses. I cannot recall the work of the second one, but the third artist, Loraine, had an exhibition entitled *Power, Love, and Rape*, in which she explored the relationship between Sally Hemming and Jefferson. The *Radcliffe Magazine* covered the exhibition but mentioned only two women, totally ignoring Loraine's work as if neither she nor her exhibit existed. When some of the women at the Bunting Institute sent a complaint letter, the magazine insisted that the article was intended to give a few examples of the work and couldn't possibly cover all of the artists.

That experience left a bad taste in my mouth and made me wonder if it was the right place for me. But I kept reminding myself how fortunate I was to have a one-year paid fellowship, a fellowship that would not only help me figure out what I wanted to do next, but would also position me to find the exciting and stimulating job I was searching for.

As outlined in my application, I planned to spend my time at the Bunting Institute researching the impact of the Oslo Peace Accords on Palestinian civic society and its nongovernmental organizations (NGOs.) Many of them had played a significant role in supporting the Intifada. After Oslo, these organizations lost their funding, as the US government, along with its western allies, rechanneled their financial support to the Palestinian Authority.

The only requirement of the institute was that each resident-fellow give one lecture about her work. Mine, entitled "Conflict in Peace," was scheduled for the second semester. As I entered the large lecture hall fifteen minutes early, I was surprised by the packed room. Every seat was already taken, and dozens of people were standing or sitting on the floor. My forty-five-minute presentation was very well received and I got a standing ovation.

The day after, I walked to my office feeling high from the night before, only to learn that a few of the women from my cohort complained to the director for having an anti-Semitic fellow among them. I was stunned. For the previous twenty years I had been reaching out to Israeli and Jewish peace activists and I had organized and participated in numerous Palestinian-Jewish dialogues. I even traveled in 1983 with Israeli peace activists for an entire month on a speaking tour sponsored by the Presbyterian Church to promote the two-state solution. After all the work I had done to bring a peaceful resolution to the Palestinian-Israeli conflict, the work that made it possible for me to receive this fellowship, I was called an anti-Semite?

Furious and hurt, I just wanted to pack and leave, but I decided not to give anyone the pleasure of seeing me go. Luckily the residency did not require much mixing among the fellows, so I limited my interaction to the couple of progressive friends I made, including Shana, a Jewish physician from Doctors Without Borders.

This was not the end of the story, however. Among the traditions of the Bunting Institute was that each year the women fellows would collectively give a gift to the institute upon the end of their academic year. Coincidentally, I happened to have in my office a large piece of framed Palestinian embroidery, a gift from the Palestine Aid Society when I left. I used to get many compliments about it. My friend Shana suggested that our cohort gift could be a piece of embroidery similar to the one I had.

"You can suggest it, but I doubt the women will say yes."

"Don't be silly. Of course they will."

"If you think so, go ahead and talk to them. If they agree, I'd be happy to order one."

To my friend's disappointment, many of the women rejected the idea as being anti-Jewish and anti-Israel.

"I cannot believe this. It is ridiculous. I am so ashamed," Shana said, almost crying.

"It's OK, my friend. You tried, and that's all you can do."

WHILE MY EXPERIENCE at the Bunting Institute was not as pleasant as I had hoped for, I did enjoy all of the amenities that came with it, including the endless cultural and intellectual offerings of Cambridge and Boston, such as lectures, films, exhibits, concerts, and live performances, as well as the beautiful parks and riverfront. Being in Cambridge also helped me reconnect with Dr. Elaine Hagopian, for whom Palestine was as close to her heart as it was to mine. From the first day I arrived, Elaine, a sociologist at Simmons College whom I'd known since I arrived to the US, adopted me like her own younger sister and introduced me to many activists in the area. Elaine and I became lifelong close friends, and for me, that was the best thing I gained from my time in Cambridge.

Before the end of my fellowship year, I applied for the position of Visiting Scholar at the Center for Middle Eastern Studies at Harvard University, and to my delight I got it. Then, only two months into my first semester, I got a phone call from my brother-in-law, Salim Tamari. Salim, the husband of my sister Suad, was living in Ramallah and working in East Jerusalem as the director of the Institute of Jerusalem Studies. Although Salim and I had a very nice relationship, I was not used to having him call me long-distance just to chat. After exchanging the usual greeting, I said, "*Khair Inshallah*, what's up Salim? I hope everyone is OK."

"Everyone is just fine." He paused a few seconds, then reluctantly said, "I want to ask you for a big favor."

"What kind of favor?"

"I got a teaching job at Columbia University in New York. I really want to go, but the Institute's board of directors won't let me leave unless I find an interim director."

"You mean you're looking for someone who would be willing to give you back your job when you return?"

Salim's laughter vibrated through the telephone line. "You got it. I know it's a lot to ask, but Suad said, 'You never know…Anan loves it here, and she would probably enjoy the work.' She encouraged me to call you."

"When do you want me to be there, and for how long?" I asked, without hesitation.

"Only one semester. January to May."

"That means I have to leave here by the end of this semester?"

"Yes. That's why I was reluctant to ask."

"Well, let me think about it."

"When will you let me know? I need to get back to Colombia soon."

"Give me one week."

I did not need a week, not even a day, to make up my mind. Within the hour I knew I was going to Palestine. But I kept telling myself, *Anan, don't rush into this. Think about it. You're at Harvard. You're not going to give this up for a five-month job in Palestine. Harvard will help you in the future. Don't waste this once-in-a-lifetime opportunity.*

No matter how much I tried to convince myself to stay, I was missing grass-roots organizing and community work. When Salim called, I was almost positive that neither Harvard nor academia was where I wanted to be. I wanted to be in Jerusalem, my childhood city. I wanted to reconnect with the friends and organizations I knew in Palestine. And I wanted to spend some time with my sister.

The prospect of being in Palestine was very exciting. But my appointment in Jerusalem was only for five months. By the end of it, it would have been four years since I resigned from the Palestine Aid Society. My initial plan was to take a one-year sabbatical to figure out what to do next. However, after all the floating around from one place to another, I was still undecided.

On the love front, I was a just as ambivalent. Noel and I continued our long-distance relationship during my time at Cambridge. Meanwhile, he was trying to convince me to move to Detroit once I was done with my one-year appointment at Harvard.

"You know the city, you have many friends here, and I just bought a large house. It's beautiful on the Detroit River. It would be the perfect place for you to pursue your writing, which you seem to enjoy a lot."

My mind drifted to Dr. Payton. She was correct. My sabbatical did provide me with many opportunities, including venturing into creative writing, something I always wanted to do, but never had the luxury. It was during that time when I started to draft some of the stories in my first book, *The Scent of Jasmine: Coming of Age in Jerusalem and Damascus*, as well as some of the vignettes in this book.

"I can't make a living as a writer. I'm also not ready to live with you or move to Detroit, especially without having a job. I've been there, done that, and failed miserably."

"After being at Harvard, I'm sure you can easily find a job in academia. Maybe Wayne State University where you taught before."

"That was ages ago. Besides, I'm not sure I want a job in academia. I miss grassroots community work."

And so went our conversation for a few months. Then came the unexpected offer from my brother-in-law for a temporary job in Jerusalem. Reluctantly, I picked up the phone and called Noel to tell him about my new plan.

"I thought your appointment at Harvard was until the end of this academic year."

"It is. But I'd rather be in Jerusalem."

"And what are you going to do after that?"

"I'm not sure. I'll figure it out."

"Suit yourself." I could detect disappointment in his voice.

"You can come and visit. You love it there."

After I hung up the phone, I started to wonder if I was pushing my luck with Noel. By then it was more than three years since we started dating and Noel had been extremely loving and supportive. And while I did not want to take advantage of his kindness, I just could not pass up the opportunity to be in Jerusalem.

Before long, Noel called to tell me that Ismael Ahmed, the executive director of ACCESS wanted me to call him.

"Call him about what?"

"I think he wants to offer you a job at ACCESS."

"Just like that? What kind of a job is he talking about?"

"Their Director of the Cultural Arts Program is leaving..."

"But I'm going to Jerusalem," I interrupted.

"I know that. Just let me finish what I have to say."

"Sorry, go ahead."

"Today I was having lunch with Ish. I told him that I've been trying to convince you to move to Detroit, but you won't come unless you have a job. The minute I mentioned it, he said, 'I'd love to have Anan work with us. Have her call me.'"

At the time, Noel was president of ACCESS's board of directors, and I was alarmed by the unsolicited offer from Ish.

"Did you ask Ish to give me a job? Is he doing this as a favor to you? I don't want such favors."

"Anan, I'm really disappointed, I thought you would know me better by now. This is Ish's idea; I had nothing to do with it."

"Let me think about it."

"You've been telling me you miss working with the community, and won't move to Michigan unless you have a job. Now you want to think about it? You know Ish. Just call him and find out what he has in mind."

Noel was right. I'd known ACCESS and Ismael Ahmed, or Ish, as people called him, since I came to the US in 1974. He, along with his grandmother Haja Aliya Hassan, played a major role in establishing the organization, which had grown a lot since I left Detroit. As two Arab American activists, our paths often crossed. Even after I left Michigan, I would run into him at various national events. I liked and respected Ish, and I knew he felt the same toward me.

I decided to come to Detroit to see Noel and also to talk to Ish before heading to Palestine. Ish asked me if I would be interested in working with

ACCESS as the Director of the Cultural Arts Program. "The current director already submitted her resignation. I think you'd be great in that position."

"But I'm going to Palestine and won't be back until late May. That's six months from now."

"If you're interested, I will not hire anyone until you come back. But I need a three-year commitment."

"I need to know more about the job and about ACCESS. It has been a long time since I visited the organization."

Ish took the time to tell me about the job and handed me a job description. I asked him to give me a few days to think about it.

Before I left for Palestine, I saw Ish again. He gave me a tour of ACCESS, introduced me to some of the staff, and then we sat in his office to talk. By the end of our conversation, we shook hands. It was a word-of-mouth agreement, but we both knew we would honor it.

In December 1996, I submitted my resignation letter to Harvard, and for the first time in my life I celebrated the New Year in Ramallah and was ready for a new adventure.

MY STAY IN Palestine was not as glamorous as I'd hoped. My sister Suad, an architect, was extremely busy with a new, large project. When I first arrived, she made a point to spend time with me. Although cooking was not her favorite activity, she did have a large dinner at her home in my honor. She took me to new restaurants and on long walks. But soon the reality of her demanding job caught up with her. After only a couple of weeks she hardly had any time for me, or anyone else. She even missed most of the aerobic classes we both signed up for. But my biggest disappointment was when I was struck with pneumonia the day Noel arrived to spend ten days with me. I had been anxiously waiting for that day and had been telling him about the elaborate plans of our ten days together. The poor man had to find a way to entertain himself. He slept on the couch during his whole visit. He came to Palestine hoping to ask me to marry him, but he was banned from even entering my bedroom. Knowing how scared I was to get married, he said, "I guess I scared you to death. You don't have to get that sick to say no."

On the day he left I wouldn't let him come close to me. "I'm sorry, Noel, there is nothing I want more than to hug you, but the last thing I want to do is give you my sickness."

"But I want to hold you, to kiss you. I hate to leave while you're this sick."

"Don't worry, I will make it up to you when I come to Detroit."

I was heartbroken to say goodbye, but I knew that soon we would be together in Detroit.

Of course, the Israelis had to top it all off. After Oslo, the settlements started to spread like a plague, swallowing more and more of the Palestinian land. My daily commute from Ramallah to Jerusalem, only twenty kilometers, would take one to two hours. It depended on traffic congestion and, more importantly, the mood of the Israeli soldiers at the checkpoints. Palestinians were banned from entering Jerusalem unless they had a permit, which was almost impossible to obtain. With an American passport, I had no problem, other than the daily embarrassment of being allowed to go while my fellow Palestinians, with whom I shared a commuter van, were questioned, humiliated, and, more often than not, sent back.

Twenty years later, as I'm writing this, I can still see the tears and hear the agony of an older Palestinian woman. She was carrying her four-year-old granddaughter with traces of blood on the child's face. The woman kept pleading with an Israeli soldier to let her through.

"Have mercy on us. My grandchild fell and has a bad eye injury. Please. I need to get her to the hospital in East Jerusalem."

"I said go back or I will arrest you," yelled the soldier, while pointing his big machine gun at her. He couldn't have been more than twenty years old. The old woman wept as she accepted her fate. She carried her child and walked slowly to the other side of the checkpoint.

Although I used to chuckle when my friends teased me about being the privileged US citizen who could go to Jerusalem any day, at that moment I felt so ashamed as I presented my American passport and was ushered across.

In East Jerusalem, and to my utter disbelief, the Institute for Jerusalem Studies was in the Sheikh Jarrah neighborhood, only a few houses from my childhood home. During my previous trips, I had avoided visiting the house, but this time it was staring me in the face. Its three floors were occupied by the

Turkish Consulate. Not only did I work only a few meters away, but I passed by the house almost daily on my way to the Old City or to lunch.

One day, I gathered my courage, checked my emotions, and walked the short distance from my office. With my heart pounding, I knocked at the door.

"May I help you?" said the Consulate guard. He was rather friendly.

"I lived in the second flat of this house when I was a child. I would greatly appreciate it if you let me see it."

"There's not much to see. Only offices."

"It doesn't really matter." Recognizing his reluctance, I added, "I came all the way from the US. I promise I won't stay long."

"If I let you in, I must accompany you."

"That's fine."

I stepped inside and leaned against the cold metal entrance door to steady myself. I was shaking while trying to take it all in. The yard looked much neater with trimmed shrubs and elegantly designed flower beds. I looked for the jasmine my mother had brought from Damascus and planted by the house entrance. It was not there. I took a deep breath to ease the tightness in my chest. The guard must have felt the intensity of my emotions. He walked away and stood by the house's entrance, waiting.

I appreciated him leaving me alone for a few minutes. I had been dreading the visit, not knowing what it would evoke in me. With wobbly knees, I walked slowly toward the guard. Together, we entered the middle floor. The flat we lived in did not look anything like home, but I still wanted to see it.

Sensing my grief, the guard asked, "Can I get you some water?"

"Thank you. I'm fine."

I walked slowly, looking around. The place was much smaller than I remembered, but it was just as bright and sunny. My bedroom veranda, from where my mother, sister Arwa, and I had watched the birth of a baby lamb, overlooked dense settlements that filled what once was a beautiful, open green space.

Five months after I arrived, I left with a broken heart, not knowing when I would be back or if I would live long enough to see peace return to my beloved Palestine.

* * * *

ONLY A FEW days after I came back from Palestine, I started my new job at ACCESS. It was June 1, 1997. Noel wanted us to tie the knot, but my fear of being married again never left me.

"Noel, I love you but I'm not ready to get married."

"I've been chasing you around the world, from DC to Cambridge to Palestine. You didn't want to move to Michigan unless you had a job, and now you have one. We've known each other for ages and we have been dating for four years. Are you ever going to be ready?"

"To tell you the truth, I'm scared of being married again."

"Well, I'm scared too. Why do you think I've stayed single for almost fifty years?"

"Let's live together for one year, then we'll take it from there," I suggested.

My return to Detroit went much smoother than I anticipated. Many of the friends I had from PAS and other progressive groups were also Noel's friends. They welcomed me with open arms and were happy to see Noel and me together. Noel also introduced me to his friends whom he'd known since his early years of involvement in the civil rights movement. It did not take me long to know that I finally found my soul mate, and my fear of being married again was evaporating. In spite of the many years I had known Noel as a friend, colleague, and partner, I was still taken by his kindness, unconditional love, and support. He was not only able to understand me, but also to respect my independence and my need to have my own space.

Ten months after I moved to Detroit, on a beautiful early spring April Fool's Day, Noel and I got married. A female judge and friend of Noel married us in the backyard of her elegant house in Detroit's Indian Village. The two of us, along with Noel's mother and our two female friends as witnesses, Pauline Everette and Angelita Espino, stood by the blooming Magnolia tree as we exchanged our vows.

WHILE MY RELATIONSHIP with Noel had a happy ending, my job at ACCESS wasn't going as well. It was neither exciting nor challenging. I started to wonder if I took the job just to be with Noel. By the time we decided to get married, I was already regretting making a three-year commitment to Ish, and knew I wouldn't be staying beyond those years. My mind and heart were already set on moving back to Washington, DC, but I wanted to be sure that Noel would be willing to leave with me. So, in exchange for me saying "I do," Noel agreed to sign a prenuptial agreement stating that in three years, if I decided not to stay in Detroit, he would be willing to move to a city of my choosing! After having a taste of life in the more cosmopolitan cities of Cambridge, Boston, and Washington, DC, it became harder for me to adjust to life in Detroit, even though I loved the city. After all, it was where I started my life in the US and where I had many close friends, as well as sad and happy memories.

To be fair, I was extremely impressed by the work of ACCESS. It had grown from the small service storefront I once volunteered with to the largest Arab American organization in the US with multiple programs and locations. It was my job that I wasn't thrilled about. While it was unconventional for a social service organization to have a Cultural Arts Program, it was the smallest department at ACCESS, with less than a $150,000 annual budget, and just two and a half staff members. All other departments were larger, and provided what was thought of as "real" needed services, such as employment, education, and health. Beyond Ish, not many in the organization seemed to care much about my department. Initially, I didn't seem to care that much about it either. It was not the kind of job I had envisioned for myself after a long-winded sabbatical. It paled in comparison to my work with PAS, a national organization with four regional offices, fourteen chapters in the US and Canada, and over four thousand members. Although there was no legally binding agreement for me to stay for three years, I was going to honor my promise to Ish and try to make the best of it. Hopefully, by the end of the three years, I would be able to find the elusive, more exciting, and challenging job I'd been searching for since I left PAS in 1993.

Little did I know that the dream job I was searching for was within my reach. Inspired by ACCESS's growth, I began to explore ways to expand the Cultural Arts department, to build on the strong and innovative programs that were already in place, and to make them more impactful. In my second year I recall telling Ish, "It shouldn't be the fate of Cultural Arts to stay with two or three staff members forever, or with such a small budget."

"I agree with you. It's your department, and you are free to make it as big as you can."

Meanwhile, I was closely watching ACCESS's first capital campaign to build an Employment and Training Center, which was launched shortly before I joined the organization. The success of the campaign and its completion ahead of schedule encouraged me to push the envelope and to dream big. I started discussing with Ish the possibility of expanding the Cultural Arts Program, to have our own space beyond one room in the administration building. Ish, an avid believer in the power of the arts, was more than receptive to the idea. "I'm with you, sister, but we need to first build a center for the community health department and one for the youth and education.

"But that will take years."

"I know, but ACCESS has its priorities."

Being stubborn and persistent and having the experience of establishing PAS from scratch encouraged me to keep pushing. Then, in September 2000, came the golden opportunity to purchase a boarded-up furniture store on Michigan Avenue in Dearborn, across the street from Dearborn's City Hall. ACCESS's initial plan was to house its Community Health Center there but the mayor of Dearborn wouldn't allow it. He did not want poor people lining up across the street from his office. However, the mayor was open to the idea of building a cultural center. We grabbed the opportunity and ran with it. In less than five years we managed to demolish that building and replace it with a beautiful state-of-the art museum facility. On May 5, 2005, ACCESS, along with our local and national community, celebrated the inauguration of the first-ever Arab American National Museum, dedicated to the history, culture, and contributions of Arab Americans. And I was proud to be its founding director, a job I held until my retirement in May 2013.

CHAPTER 28
A LEARNING MARATHON

DETROIT, 2000-02

Despite my euphoria that an Arab American museum would soon become a reality, it didn't take me long to grasp the enormous challenges such a project presented. Suddenly, I found myself moving from managing ACCESS's small Cultural Arts Program with three staff members to establishing a full-blown museum. I couldn't tell what was more overwhelming: my excitement or my fear.

"I guess I got what I've been asking for," I told my husband. "But honestly, Noel, I'm terrified. What do I know about museums, let alone the process of creating one?"

"I'm sure you will do an excellent job."

"But how are we going to transform this ugly boarded-up building into a beautiful space?"

"*Saber,* my wife, *saber.* Be patient. It's too early to think about that. Besides, there is nothing money can't fix."

I had expressed a similar fear to Ish and received the same response. I have to be thankful for both. Their trust in me never wavered during the five years it took to create the museum, or the eight years of being its director.

Fundraising for the museum fell mostly on ACCESS's leadership, above all the organization's CFO, Maha Freij. I, however, still had to help, especially when it came to raising money from foundations. Additionally, much of the content of the museum and its exhibits fell on my shoulders. Before I knew it, the museum became my new obsession. I literally started to lose sleep over what an Arab American museum might look like. *What kind of exhibits should we have? What and whose stories should we include, and more problematically, what should we exclude?*

One day, as I was exploring these issues with Ish, he told me, "You can build upon the programs and exhibits we already have."

"I'm planning on it. But what we're venturing into is a much more expensive and complex project. Let's face it, Ish, ACCESS is a social service organization. Neither you nor I know much about museums. I am worried we might end up making serious mistakes. We need to consult with experts and hire someone with museum expertise, like a museum curator."

"Let me reach out to Steve Hamp, president and CEO of the Henry Ford Museum and Greenfield Village[17] and ask his advice."

Steve Hamp's generosity exceeded our expectations. After Ish and I met with him, he immediately assembled a team of his senior staff and made them and himself available to us throughout the planning years and even after we opened the museum. Encouraged by Mr. Hamp's response, we started to reach out to others. To our delight, not a single person in Michigan or elsewhere, whether a scholar or a museum professional, Arab or non-Arab, turned us down!

Fearful I wouldn't do it right, I began voraciously reading books and articles, searching the Internet, and looking at museum websites. I visited dozens of museums around the country, including a few ethnically specific ones, examining not only the content of their exhibits, but also the length of text and size of exhibit fonts. I took pictures of their donor walls, and left with copies of every brochure and flyer I could get my hands on. I had a lot to learn, and I had to learn it fast. It felt like a learning marathon, having to go from kindergarten to graduate school in a couple of years.

My poor husband had to hear about museums day and night. It was what I talked about first thing in the morning, when I came back from work, at the dinner table, and before I went to sleep. Many nights I kept him awake, in spite of his love to sleep, telling him in minute details about my day, or a trip I just took, or some new, crazy idea I had.

ANAN AMERI

"You know, Noel, I need to find some museums that might share our vision and core values, museums that have strong connections to their communities. There must be some out there."

"With your persistence, I have no doubt you'll find them."

"But what if…?"

"Anan, you need to stop worrying, and I need to get some sleep."

Noel was right. In Seattle, I found the Asian American Wing Luke Museum. In many ways their community resembled the Arab American community in terms of its national, religious, and socioeconomic diversity, as well as immigration background and timeline, which was encouraging.

I picked up the phone and called. After introducing myself, I said, "I would like to visit your museum and if possible, spend some time with your director, Mr. Ron Chew."

"Mr. Chew is out of town. Can I get back to you when he returns?"

After I hung up the phone, I wondered if I was asking too much, or if they would really get back to me. Sure enough, within a week, I got the call I'd hoped for.

"I just landed on a museum that might be of great help to us. I'm going to Seattle," I told Ish.

"What museum?"

"It's an Asian American museum. Their director is an activist and had no museum background prior to its opening. He is also committed to involving members of his community in all of the exhibits they do."

"Sounds interesting. I'd love to hear what you find out there."

AFTER TAKING ME on an elaborate tour, Mr. Chew took me to lunch, where we sat for more than two hours chatting.

"When I visit other museums or talk to museum experts, I'm often asked what kind of a collection we have. But we really don't have one. I'm hoping to collect what we need from the community as we build the exhibits. Does that make any sense to you?" I asked.

"Of course it does. Personally, I'm not a big fan of acquiring collections for the sake of having them."

"I have another concern. How can we create a balance between being professional and continuing to be rooted in our community?"

"If you involve your community in what you do and are willing to listen and respect what they have to say, you'll be fine."

I went back home feeling energized. "You have no idea how helpful and validating my trip to Seattle has been," I told Noel the minute I saw him upon my arrival at Detroit Metro Airport.

ONE PROGRESSIVE MUSEUM led me to another, including the Japanese American National Museum in Los Angeles, the Tenement Museum in New York, the Women's Museum in Dallas,[18] and the Civil Rights Museum in Memphis, among others. I was like a kid enjoying these explorations. But the more I learned, the more challenging certain issues became. For example, once we announced our plans to build the museum, I would often say, "We want to establish a museum that tells our own story from our own perspective." Or, as Ish used to put it, "Our story has been told by others, and often with malice. We need to tell our own." That was the mantra we chanted over and over again. But the more I said it, the more I pondered, *What is our story? Do we, as Arab Americans, have a different story than other immigrant groups? Are we unintentionally reinforcing the view that Arab Americans are the "others" and not part of the American story? Will having our own museum provide further justification for our exclusion from mainstream museums? Why should we assume that ACCESS, or I, know the Arab American story or are qualified to narrate it?*

Claiming that we needed to tell our story in our own voice assumed that Arab Americans had one voice and one story. But Arab Americans are as diverse as the Arab world they come from. During my long years working with the Palestine Aid Society (PAS) and the national Arab American community, I came to witness firsthand the extent to which our community is diverse in every aspect of life one can think of. For example, some came to the US as early as the 1800s and their offspring assimilated to the point of not thinking of themselves as Arab Americans. Others are recent immigrants and have a much stronger Arab identity. Some came from rural backgrounds with little formal education and ended up joining the American working class, while others came from cosmopolitan cities like Cairo and Baghdad, and are highly educated professionals. Some live in their own ethnic enclaves, others live in the rich suburbs. Compounding all of this are the complexities of different religious affiliations and physical appearance. Arab Americans can be blond with blue eyes, and thus "pass" as European Americans, while others are brown and are often subjected to racial profiling.

So what does it take to create a museum that reflects this enormous diversity with its vast religious, national, professional, socioeconomic, and lifestyle differences? How do we create a museum that will make someone like my husband, Noel, a third-generation Christian whose grandparents came from Lebanon, and someone like myself, a newly arrived Palestinian Muslim immigrant, feel that the museum tells their stories? Or what does it take to make someone like Diane Rehm, a highly accomplished NPR host and daughter of Egyptian immigrants, and my friend Hala, a recent Iraqi refugee, feel that the museum equally respects and reflects their experiences?

An additional challenge was *constructing* an Arab American identity. Should we choose our own definition, a scholarly definition, or the public media construct of Arab identity? For example, while some Egyptian Copts, Lebanese Maronite, Iraqi Chaldeans,[19] and children of mixed marriages don't identify as Arab Americans, others do. Once, before heading to Los Angeles, I asked my friend Nizar to help me organize a few meetings with various segments of the Arab American community. Nizar, whom I knew from the days of the Palestine Aid Society, lived in LA, and was a well-respected activist. A few days before my trip, Nizar called.

"I have managed to arrange a few meetings. But I couldn't get you one with the Egyptian Coptic community," he said.

"But this is an important community. I need to hear their perspective and hopefully meet people who are interested in sharing their personal stories."

"I talked to more than one person, but I was told they are not Arabs and don't want to be included."

"What do you mean they're not Arabs? I had a similar meeting with the Coptic community in Michigan. I lived in Egypt for a few years. I've never heard that Egyptian Copts are not Arabs."

"Sorry, Anan. I am just telling you what happened."

Later, I had similar experiences with some Lebanese Maronites in Texas, Chaldean Iraqis in Michigan and California, and children of mixed marriages. The fact that we were trying to connect with these groups shortly after September 11, 2001 did not help. Arab and Muslim Americans became—in the eyes of law enforcement and the general public—guilty by association. Consequently, some tried to hide their Arab identity, or reinforce their Christian affiliation. All of a sudden, the cross necklaces worn by men and women or hung on car rearview mirrors became bigger and shinier.

As I was briefing Ish and the staff about my trip, one staff member said, "Well, if they don't want to be included, that's their loss. It's not like we don't have enough Arab American groups to include."

"But how about those who identify as Arab American and want to be part of this project. Do we ignore them?" asked another staff member.

After long debates and consultations with scholars and community members, we decided to include those who define themselves as Arab Americans. Many were delighted to share their stories. A few were not, and we respected their choices.

Then came the issue of documenting Arab Americans' contributions. While I realized the importance of including individuals such as Dr. Ahmed H. Zewail, the recipient of the Nobel Prize in chemistry, or Christa McAuliffe, who died in the Space Shuttle Challenger disaster in 1986, I felt that the contributions of ordinary people such as automobile, railroad, and mine workers, as well as community activists, were equally important, if not more. The same applied to Arab Americans who served in the military. Should there be more recognition given to those who reached a high rank in the military, such as General George Joulwan of NATO or Vice Commander William Jabour of the Aeronautical Systems Center, than to foot soldiers who died in the field?

Whether high-ranking or not, people who served in the US military were very proud of their service, and were the most forthcoming in sharing their stories. However some, especially Muslims, felt unappreciated or even betrayed. As a third-generation Lebanese Muslim American in Brooklyn told me, "My grandfather fought in World War One, my father fought in World War Two, my two brothers and I fought in Vietnam. Except for one brother and myself, all were injured or suffered mental challenges. Still some don't think of us as patriots or 'real' Americans. What more are we supposed to do?" These and similar comments I heard from so many Arab Americans prompted us later to create a special traveling exhibit entitled *Patriots and Peace Makers: Arab Americans In Service to Our Country,* which highlighted servicemen and servicewomen in the US military, Peace Corps, and State Department's diplomatic services.

To complicate our lives even more, we soon realized that people who were most inclined to share their stories and donate artifacts and historical documents were second- and third-generation professionals with high levels of education and income. In Boston, the late Evelyn Menconi was eager to give me some of the merchandise her peddler grandfather sold. Journalist Helen Thomas gave us her first typewriter. Vicki Tammoush from Los Angeles gave us some Mexican pesos her grandfather brought with him when he emigrated from Mexico. And Senator James Abourezk gave us a gift he received from Native Americans in appreciation of his support to their causes, to mention only a few. On the other hand, new immigrants did not feel as comfortable sharing their stories. They were more concerned about basic needs like finding jobs, or they were afraid to tell their stories, or did not think they owned anything worth being in a museum. A Moroccan immigrant in Washington, DC told me, "I don't have time to worry about your museum. I need a decent job. I came here to secure the future of my children, not to be in a museum." A Sudanese woman in Minneapolis said to me, "Are you serious? You want to spend money building a museum while our people are fleeing war zones and searching for a safe life in America? Why don't you spend the money helping them?" When I tried to tell her about all the services ACCESS provided, she said, "That's in Michigan, what good does it do us here?"

As if our job was not hard enough, one year after we started, the tragic events of September 11, 2001 happened. At the time, Noel and I were on a vacation in Paris. We spent the day in our hotel room watching in horror as the events of that day unfolded. Noel was still the president of ACCESS's board. We both felt the need to rush back home.

Neither Noel nor I were surprised to find that many Arab Americans felt under attack, or that fear and apprehension dominated our community. Already subject to negative stereotyping, our community encountered even greater hostility. Many faced loss of employment as well as harassment and detention by law enforcement agencies. Even Ish, ACCESS's executive director, a great grand-child of Lebanese immigrants born in Brooklyn and a well-known and respected leader in Michigan, was attacked as he stopped at a red light in Dearborn.

On the other hand, we received many supportive e-mails, calls, letters, and visits from many non-Arabs, some of whom we knew and many we did not. I'll forever remember sitting in my office, moved to tears, as I read the website editorial of the Japanese American National Museum (JANM) in Los Angeles by their executive director, Ms. Irene Hirano. She was addressing the aftermath of 9/11, stating that it was the moral responsibility for every Japanese American to stand up and assure that what happened to Japanese Americans during WWII would never happen to Arab or Muslim Americans.

I picked up the phone and called Ms. Hirano and thanked her. Soon after, she called. "I have an idea I want to share with you. How about we have a joint program in Dearborn about 9/11 and the Japanese Internment Camps?"

"That is a great idea. Thank you for suggesting it," I said.

Sure enough, Ms. Hirano, along with JANM board member Senator Daniel Inouye, flew from Los Angeles and Washington, DC. They spoke at a joint public event expressing their solidarity with our community. That was our first public function in the name of the Arab American National Museum. Little did I know that we had discovered a gold mine, and found the most support-ive friends, mentors, and allies anyone could ever hope for. The support of the Japanese American National Museum and its staff and board, including Sena-tor Inouye, continued. Ms. Hirano and I were able to immediately bond as two activist women of color whose communities were unfairly treated because of our ethnicities and ancestral backgrounds. Thanks to Irene and the wonderful staff of the JANM, the bond that was created between us was extended to our insti-tutions and continues to flourish until today.

THE EVENTS OF 9/11 had also left its mark on Noel and I in more than one way. A few months after 9/11, Noel came home telling me, "I got a call today from Kary Moss, the director of the American Civil Liberties Union of Michigan. They want me to take a two-year full-time position with them to address the threat to civil liberties in the aftermath of 9/11."

"That's great. But what about your law office?"

"I am thinking of closing my office and quitting private practice."

"What happens after two years?"

"I'm not sure. I'll cross that bridge when we get to it."

"This is the perfect job for you. Go for it."

Sure enough, Noel closed his practice and started his new job at the ACLU. Both of our jobs required lots of travel and community meetings, and we were both dealing with the impact of 9/11 from our respective positions. At the dinner table we often discussed what we encountered during our day or weekend. It was during these hard times that my relationship with Noel grew even closer, and I came to realize the extent to which we shared the same values and concerns.

On my end, as the hostility toward Arab and Muslim Americans lingered, many new immigrants were not at ease displaying their stories in an "Arab" public space. An Iraqi American from Cleveland—who indicated in his initial story that he left Iraq because of the US economic embargo after the first Iraq war, wanted me to return all his material. When I asked him why, he said, "I don't feel safe sharing my story with the public." A Palestinian American from Santa Fe, New Mexico called me one day saying, "I'm sorry, but I lost the materials I was planning to send you." Some even questioned the sanity of building an Arab American museum in the existing political climate. It wasn't surprising that the most reluctant were newly arrived Palestinians and Iraqis who had left their countries because of the Israeli occupation or US-led wars in Iraq. While I understood their fear and respected their choices, it did make my already challenging job even harder.

However, as I look now at the larger picture, the overall response was very encouraging. Despite the fear and apprehension, the hundreds of valuable artifacts, historical documents, photos, and oral histories that we included in the permanent exhibits were all donated. We did not have to purchase a single item.

IN 2002, WITH the impact of 9/11 still raw, I decided to hit the road and find out what our community would like to see in a museum. I called people we knew in various cities, including members of PAS with whom I maintained friendships over the years and said, "I need your help. Can you arrange a few meetings with various segments of the Arab American community? I want to talk to them about the museum project."

For over eight months, I traveled, sometimes alone, other times with a colleague, from one city to another. In the beginning, I wasn't really sure what exactly I was looking for, but assumed that things would get clearer as I discussed the museum with the community. People, however, were giving me all kinds of advice about what I should or should not do. After a couple of meetings, I tried to ask more specific questions like, "What would you like to see in an Arab American museum?" or "How might the museum reflect your personal and community experiences?" People were more than willing to share their thoughts, and had a plethora of ideas. Every night, I would sit in my hotel room for hours, trying to sort through pages of notes, wondering how to make sense of what I had, and how to reconcile the often contradictory ideas I heard.

I recall one meeting in Orlando when a person told me, "You should have twenty-two rooms, each dedicated to one Arab country." "That's not right," said another. "You can't have the same size room for a small country like Dubai and a country as big as Egypt or Morocco."

"This museum is about Arab Americans and not the Arab world," I would explain.

"But that's where we come from," protested one person.

"Forget about the Arab world. We're American now," said another. "The name of the museum should be American Arab, not Arab American; we're American first."

After a few meetings with similar passionate discussions, I started to question the wisdom of my methodology and the validity of this "democratic grassroots" approach. But my gut feeling told me to keep going, to visit one more city, to have one more meeting, and I did. However, the more meetings I had, the bigger the burden and the expectation seemed to be, which made me question if the path we were taking would lead us to where we needed to be.

CHAPTER 29

TELLING OUR STORY...THE AMERICAN STORY

DEARBORN, 2005

My intuition to keep meeting with members of our community and hear what they had to say ultimately paid off. After numerous meetings in various cities, I began to observe certain consistencies in community members' feedback and a consensus was emerging. There were a few ideas that came up over and over again. "The museum should reflect the beauty and richness of Arab architecture and be modern at the same time." "We should have a section about the contribution of the Arab world to world civilization." "We have been in this country and part of the fabric of the US since its inception," and "We have fought and died for this country since the War of Independence." We also heard the agony in the voices of so many Arab American women: "We are tired of being portrayed as weak and submissive. You've got to do something about that." A visit to the museum clearly reflects the extent to which these messages were critical in shaping the building, exhibits, and public programming.

These road trips took me and my colleagues to many cities and towns. We met with new immigrants and third- and fourth-generation Arab Americans. One of these trips took us to Delano in California's San Joaquin Valley where large numbers of Yemeni farm workers resided. As we sat in one home, I asked the family if they had any items they brought with them from Yemen. We were particularly looking for suitcases for one exhibit.

"I have a very nice one I can give you."

Before I had a chance to respond, he rushed out of the living room and came back with a large red Samsonite.

"It's brand-new. I just bought it to take on my next trip to Yemen. You can have it. I can buy another one."

"Thank you. You're very generous. But I'm looking for one you or your wife brought from Yemen when you first came to the US. Do you still have one?"

"I do. But it's a cheap one. I didn't have much money then."

"Do you mind if I look at it?"

"You can. It's in the backyard. I'm ashamed to give it to you. Why don't you take the new one?"

We walked to his backyard. It was a 110-degree, steamy, hot afternoon. There sat a small metal suitcase decorated with colorful labels. It was filled with garden tools.

"What are these labels?" I asked.

"They're from the farm where I worked when I first came. I used the vineyard labels to decorate my room and I put a few on my ugly, cheap suitcase."

"I think it's beautiful. Would you be willing to donate this to the museum?"

"Are you sure? It's old and dirty."

"Don't worry about it; we can clean it."

He and his wife wouldn't hear of it. After emptying the trunk, they took a brush and hose and started cleaning it while my colleague and I stood watching, begging them not to damage the colorful labels."

Thanks to my long years of activism, coupled with ACCESS's connections and contacts from friends of friends, my colleagues and I were able to connect with hundreds of Arab Americans. We collected stories, artifacts, and historical documents from every state. Like the Yemeni suitcase, each acquisition had its own story narrated by Arab Americans, their children, and grandchildren. We also managed to acquire many recorded oral histories from families, libraries, and historical societies, including the Ellis Island National Monument.

During the years leading up to the museum's opening, I attended and spoke at community gatherings, reunions, and conferences to rally support for the museum project. At one of these conferences, held at the University of Maryland, I faced many challenging and sometimes hostile questions such as: "Are you or ACCESS really qualified to build a museum?" "Why do you want to build it in Dearborn, and not Washington, DC?" "What makes you think you will be able to raise sixteen million dollars?" and "Is this the time, right after 9/11, to build a museum?"

After the session, the late Richard Shadyac Sr., the chief executive of ALSAC[20] the fundraising arm of St. Jude Children's Hospital—walked up to me and said, "Congratulations. You're on to a great project."

"I'm sorry I got defensive. To be honest with you, some of these people intimidated me. I'm not sure I handled them well."

"Don't let anyone discourage you. I was with Danny Thomas when we started St. Jude. We were told the same; 'You can't do it. How can you raise this kind of money? And who is going to support Arab Americans building a hospital?' But we kept going. And look at St. Jude now."

"Thank you, Mr. Shadyac. I am going to remember what you told me every time I get frustrated or discouraged."

From the very early stages of establishing the museum, we hired the best architecture, construction, and museum firms we could find. And we assembled a local advisory board that included activists, community leaders, scholars, and museum experts. Two iconic Arab American scholars and personal friends, Dr. Michael Suleiman and Dr. Jack Shaheen, provided free advice throughout the founding years and beyond. I am grateful to all of them. But the people who really shaped our museum—who gave it its unique character and charted its future path—were members of our community.

The museum took five years to build. To people in the museum world, that is a rapid pace from planning to opening. But to me and my colleagues, it seemed like a long and arduous journey that was both exciting and dreadful. It was a once-in-a-lifetime opportunity to create something memorable that our community would be proud of. Later, I came to realize that our lack of museum background might have served us well. It freed us from preconceptions of what we could or couldn't do, or what should or should not be included in a museum. I recall Harold Closter, the Director of Smithsonian Affiliations, telling me after he toured the museum, "Had you come to me at the early stages of building the museum, I would have asked you first about your collection. And had you said you didn't have any, I would have definitely said you weren't ready."

* * * *

SIX MONTHS BEFORE the museum's scheduled opening we hired consultant Maud Lyon to help us develop a timeline for what tasks needed to be completed by the opening date, which was set for early May. Irene Hirano from the Japanese American National Museum invited the museum staff, along with Maha Freij, ACCESS's CFO, to a one-week training at the JANM in Los Angeles. As we celebrated the holidays at the end of 2004, we came back to work energized, looking forward with much anticipation to the opening date. We were ready to tackle the long list of challenging tasks that needed to be done in the final four months, from filling all of the needed positions, finding and purchasing store merchandise, setting up the library, and furnishing the building, to hosting dignitaries and planning the opening celebration.

On January 29th, 2005, three months before the opening, I received a call from my sister Arwa telling me that my mother had a stroke and might not be with us for long. I took the first flight to Amman and headed immediately to the hospital. My sisters warned me before I entered my mother's room, telling me, "Mama is in a coma."

I held Arwa's hand and walked in. It was early evening, but the winter sun had already departed. A gloomy yellowish light made my mother look paler than she already was. A loud cry escaped me when I saw my strong, independent mother with her half-closed eyes lying there helpless, hooked to machines with tubes coming out of different parts of her body.

"I'm sorry," I told Arwa. "I hope she didn't hear my cry."

"Don't worry about it. I'm sure she didn't."

"What are the doctors saying?"

"We keep asking and all they've told us is, "We have no idea how long she will stay in a coma or if she will ever wake up.""

In Amman I spent most of my time at the hospital with my brother Ayman, two sisters Suad and Arwa, my nieces Diala and Alma, and two close friends Muna and Najwa. Every morning I got up early and headed to the hospital, hoping my mother would be awake. I would quietly walk into her room, kiss her, touch her face, and hold her hand saying, "Mama. This is Anan. I came all the way from Detroit to see you. Do you hear me? Do you know I am here?"

Sometimes I would cry or get angry and yell at her, "Please, Mama, talk to me." But I never got a response. In spite of being nonreligious, I found myself reciting verses from the Quran, hoping for a miracle. I was torn between staying in Amman and coming back. We were only three months away from the opening of the museum and a lot had to be put in place. After ten days, with a heavy heart I decided to come back.

On February 28, less than three weeks after I returned, I got the call I was dreading. My mother had died. Noel and I flew to Amman. After ten days, I said goodbye to my siblings, nieces, and friends. I left knowing that Amman would never be the same, and our home would never be home again.

AT LAST THE long-awaited day arrived. On May 5, 2005 at 5:00 p.m., our community celebrated the inauguration of the first Arab American National Museum.

"Are you OK?" Noel asked as we walked from the parking lot to Dearborn City Hall where the celebration was about to start.

"Of course I am."

"You look kind of subdued."

"I'm fine," I said, but was unable to hold my tears.

"What's wrong? These don't seem to be happy tears."

"I miss my mother. She had followed my news about the museum and kept telling me how proud she was. I wished she had lived to witness this."

"I wish she was alive too. But this is your big day. You should be happy. Focus on the great job you've done. That's what Um Arwa would have wanted and expected."

I tried to focus on what Noel had told me, to remind myself of the historic occasion and the role I played in making it happen, but I couldn't get rid of the image of my mother lying in a hospital bed unconscious. I missed her and I missed my father, who had died more than twenty-five years ago. I wanted them to be there with me, to witness this moment. Noel wrapped his arm around me, and said, "Let's go." Together, he, as the president of ACCESS's board of directors, and I, as the founding director of the first-ever Arab American National Museum, entered Dearborn City Hall. Local and national dignitaries, officials,

Arab ambassadors, and representatives of major cultural institutions filled the reception area. The festive mood and the big smiles that surrounded me brought me back to the wonderful reality we were about to celebrate.

With our guests, we walked slowly on a red carpet that stretched across Michigan Avenue to the museum's entrance a few minutes shy of 5:00 p.m. Thousands of people formed a wall of human bodies, clapping and cheering as we crossed the road and cut the ribbon. The symbolic location, across the street from Dearborn City Hall, added to our pride. It was, in many ways, a celebration of the triumph of our community in the face of a city that has been, throughout its history, hostile to ethnic and racial minorities. One of the most memorable moments of that day was when an elder from our community stood at the museum's third floor terrace, looking across the street at the statue of Mayor Orville Hubbard[21], and said, "Mayor Hubbard, eat your heart out. We are here."

ESTABLISHING THE MUSEUM was a difficult and sometimes painful journey, but a journey that has greatly enriched my life. As a sociologist by training, I often wondered if we would actually pull this together. As the saying goes, "It takes a village to raise a child." It took hundreds of people from all walks of life to actualize this dream by giving generously of their time, money, and family treasures. Together, we were able to share a vision and create a home for all Arab Americans, and build an institution that tells our story from our community's diverse voices and perspectives. This is a place where Arabs and non-Arabs can share and learn more about the Arab American story, which, in fact, is an American story.

ACKNOWLEDGMENTS

Writing a book, especially a memoir, is a tedious and lonely process, but it is also reflective and healing. It often evokes intense emotions and brings to the surface what we would rather forget. To assure that my emotions or nostalgia would not impact my judgment or color my narrative, I had to dig deep into piles of hard copy and computer files, and to look at publications and photographs. While doing so, I was taken by the tears that often clouded my vision, and the smiles that spread over my face. It brought a flood of sad and happy memories, as well as the voices and faces of the hundreds of comrades, friends, and colleagues.

As I reflect on my life, my biggest gratification and pride comes from my activism and community involvement, as well as the wonderful people who walked that path with me. The work I have done throughout my years in the US required collective efforts, collaboration, and camaraderie. It was the kind of work that no one person can accomplish alone. While these friends might not have contributed directly to this book, without the work we have done together, I wouldn't have much to write about. First and foremost, I am so indebted to all of those who accompanied me on the long and challenging journey of the Palestine Aid Society of American (PAS). It was your faith and trust that set me on a lifelong career in the nonprofit world. Thank you for giving me the honor of leading this wonderful organization. Thank you for your enduring friendship, and thank you for hosting me in your homes. Whether I have slept on your couch, in your child's bedroom, or the guest suite, your warmth and love has sustained and given me precious memories that will last a lifetime.

I am also grateful to my friends and colleagues at ACCESS. While PAS was my training ground in nonprofit management, fundraising, and community organizing, it was the trust and support of ACCESS's leadership, including senior staff and board, that provided me with this once-in-a-lifetime opportunity. Establishing the Arab American National Museum took an army of committed individuals. I want to thank all of you, including the Museum's staff, members of the Task Force, the Advisory Board, and the Friends Committee. It's your dedication, along with invaluable community support, that made it possible for us to make our dream of creating the AANM a reality. Thank you for allowing me to lead the efforts of establishing the first ever Arab American National Museum, and to become its founding director.

Like my first book, *The Scent of Jasmine: Coming of Age in Jerusalem and Damascus*, I started drafting some of the vignettes of this book in 1993, when I took a one-year sabbatical after leaving the Palestine Aid Society. But soon after, I had to give up my writing to pursue a new career. However, my friends and family never gave up on me. They kept telling me, "You need go back to writing." "This is too important." "You should put it on paper." Thank you for the encouragement, and sometimes annoying nagging. Without you, *The Wandering Palestinian* would have never seen the light.

My heartfelt gratitude goes to my husband Noel Saleh, who has repeatedly read every single word of this book, spending endless evenings and weekends reading, editing, and brainstorming with me. His priceless feedback, patience, and wisdom have been extremely helpful. I am most thankful to my sisters Suad and Arwa, my nieces Diala and Alma, and my friend Rabia Shafie, who kept pleading with me to keep writing.

Last, but not least, I want to acknowledge my dear friend Barbara Kessler for reading the manuscript and giving me her invaluable critique and advice; my friend and writer pal Dr. Evelyn Alsultany, my friend and colleague Greta Anderson Finn for her keen eye and excellent copyediting; to Zilka Joseph for her insightful reviews and suggestions; and to all the members of the Ann Arbor Area Writers Group at Nicola's Books—your honest comments and reassurance made me a better writer.

GLOSSARY

A'ama: Blind

Ahlan wa Sahlan: Welcome

Aini: My eye; a term of endearment

Al-Hurreyah: The Freedom; the name of a magazine

Allah: God

Allah Yerhamoh: May God have mercy on him, or bless his soul; an expression used after a person's death

Ameerca: Arabic pronunciation and word for America, referring to the USA

Arak: Colorless liquor made of anise

Arba'een: Forty; a ceremony held forty days after a person's death

Aza: Condolences or funeral services

Baba: Father

Carawyeh: Pudding made of certain spices and mixed nuts served in celebration of a baby's birth

Dabkeh: Traditional line dance

Doctora: Female doctor

Eib: Shame

Eid: Holiday. In Arabic the word means any holiday, religious or secular, while in the West, it is often used to refer to a Muslim holiday

Elhub: The love

Eretz: Land (Hebrew)

Fellaheen: Peasants

Habibti: My love (for a female); *habibi* for a male

Hajja: Refers to a woman who has performed al Hajj (the pilgrimage to Mecca); also used as a term of respect to the elderly

Hathi madanieyeh: She is a city girl

Imam: Muslim cleric

Inshallah: God willing

Inti bint meen: Whose daughter are you?

Kartooneh: Cardboard; my mother used it to refer to a university certificate

Katib al Kitab: Muslim marriage

Khair Inshallah: Good news God willing

Kibbeh: A dish made out of cracked wheat and meat

Kussa: Zucchini

Mabrook: Congratulations

Mansaf: A traditional Palestinian and Jordanian dish served at weddings or large dinners. It is made of lamb, rice, yogurt, and nuts

Marhaba: Welcome

Marqook: Paper-thin bread

Muhtaramah: Respected

Mujadarah: A traditional dish made of onions, rice, and lentils

Nakba: Disaster; Palestinians use the word to refer to the 1948 creation of Israel and the Palestinians' expulsion from their homeland

Nye: Musical instrument similar to a pipe

Oroob: Arabs; a colloquial term used by villagers and earlier immigrants

Oud: Musical stringed instrument similar to a guitar

PLO: Palestine Liberation Organization

Qanoon: Musical instrument

Quran: The Islamic Holy Book

Saber: Patience

Saj: Similar to a thin, inverted wok but larger and used to bake *marqook* (paper-thin bread)

Serveece: A shared taxi that runs certain routes within a city

Sharaftina: You honor us with your presence

Sharru al balliete ma yudheck: It's so bad it's funny

Souq: Market

Um: Mother

Um Khalid: Mother of Khalid; a traditional way of calling a woman by the name of her firstborn son

Wallah: I swear by God

Ya Allah: Oh God

Ya binti: My daughter

Ya binti, ya habibti: My daughter, my love

Zaatar: An herb similar to thyme

ENDNOTES

Chapter 3

1. When I came to the US in 1974, people could walk all the way to the airplane gate to meet passengers.

2. The Detroit rebellion, also known as the uprising, took place in the summer of 1967. It was one of the largest and most violent race rebellions in US history. It was sparked by a police raid on an African American bar and resulted in a five-day confrontation between predominantly African Americans and Detroit police. The rebellion was also the result of growing anger within the African American community about racial oppression.

3. ACCESS, the Arab Community for Economic and Social Services, was established in 1971 by Arab Americans and new Arab immigrants in the South End of Dearborn, a working-class neighborhood. ACCESS serviced the large number of recent Arab immigrants mostly from Palestine, Lebanon, and Yemen.

Chapter 4

4. The tradition in the Arab world is to call the parents by the name of their firstborn son, Um Khalid, the mother of Khalid, and Abu Khalid, the father of Khalid.

Chapter 9

5. OAS, the Organization of Arab Students, was a national organization, with many chapters throughout US university campuses. It also had a national executive committee elected each year at the organization's convention.

Chapter 10

6. The Ford Motor Company Rouge Plant was the largest industrial complex in the world. Construction began in 1907 and was completed in 1928. In 1930, it employed over one hundred thousand people.

7. After 17 years (1971-1988) of legal battles, the US Federal Court of Appeals ruled in favor of the community against the City of Dearborn. It found the city's action in violation of the community's civil rights and a denial of due process of law.

Chapter 11

8. It was through Abdeen, and mostly at our home, where I met people like Edward Said, Jack Shaheen, Michael Suleiman, James Abourezk, Ibrahim Abu Laughed, James Zogby, Elaine Hagopian, Ismael Ahmed, Congressmen John Conyers, and George Crocket, among many others.

Chapter 12

9. The presence of the PLO and Palestinians, most of whom were refugees since 1948, was at the core of the Lebanese Civil War. The Lebanese National Front, a coalition of nationalist and leftist political parties, sided with the PLO and the Palestinians, while the right-wing parties led by the Phalangists opposed the PLO presence in Lebanon. The Sabra and Shatila are two adjacent Palestinian refugee camps, on the outskirts of Beirut. It housed Palestinians who became refugees after the creation of the State of Israel in 1948. A few poor Lebanese Shiites also lived there. On the evening of September 16, 1982, the Lebanese right-wing Phalange party militias stormed the camp on a killing rampage, under the watching eyes of the Israeli army who had been occupying Lebanon since June of that year. By the time the Phalange militias left, thirty-eight hours later, they had massacred an estimated 2,500-3,000 civilians, including a large number of the elderly, women, and children.

Chapter 15

10. In 1947, the United Nations voted to create two states: Israel and Palestine. The Communist Party, the only party that included both Palestinians and Jews, accepted the UN resolution, while the majority of Palestinians did not.

11. The Muslim Brothers are a political party that advocate for Islamic laws to govern family, society, and government; they are against secular states or the separation between state and religion.

12. *Decembrists* is a term used to reference revolutionaries. The Decembrists movement was a discrete revolutionary movement that evolved in the Russian Empire in the first quarter of the nineteenth century. It culminated in an unsuccessful revolt in Saint Petersburg on Dec 26, 1925, from which the term "Decembrists" is derived.

13. Emil Habibi was kind enough to give me his handwritten speech, which I still have.

Chapter 20

14. The Palestine Red Crescent Society is part of the International Red Cross Red Crescent.

Chapter 23

15. About a dozen years later, Dr. Peterson was shot and killed in his office by an angry patient.

Chapter 26

16. In the aftermath of the Iraqi invasion of Kuwait and the following US war against Iraq, the Kuwaiti government arrested hundreds of Palestinians, without any charges, many of whom had been living and working there for dozens of years. Later the entire Palestinian community, estimated at 350,000, were forced to leave the country.

Chapter 28

17. Renamed The Henry Ford.

18. The Women's Museum opened in Dallas, TX in 2000 but closed in October 2011.

19. Chaldeans, a Christian minority in Iraq, have their own church and their own language.

Chapter 29

20. American Lebanese and Syrian Associated Charities (ALSAC).

21. Mayor Orville Hubbard was the mayor of Dearborn, Michigan for 36 years from 1942-1978. Sometimes referred to as the "Dictator of Dearborn," Hubbard was the most outspoken segregationist north of the Mason-Dixon line. During his administration, nonwhites were aggressively discouraged from residing in Dearborn. Hubbard's long-standing campaign to "Keep Dearborn Clean" was widely understood to mean "Keep Dearborn White." In 2017, his statue was removed from what used to be Dearborn's City Hall, which is across the street from the Arab American National Museum.

ABOUT THE AUTHOR

D r. Anan Ameri is a scholar, author, activist, and community organizer. She is the founding Director of the Arab American National Museum (AANM) and Palestine Aid Society of America. She holds a BA in Sociology from the University of Jordan, an MA from Cairo University, and a Ph.D from Wayne State University in Detroit. She was a fellow at the Bunting Institute of Radcliffe College, a visiting scholar in Middle Eastern Studies at Harvard University, and served as Interim Director of the Institute for Jerusalem Studies.

The recipient of numerous awards, Anan was inducted into the Women's Hall of Fame in Lansing, Michigan in 2016 and received ACCESS's Arab American of the Year award in 2020.

She enjoys writing and has authored and edited several articles and publications.

CPSIA information can be obtained
at www.ICGtesting.com
Printed in the USA
LVHW091657160321
681690LV00022B/185

9 781643 971315